Williams

Williams

MAURICE HAMILTON

FOREWORD BY
SIR FRANK WILLIAMS

EBURY
PRESS

1 3 5 7 9 10 8 6 4 2

Published in 2009 by Ebury Press, an imprint of Ebury Publishing
A Random House Group Company

The Random House Group Limited Reg. No. 954009

Addresses for companies within the Random House Group can be found at
www.randomhouse.co.uk

A CIP catalogue record for this book is available from the British Library

The Random House Group Limited supports The Forest Stewardship Council
(FSC), the leading international forest certification organisation. All our titles
that are printed on Greenpeace approved FSC certified paper carry the FSC logo.
Our paper procurement policy can be found at www.rbooks.co.uk/environment

Mixed Sources
Product group from well-managed
forests and other controlled sources
www.fsc.org Cert no. TT-COC-2139
© 1996 Forest Stewardship Council
FSC

Designed and set by seagulls.net

Printed and bound in Great Britain by Clays Ltd, St Ives PLC

ISBN 9780091932671 (hardback)
ISBN 9780091932688 (paperback)

To buy books by your favourite authors and register for offers visit
www.rbooks.co.uk

CONTENTS

FOREWORD

Williams is a team that has my name over the door, something that for three decades has made me truly proud. However, I do hope this is not misplaced vanity on my part, as I know only too well that Formula 1 is not about any one single person.

In our sport, we often look to the racing driver as the solitary embodiment of our hopes and abilities, and goodness knows, I have more respect than most for what they do behind the wheel. But, like the person who lends his name to the team, they only do so much. The vast majority of the iceberg is below the water, and that has meant over the past thirty years that literally thousands of people have contributed to the team's achievements, whether it be our sixteen World Championships and 113 race wins, or the less noteworthy but no less valid individual and daily triumphs that have kept us buoyant.

While my lifelong compulsion with Formula 1 might seem to be about the blur of speed, the noise and the smell of burning metal, hot rubber and consumed fuel, this sensory assault is transient – perhaps a couple of hours twenty or so times a year. In reality, a stronger fascination for me has been the continuous variety of people drawn to us by our sport. They come from all corners of the earth, but to a man, and despite their diversity, they have all been people with a driven sense of purpose, all willing to make huge personal sacrifices and commit incredible energy and effort in the pursuit of the highest achievement on the race track.

That is what has driven me all these years. It is the reason that, although into my sixties, a gentle retirement never crosses my mind. I have been given the extraordinary privilege of seeing the ebb and flow of remarkable human talent across the Williams threshold.

As well as drawing all manner of talent into our organisation, Formula 1 also attracts the attention of people of rank and note from across the world. Here again I have enjoyed a life of great fortune thanks to meeting and taking pleasure from all kinds of engagements with statesmen, sportsmen, business leaders and all manner of aficionados of our sport. This has been a constant stimulus to me.

Because my time at Williams has been defined by the contributions of so many others, it would be inappropriate to bear reference to any one person, but in this respect I make one exception.

Patrick Head has been my friend first, but also my business partner and major contributor to the success our organisation has achieved. He is a genuinely gifted person and a brilliant engineer. He has coupled his inherent talent to endless energy and together we have found a common desire to achieve success in Formula 1. This has been the basis of our partnership of over thirty years. It is a genuine privilege to have shared the stewardship of our organisation together on what I hope you will agree has been, and I expect will continue to be, an extraordinary journey.

Frank Williams
May 2009

INTRODUCTION

Patrick Head summed it up: 'I have to say, when we win a race, it goes out of my head, even the details of it. Whereas the things that stop you winning a race, I remember all of those.' Considering Williams have won more than a hundred Grands Prix – a staggering number when you think about it – Patrick can be forgiven for being unable to recall the champagne moments. But that would be missing the point. Head was not being unduly modest or forgetful; he was merely expressing a core value that has been evident ever since he and Frank Williams began Williams Grand Prix Engineering in 1977. The whole point about taking part in a motor race is to win it. Cross the line first and it's job done. Now move on to the next race. Such a straightforward principle still applies today, despite or perhaps because of the accumulation of seven drivers' world championships and nine constructors' titles.

The Williams team is devoted to winning. Other racing organisations trot out that mantra as a matter of habit rather than careful thought about its true meaning. At Williams racing is the *only* thing. There are no distractions – no associated enterprises or peripheral partnerships. In a sport driven by corporate affiliations at the highest level, Williams remains a down-to-earth independent team of racers, a David among Goliaths. That is why there is arguably more widespread affection – as opposed to clannish support – among Formula 1 fans for Williams than for any other team. And that is why it is appropriate to mark the thirtieth anniversary of its first Grand Prix victory by relating the growth of this fond attachment during a fascinating roller-coaster ride through the decades.

It is a compelling story but writing it was going to be difficult because Williams and Head have always preferred to look forward rather than back. Frank encapsulated the philosophy perfectly at the launch of the 2009 Williams-Toyota: when asked if he would be recalling the thirty years since that emotional day at Silverstone, he said the only span of time that interested him was the five years since the team's last victory. And that was not something to be celebrated.

The best way to proceed, it seemed to me, was to let this book gather its own unstoppable momentum, to reach a point where Head and Williams, for all their genuine dislike of celebrity, would have no option but to accept that theirs is a story worth telling. The most practical solution was to allow those who know the team best to articulate their sense of attachment to a professional company possessing a unique and attractive quirkiness that comes with being British and proud of it. Setting off on this voyage of vocal discovery, I had no idea that the response would be so fulsome, genuine and deeply caring. I have been overwhelmed by emotion that says everything about the two men who inspired it. Frank and Patrick may not always be the easiest people to work for, but they are steadfastly honest and incredibly passionate about their team and the business which has absorbed everyone within in it for more than three decades.

Respect is a word much abused these days, but within Williams it has proper and genuine roots. On that note, it is not a slack omission or a sign of impertinence that Sir Frank's title has largely been disregarded in the narrative. Rather, it is a measure of the man that he would be appalled if protocol stifled the perfect blend of informality that has been his hallmark.

As this project gathered speed, it generated an enthusiasm which has been a privilege to experience as well as providing a vehicle for its rightful exposure. It has been a revealing and at times a touching journey.

There have been occasions when it was difficult to prevent a lump in the throat; moments of delicious humour as anecdotes emerged; a wonderful dinner with Patrick in an appropriately noisy Italian restaurant; an hour when time seemed to stand still as I enjoyed a cup of tea with Frank and reminisced in his office on a peaceful Sunday afternoon.

This book has not so much been written as managed. These are the words of the people who matter.

Maurice Hamilton
Cranleigh, 2009

ONE

The Thrill of Movement

B orn in South Shields on Thursday 16 April 1942, Frank Williams would come to epitomise the old saying, 'Thursday's child has far to go.' But it would be a tricky and unconventional journey. Francis Owen Garbett Williams arrived in the middle of World War II and you could argue that he has been fighting private battles ever since.

Frank's father flew Wellington bombers and left home before his son was one year old. Mrs Williams, faced with single parenthood and trying to make ends meet, worked hard to ensure her boy had a decent upbringing and education, something for which he would always remain grateful. Frank's friends would later note that the relationship between mother and son appeared to lack a certain warmth. That could be accounted for by the fact that Frank was cared for by his grand-parents for much of the time while his mother was heavily involved with teaching children with learning difficulties, a vocation which might have made it difficult for her to relate to a perfectly healthy son.

Frank spent three years at a convent school near Liverpool, followed by a year at day school in Jarrow. In the meantime, his mother had scraped together enough money to find him a place at St Joseph's Roman Catholic boarding school in Dumfries. It was here that he would learn a great deal about himself as well as experiencing the first flickers of interest in a sport that would quickly become an all-consuming passion. It was a tough regime that lasted through his early teenage years and did much to mould a determined and competitive personality. As one of a number of English boys in a Scottish school, Frank's national pride was developed by banter over sporting contests, none more so than motor racing.

In the early and mid-1950s the Le Mans 24 Hours was as prestigious as the Formula 1 World Championship, then in its infancy. If the dominance of Alfa Romeo and Ferrari pushed Formula 1 into the margins of British newspapers, Jaguar captured the headlines thanks to success at Le Mans. Jaguar was represented by a works team, operating from Coventry, and a highly professional private entrant bearing the cleverly alliterative title Ecurie Ecosse, based in Edinburgh. The Jaguar teams shared most of the wins between 1951 and 1957, Frank's fascination with motorsport expanding rapidly alongside an intense interest in anything on four wheels.

By the age of ten, Frank could recite the specifications of almost every road car listed in the *Autocar* and the *Motor* weekly publications. His fascination with cars was fuelled by sights of the latest models as well-heeled parents swept up the school drive to collect their offspring. Mrs Williams, meanwhile, would arrive by train. Rather than cause embarrassment, this reinforced Frank's appreciation of the hardship his mother was prepared to endure while, at the same time, heightening an awareness of the prestige value of fine cars and his longing to ride in them. Temporary relief from the latter was provided one day by a school friend's father who was the owner of a Jaguar XK150S. When offered a ride in what was unquestionably *the* sportscar of the day, Frank admitted he was virtually speechless with excitement.

Frank's passion for motoring is highlighted by the fact that whenever possible he would hitchhike rather than go by train. It saved money but also it allowed him to experience the thrill of movement on four wheels. His mother was now in charge of a village school ten miles outside Nottingham, and during school holidays Frank would frequently hitchhike from Nottingham to Newcastle upon Tyne, his reward being a ride in an exotic car at the end of the journey courtesy of Francis Holmes, a school mate from a family of motor traders. Mrs Holmes would invite Frank to stay during half-terms and he would seize the opportunity to inspect whatever cars Mr Holmes had in stock. Even better, cars were sometimes bought at auction in Glasgow and, if he went along for the trip, then a ride back to Newcastle was on offer in the tastiest purchase of the day. This was such a big deal for Frank that, if necessary, he would use his thumb to travel from Nottingham, have a wash and brush-up in Newcastle Central railway station and then present himself at the Holmes residence ready for the trip to Glasgow. The delight of the three-hour ride back to Newcastle in the passenger seat of some exotic car would be enough to sustain him as he said his cheery farewell and hitchhiked all the way back to Nottingham.

Quite what Mrs Williams made of all this is not known. In the 1950s teenagers enjoyed freedoms that would not be countenanced today. Frank's trips were probably considered normal for a motor-mad lad who would take every opportunity to drive his mother's Morris Minor 1000 around the school grounds before he was legally permitted to do so on public roads. It was also no surprise that Frank passed his driving test at the first attempt and that he left school at seventeen with no idea about his future except to say that he did not wish to go on to university. Mathematics may not have been his strong point but his gift for languages would stand him in good stead in the years to come. For now, though, the only language he wanted to understand was automotive with, if possible, a strong accent on racing. His journey on four wheels was about to make a humble but noisy start.

In early 2009 an Austin A35 was advertised on eBay for £2,990. The dumpy little two-door car, affectionately known as the Baby Austin, was manufactured by the British Motor Corporation at Longbridge from 1956. It was very popular at the time as family transport but the A35 also provided a reasonably inexpensive competition car for amateur racers. Frank Williams was not yet such a racer, despite his passion for cars. He was a wide-eyed enthusiast earning £3 10s a week as a management trainee with a car and commercial vehicle distributor in Nottingham. Williams scraped together every last penny to pay £350 for a tuned A35, more as a means of catching the eye of girls rather than going racing. Had he known then what his pride and joy would be worth nearly fifty years later, he might have taken greater care of it.

But, then again, probably not. Frank could not resist rapid movement in a motor car, much to the alarm in the years to come of most of his passengers, including his future wife, Virginia. It would be his undoing in more ways than one. And yet the Baby Austin would also shape his future in a manner that would have been beyond the wildest dreams of a car-mad nineteen-year-old. Frank's A35 had been tuned for racing by Speedwell Conversions, a company owned by Grand Prix driver Graham Hill and therefore instantly credible in the eyes of the car's new owner. Despite a noisy exhaust which would not pass muster today, the Austin was street legal, Williams making good use of it to go about his business in and around Nottingham. When someone enquired if Frank had ever considered racing his sporty little device, he thought it might be worth a try, nothing more, and he drove the car to a minor club event at Oulton Park in Cheshire in April 1961. Finishing his first-ever race would turn out to be something of an achievement, but transmission failure, which stranded Williams by the side of the road on his return journey, would be more indicative of what was to come.

By today's standards, club racing with your road car in the early 1960s was a relaxed affair. You taped up the headlamps (to prevent broken glass from littering the track), stuck competition numbers on the door, donned a basic crash helmet and raced in the clothes you had put on that morning. For some a collar and tie were essential, while a polo shirt of the sort favoured by Stirling Moss, a true British hero on the international Formula 1 scene, was considered distinctly racy. Seat belts were non-existent and it was something of a step forward to carry a fire extinguisher. Racing in club events at circuits such as Oulton Park, Snetterton and Brands Hatch was purely for pleasure. There was no sponsorship and the only reward was a possible mention in the motoring press.

On Sunday 2 July 1961 Frank Williams made it on to the pages of the weekly magazine *Autosport* for all the wrong reasons. Entered for a saloon car race at Mallory Park in Leicestershire, Frank's enthusiasm got the better of him in conditions made treacherous by unseasonably heavy rain. *Autosport* reporter Francis Penn wrote, 'As the cars lined up, the rain stopped. First away was P. Eva (Mini Minor), only to lose the lot at the Lake Esses. He continued, trailing a damaged exhaust pipe. Spins in this event were plentiful, the worst being F. O. Williams.' Frank lost control at Gerards, a fast right-hander where he heavily modified the little A35 against the bank. With no hope of continuing, Williams scrambled up the bank to join another wayward amateur, Jonathan Williams, who had crashed earlier at the same spot. Meeting for the first time under adversity, the two at least had something in common with which to start up a conversation while waiting for the race to finish. It was the beginning of a friendship that would have far-reaching consequences.

Jonathan had been accompanied to Mallory Park by Piers Courage, another would-be racer but from considerably more substantial stock than either Williams. The son of Richard Courage, chairman of the Courage brewery, Piers had been to Eton but failed his crammer course for Cambridge, the slim and engaging nineteen-year-old preferring the company of students at the Chelsea College of Aeronautical and Automobile Engineering – affectionately known as the College of Knowledge. Jonathan was studying there, as was Sheridan Thynne, later to become a driving force behind commercial affairs at Williams Grand Prix Engineering but at the time a friend of Courage from their days at Eton, where Thynne had been secretary of its very active Automobile Society.

Courage had become enthused with cars and motorsport to such an extent that he had entered an unsanctioned race in an equally un-authorised racing car, his mother's Morris Minor Traveller, the estate version of the Minor 1000 which featured mock-Tudor wooden trim. In much the same way as a group of like-minded enthusiasts in search of a venue immediately after World War II had discovered Silverstone airfield as a possible venue, Courage had joined fellow Etonians to sneak into an ex-RAF base at Chalgrove and race at the weekends. Courage's appetite for racing on a grander scale had been whetted by visits as a spectator to the Italian Grand Prix and the Le Mans 24 Hours. It therefore seemed a fun thing to do to come along for the ride with Jonathan Williams to Mallory Park.

Accompanying their damaged cars back to the paddock, Jonathan introduced Frank to Piers – although Frank now believes he met Courage either in London or at another race meeting. Whatever the circumstances, a bond was formed and Frank had met the group associated with the College of Knowledge. He would have very little influence on Jonathan's future career as a talented driver for Ferrari, but the introduction to Piers Courage led to one of Frank's greatest friendships and his future as one of the most enduring and popular team owners in Formula 1.

FRANK WILLIAMS

I was always interested in cars from the age of eight or nine. I was at a boarding school and once in a while a wealthy family would turn up with their Jaguar XK and I'd drool; it's one of those things I've never forgotten. St Joseph's school was hard. The emphasis was on attainment, and that rubbed off on me during ten very formative years at the school. There were 320 boys, split evenly between English and Scots since we were pretty close to the English border. At first I couldn't understand a word some of the Scots were saying but I quickly developed a pride in my nationality which I would never lose.

There was a lot of rivalry between England and Scotland: 'We scored more goals than you' or 'We built the last big battleship.' 'No you didn't!' Or 'We built the *Queen Mary* or *Queen Elizabeth*.' 'You didn't!' Endless stuff like that. But when Ecurie Ecosse began racing Jaguars and won Le Mans and then Aston Martin took over, I was just so pleased. I became so involved and I was happy supporting a Scottish team. I became very interested in Le Mans, more than Formula 1 at that time. I never really understood motor racing very much. It was a link to my love of cars and I was desperate to get behind the wheel. It all began at school. I was off; that was the escalator. But I did not leave school saying I was going to be a racing driver or saying that I was going into Formula 1. Absolutely not.

It was not until some time later that I began to take notice of Formula 1. My mother's school was about ten miles north of Nottingham city centre – very much countryside then, probably built up now. I hitchhiked because I had no money and I was desperate; I just wanted to go to the races and to ride in cars.

I remember the father of one of the boys at school was a successful bookmaker in Glasgow. He turned up at school in a convertible XK150S and took me for a ride up these narrow roads. Phew! About 90 mph. He must have been aged about sixty-five and he was showing off. But I just couldn't get over it. He was very kind to me. I never saw him again.

On one of my trips to Newcastle I got lucky. A very wealthy young man in a Triumph TR3A stopped. It was a two-seater sports car and he'd just got it. Off we went, top down, 100 mph, overdrive, four-speed gearbox. My eyes were on stalks. I've never forgotten it. I'd never had a thrill like it in my life. Getting rides in cars was such a big part of the fun. It was all about the speed and the movement, going quickly on the road.

When I went to races, I either arrived very early before anyone got there, so you could just walk in, or I would arrive after the racing had begun and slip in that way. The first proper race I ever went to was the 1958 British Grand Prix at Silverstone. I left Nottingham at 5 a.m. on a beautiful summer's morning in the middle of July. Walked about three miles to the main road, got a lift for five miles, spent an hour waiting for another lift, and so on. I got as far as Towcester and walked to Silverstone from there. I arrived at about 2.30 p.m. and walked in through a car park for free. The first race I saw was for touring cars – amazing Jaguars, little A35s, big American Ford Galaxies. I loved it. The Grand Prix wasn't so exciting, as it went on for about three hours. Peter Collins won, an Englishman in a Ferrari. That impressed me. A couple of weeks later he was killed at the Nürburgring. These things stick in your mind.

In 1961 I persuaded my mother to lend me eighty pounds to buy a little Austin A35. She put up the deposit; left the rest to me. It had been used for racing but I only wanted it for the road. It had roundels [for competition numbers] on the doors, plastic windows, no trim inside, lots of noise. I thought, *That'll do me, I'll soon pick up the girls with this.* I took it to work every day even though it wasn't ideal for that because it had a very delicate engine. But it was fun. And then somebody at work said, 'Why don't you race it?' Until that point it had *never* crossed my mind for me to race. I bought it as a road car: great little car, attracted attention, really quick. I could show off in it all day long.

I went to Mallory Park. It rained for race day. I don't know where I qualified, midfield or something. On lap six or seven at Gerards, off I went and rolled it. I finished up parked on the inside, climbed out the back window and this very laconic, posh voice said, 'Oh hello. Come up here, old boy, I thought you'd join me some time!' It was my first meeting with Jonathan. He was a very bubbly, charming person and made everyone around him laugh. We got on well straight away. Then I met Piers, who clearly came from a very different social background but we all lived for motor racing. That was the start of it.

VIRGINIA WILLIAMS

I remember meeting Frank's father and mother. His father turned up at a race one day. He looked *exactly* like Frank but with a lot of hair – quite extraordinary. Frank was very driven, as was his mother. His mother was a teacher and I have to be careful how I say this, but I think that Frank was probably secondary to her pupils in some ways. Frank's father was an RAF pilot and they were together during the Second World War, so it was a pretty flaky relationship.

I know Frank's father was terribly upset because, in my book[1] Frank had said to me that his father had left before he was born, but in fact he didn't. He left when Frank was just under a year old and he took offence at the suggestion that he had left before then. He was upset to have been depicted as someone who would have left a pregnant woman.

---

1. Virginia Williams with Pamela Cockerill, *A Different Kind of Life*, Doubleday, 1992

But it would have made no difference to Frank whether his father had left before he was born or if he was eleven months old; either way, Frank did not have a father at home.

Frank had to be shunted off here and there so that his mother could get on with her career. I think she received an MBE for looking after retarded children but, because she took schooling very seriously indeed, Frank had a fabulous education as a result. When you think about it, it's quite extraordinary that someone should have come out of any sort of English education speaking three foreign languages. But it's difficult to understand where his passion for cars came from. I don't think his mother drove that much and there was no other motoring background. But I seem to remember his mother saying that Frank used to sit in the bus and stare at the driver. He was enthralled by anyone who could drive anything. Even a bus.

JONATHAN WILLIAMS

I remember watching Frank driving and thinking he was a right lunatic. But when he joined me on the top of the bank, I could tell straight away that he was just like the rest of us. A perfect fit. We were all mad on motor racing. We would rather not have eaten if it meant going somewhere and racing something. We couldn't wait until the next Sunday before we could go and do it again. We always felt there should be races on a Wednesday as well. We hadn't got much money – Frank had even less than that. When we raced subsequent to that day at Mallory, generally I had the upper hand, but only because I tried to avoid spinning off! Frank was clean to race with, very fair. But he was a daredevil and, unfortunately, had no self-control. I don't think any of us had any race craft whatsoever in those days – you just went fast! The trouble was, Frank didn't know when to stop.

TWO

Souped Up

The issue of *Autosport* which reported Frank's exuberance at the wheel also carried a number of classifieds at the back. Under the heading 'Carburetters' (*sic*) a three-line advert offered a Weber twin-choke downdraught for twenty pounds, a princely sum in the days when the same columns presented 'fantastically powerful twin air horns – new from France! – must be the loudest ever' for £3 16s 6d and a seven-day coach trip to the Italian Grand Prix which would set you back sixteen pounds, all included.

Frank spotted that carburettor ad or one similar, and saw it as an investment for the A35. He hammered out the dents, straightened the bodywork and took the Austin to a tuning company in Wiltshire. It became something of a rush job when Frank realised he only had four hours in which to return north to sign on for a race at Oulton Park. Carried away by the boosted performance and forgetting his semi-bald racing tyres, Frank's enthusiasm once again got the better of him. In the middle of Salisbury he spun backwards into a lamp post. The job which he had started at Mallory Park was now complete. The A35 was a write-off.

Undaunted – how many times will that word be appropriate in the following pages – Frank salvaged what he could from the wreckage and fitted the bits into the shell of a larger Austin, the A40. By the approach of the 1962 season Frank was ready to return to the racetrack, where one of his competitors in a similar car would be Williams, J.

Frank would make regular visits to the flat shared by Jonathan Williams and Sheridan Thynne in London's Lower Sloane Street, a handy location for Brands Hatch. Once the fun on the track was over, Frank would motor up from Kent, park the A40 outside the flat and, being short of petrol money, hitchhike overnight to Nottingham in time to start work on Monday morning. Sometimes he would thumb his way to London for the weekend and stay with Jonathan and Sheridan. They would be joined by Piers, who was focusing more on racing than the qualification in accountancy hoped for by Courage senior.

Frank's job with the vehicle distributor had come to an end when he failed to show up for a day-release course on the understandable grounds that classes including rudimentary English were unnecessary for someone already in possession of an A level in the subject. After a stop-gap job as a filling station attendant, he became a trainee sales representative for Campbell's Soup. This brought ten pounds a week and a Ford Anglia company car and was seen as a useful move even if Mr F. O. G. Williams was required to wear a bowler hat when visiting shopkeepers on his patch in Yorkshire. Given his winning smile and polite manner, Frank's sales figures were more than satisfactory, but the job was a means to an end, and the focus of his ambition increasingly became the flat in Chelsea rather than high-class grocers in Barnsley and Rotherham. In 1963 he moved to Lower Sloane Street, his new job mechanic – in the loosest sense of the title – for Jonathan Williams.

When Jonathan and Piers had visited Frank and his mother in Nottingham in 1962 the main purpose of the trip had been to run in the brand-new Lotus 7 which Piers had built from a kit. The two-seater sports car was nippy transport for the road but mainly for Piers to race. His competition career had started with a minor sprint meeting at Brands Hatch in April 1962. Twelve months later he was ready to step up to a Merlyn, a proper racing single-seater. Meanwhile, Jonathan, with assistance from his father, a squadron leader in the RAF, had bought a

Merlyn in which to compete in Formula Junior, recognised throughout Europe as a proving ground for future Grand Prix stars. Frank may have been a 'mechanic' but his driver, along with Piers, was quick to realise that their cars needed proper care and attention if they were to finish, never mind win. It was at this point that the Sloane Square set fell in with a colourful collection of out-and-out racers inhabiting a seedy but atmospheric yard off the Goldhawk Road in Shepherd's Bush.

Motor racing at every level bar Formula 1 depended on places like this during the 1960s and into the '70s. Williams and Courage had been put in touch with Roy Thomas, known as Tom the Weld because of his prodigious ability to fix anything to a high standard. Thomas rented one of several garages in a yard at the back of a car showroom owned by Cliff Davis, a larger-than-life character who had seen it all as a prisoner of war and lived life to the full as a salesman, racing driver and organiser of outrageous stag evenings for the motorsport fraternity. Frank loved it from the moment he first set foot in the place. Added to which, a summer spent racing in Europe beckoned.

It was a gypsy existence, racing every weekend from the beginning of May to the end of September. They lived hand to mouth on the start money – as much as a hundred pounds, a considerable sum in 1963 – paid by the race organisers and, if they were lucky, prize money in cash at the end of the meeting. Jonathan bought a Volkswagen pickup as a means of transporting the Merlyn to and from places as far-flung as Sicily and Sweden. Once a week they would share a hotel room for a shower, a square meal and a proper bed. Otherwise they made do with the back of the Volkswagen as sleeping quarters.

When Jonathan's money ran out and he returned to England, Frank had made enough contacts to ensure he could continue living in Europe doing whatever was asked. The most useful introduction had been to Charles Crichton-Stuart at a racetrack in East Germany. Frank had been impressed by Charlie, not least because he was the grandson of the fifth Marquis of Bute and could afford the latest equipment. Charlie also owned a ground-floor flat in which he lived and let out rooms, sofas and, depending on the depth of the tenant's financial despair, floor space. This was 283 Pinner Road, Harrow, soon to become one of the most notorious addresses in the junior ranks of motor racing. Frank moved in towards the end of 1963.

Flat 6 had three bedrooms and a number of lock-up garages at the rear which proved ideal for the storage and preparation of racing cars. Crichton-Stuart, who would later be a key member in the formation of Williams Grand Prix Engineering, occupied one bedroom, leaving the other two to be shared by tenants and regular visitors, the number of occupants on any given night ranging between five and ten. Charlie used the rent to pay for a daily help, Mrs Buckland, who prepared his breakfast and generally kept him straight. Food was purchased by those who could afford it while the height of luxury was a visit to a nearby café in Rayners Lane and a three-course lunch for five shillings.

Piers Courage, having abandoned all hope of a career in accountancy, joined the Pinner Road brigade, as did Charles Lucas, also a student at the College of Knowledge, the son of a wealthy businessman and landowner. Frank was among the least well-off but his engaging enthusiasm and willingness to earn a couple of quid carried him through. One Sunday morning Crichton-Stuart bet Frank ten shillings that he wouldn't go outside naked when a Tube train was passing on the Metropolitan Line at the bottom of the back garden. Frank accepted the wager and duly startled the commuters but was then locked out. To Crichton-Stuart's alarm, Frank then went to the front of the house and began thumping his chest in a demented fashion just as the congregation was emerging from a nearby church. Frank was quickly readmitted to receive his winnings.

Among the more irreverent congregation pressed against the windows of Flat 6 was Anthony 'Bubbles' Horsley, an habitué of the flat who also worked in the yard at Goldhawk Road. Despite his substantial girth when compared to the jockey-like Williams duo and the elegance of Courage, Horsley shared the burning desire to become a serious racing driver. For the 1964 season Horsley had used a legacy to buy a Formula 3 Ausper single-seater to replace a Brabham which was in need of repair. He agreed to allow Frank to race the Brabham if he acted as mechanic and general helper when they joined the F3 trail around Europe during the summer of 1964. Frank jumped at the opportunity, particularly as there was the luxury of a van to sleep in as well as acting as a mobile workshop and towing vehicle for the double-deck trailer carrying the two cars. The elderly Morris van had seen better days as a service vehicle for Hoover and Frank began to doubt his initial enthusiasm when he picked up dermatitis thanks to oil seeping into his sleeping quarters. With a race in Sicily – one of the most financially rewarding of the season – beckoning, Bubbles decided against risking the van for the long trip south but bizarrely replaced it with a 1955 Plymouth bought from Piers Courage. It would be a disastrous trip in more ways than one.

Driving the lumbering American car and attached trailer through the Alps would prove a challenge as great as anything experienced on the racetrack. Having no brakes was one thing; having no money was an entirely different problem. Frank had left the wallet containing what little money they had on the roof of the car at a service station in Italy. There was no option but to press on to Reggio di Calabria in the hope of borrowing cash from other racers as they waited to board the ferry. Frank and Bubbles, brakeless and broke, struggled into the port to discover the ferry had already departed for Messina. There was nothing for it but to wait until their friends reappeared three days later, surviving on bread, water and grapes pinched from a nearby vineyard. The return journey, long and arduous even when things were going well, was made worse by the disappointment of no racing and no earnings. And then, for good measure, the exhaust fell off the Plymouth, the battery packed up and the power steering failed. By the time they reached Dover three days later conversation had ceased and Bubbles was demoralised. Frank, however, merely dusted himself down, ready to continue following his dream even though his progress in Horsley's Brabham had been less than spectacular.

The dream, for 1964 at least, was to reach a typically dramatic end when Frank crashed the Brabham at the Nürburgring south circuit. As Horsley rounded a corner and spotted bits of familiar green bodywork on the road, his feelings rocketed from despair to anger when he saw Frank grinning from the trackside. Bubbles was so upset at seeing half of his worldly goods deposited against a grass bank that he promptly went off at the next corner and was thrown from the spacious cockpit of the Ausper. Winded and in pain from a sore leg, Horsley looked such a sorry sight that he was loaded into the back of an ambulance, which then set off. Gathering his wits and realising this might be expensive, Bubbles took the opportunity to make his escape discreetly when the ambulance stopped at an exit gate. There was consternation when, arriving at the hospital, the medics opened the rear doors, only to find their charge had disappeared. At least it was easy to describe the large and lugubrious racing driver to the police, who caught up with Horsley in the paddock and delivered a severe dressing-down. It was no way to end a season that had promised so much.

If Frank had barely two pennies to rub together before, he was now so broke that he could not even afford to rent a sofa at Number 6 and resorted to sleeping in the back of the Morris van, which not surprisingly had failed to attract a buyer. But when it came to buying and selling bits and pieces for racing cars, Frank was entering new and potentially profitable territory.

Putting his French, German and Italian to good use, he found he could satisfy a demand from racing drivers from the continent who had bought racing cars built in England. Given the ravages of a racing season, spare parts were always needed, and in the days before credit cards drivers needed to go through a time-consuming process of telephoning Brabham or Lotus and then arranging bank transfers. With races in every corner of Europe following each other in rapid succession, there was scope for someone who understood urgency and could offer a reliable service with cash on delivery. Frank quickly filled the gap in the market to the extent of being able to not only afford a decent bed inside Flat 6 but also to install a phone line on which to conduct his business, which quickly expanded to the buying and selling of entire racing cars. Eventually, profits were such that he was able to buy cars for his own use on both road and track, although his choice of racing car demonstrated that Frank's business acumen was not yet a match for his enthusiasm. The Ford Zodiac bought from Piers Courage would prove a comfortable and trusty set of road wheels but the second-hand Cooper purchased for the 1965 season from team owner John Coombes did not go down as one of the world's great Formula 3 cars.

Initially, Frank could not deal with the Cooper's unusual handling characteristics and was further handicapped by an uncompetitive engine. In typical style, however, he persevered and scored his first international result of note by finishing fourth at Skarpnack in Sweden on 5 September 1965. Typically, Frank made the most of his brief moment of glory by selling the car to a Swedish driver and returning home with a profit. Working harder than ever, Frank borrowed money where he could and used it to buy new F3 cars from Brabham and Lola, selling them on and using the profits to keep a brand-new Brabham for himself. His money-raising knew no limits, as Crichton-Stuart discovered when he returned from an evening meal to find Frank charging passers-by one pound to view scratchy black-and-white porn movies imported illicitly from abroad. The 1966 season ought to have been a turning point for Frank Williams, racing driver, but a minor win in Sweden on 28 August notwithstanding, progress was marred by incidents such as one in Portugal where he lost control on a level crossing and destroyed the front of the car on a gate post.

Redoubling his efforts in the winter of 1966/7, Frank placed full-page For Sale adverts in *Autosport* for cars which were spread around the lock-up garages of Harrow. Such was the pressure of business that there was no time for his beloved racing in 1967, a sure sign of how successful he had become in his new career.

Piers Courage, meanwhile, had been making the sort of progress Frank had dreamed of on the racetrack. Jonathan and Piers had teamed up to run a pair of Lotus-Fords in Formula 3 (the new name for Formula Junior). Piers had picked up a couple of second and third placings as they criss-crossed Europe during the summer of 1964. The ravages of twenty-seven races took their toll on the car, Courage at one stage fixing a bent chassis by propping the tubular frame against a wall and backing into it with his Ford Zodiac. It was enough to do the job and move on to another race and more starting money. By 1965 Charles Lucas had come into a substantial family inheritance and did not take much persuasion to spend it on a Formula 3 team – with Jonathan and Piers joining 'Luke' as drivers. Courage won his first race, a major Formula 3 supporting event to the Formula 1 International Trophy at Silverstone in May 1965. Piers would finish the season with twelve wins and five lap records. He would also announce his engagement to Lady Sarah Curzon, known to everybody as Sally and much admired by the scruffy contingent at Pinner Road.

Sally may have been slightly nonplussed after her first visit – then as Charlie's girlfriend – to the shambles at Pinner Road but she was no stranger to motor racing. Her father, Earl Howe, was a pioneer of post-war motorsport and president of the British Racing Drivers' Club. Sally loved the enthusiasm and vitality of the motley crew residing in Flat 6. Twelve months later Piers and Sally were married and Piers had done enough in Formula 3 and Formula 2 to deserve consideration for occasional drives in Formula 1 in 1967. There seemed to be no stopping him but, as anyone at Pinner Road would testify, motor racing is never that simple.

FRANK WILLIAMS

The Pinner Road flat was an episode in my life I'd rather not talk about, but it wasn't as naughty as people make out. Charlie was our social and spiritual leader. He was such a gent. He had some money – not a lot – but he spent it and lived like a gentleman. Flat 6 was his place, but he wouldn't concede anything. It was, to our eyes then, a nice place with a living room and a dining room. We even had a lady come in to make us breakfast every morning, but she had to go eventually.

Depending on how much money I had, I would sleep on the sofa but eventually rose to the luxury of having my own room. Various different people lived in the other rooms, either Jonathan Williams or Porridge [Piers Courage]. Luke was there for a while, and then Bubbles moved in. It was heaven in a way because we talked about nothing but racing.

The Brabham I raced, I sort of bought from Bubbles. Some poor man had killed himself at Oulton Park in this Formula Junior Brabham. He was a London car dealer, and the story goes that when he was buried his wife turned up, as you would expect, for the funeral, but so did four other ladies and four Fiat 500s. This chap had loads of crumpet and gave each one a car. The Fiat 500 was the cheapest car you could get. You can imagine the scene at the funeral, can't you?

The Brabham needed a new chassis, which I sorted out with Bubbles, and we went off with his Ausper around Europe in 1964. I bent that Brabham and then crashed it. It hardly ever ran reliably but I rebuilt it and did quite a few races in it. I can't remember what happened in terms of results – obviously nothing special. I finished up in the fence at the Nürburgring Sudschleiffe on lap one or lap two, something useless like that. Bubbles wasn't happy, but we still remain friends to this day.

Some time in 1963, about May, Jonathan had called me and said, 'Listen, I'm setting off with my Lotus 20. I had a friend who's dropped out. I need a gofer; can you come?' I thought fantastic, and off we went with a VW flatbed that was just long enough to take the car, with the nose sticking out the front. You could buy these accessories and we had this tarpaulin arrangement, like the canvas roof cowboys had on wagon trains.

We had about two months in Europe. There weren't that many racing cars around in those days and there was a chain of events the Europeans wanted in various cities, which brought a bit of style to our lives.

People like us would turn up, get our sixty, hundred pounds or whatever, motor on to the next race. Every Sunday, after the race, we'd have a night in a hotel, a good bath and a good bed. The rest of the time, we slept between the wheels of the racing car. I'm five foot eight and Jonathan is five six. It was a tight fit but we slept like babies. Wonderful.

SHERIDAN THYNNE

There was a defining moment in 1962. It was a race meeting at one of those wonderful two-day BRSCC [British Racing and Sports Car Club] race meetings at Brands Hatch. Frank raced an A40 and I raced a Mini. There was a group of us: Jonathan, Piers, Frank and others, and we had supper just near Sloane Square, where we were living. I suppose we finished round about 10.30 p.m. or something like that and we were five minutes' walk away from where we were living.

It was July, so I was twenty-three then. We were all quite knackered and I thought that it was nearly bedtime and said so. Knowing that Frank didn't live around there, we asked him what he was going to do and he said he was going to Nottingham, where he worked. On that particular day we knew he'd had a lift back from where he'd left his race car, so we asked him how he was going to get to Nottingham. He said that one of the other guys at supper had told him that they were going to north London and they would drop him on the A1, from where he was going to hitch.

The rest of us were pretty sheltered from these sorts of difficulties at that stage and I remember very vividly thinking, *Jesus, we're knackered and, far from starting work, we were going to college the next day. We could stagger in bleary-eyed like one did at college. And here was this guy who was going to hitchhike to Nottingham, starting at half ten, and be at work the next day. He operates a different way to us.* You can understand how defining that was at that stage.

We talked about nothing but racing. We didn't think we were lucky or different, particularly. We just had a great desire to get on with it and go racing. We had come to learn that, as a driver, Frank was fairly wild. The A40 had a Formula Junior engine and a lot of people had got some sort of limited-slip diff. Frank had locked the differential in some way – presumably there was no budget for a slip diff – so it was extremely sudden. He was quick, but a bit wild.

CHARLES LUCAS

Frank was always on the move; it really was noticeable even then. He'd do anything to make a few bob. He even organised porn shows for the local police, which I thought was fairly adventurous. Don't ask where he got the film from; I have no idea. He would be out at all hours of the night, hustling.

I was only there for just under a year, and at that time Frank had no money at all. He slept on the sofa. I took him home for Christmas because he had no money and had nowhere to go. I had to lend him ten bob to buy my sister a Christmas present. He was amazing, just a totally driven guy. Things like that didn't seem to matter too much. When it came to talking about racing – which seemed to be most of the time – his eyes would just light up. And he's exactly the same now.

You meet people and you realise that their situation is going to be shit or bust. It is either going to be a total disaster – which it nearly was for Frank in the early 1970s – or a great success. When you saw what he went through at the time, it would have put a lot of people off. But when we were in the flat, I really can't claim to have thought that he would turn out to be the huge success we've seen. His nickname then was Wanker Williams, which tells you quite a lot about his haphazard existence in those days. But he had this star quality, this burning ambition to succeed – and it had to be in racing.

I remember he was staying with me in Yorkshire; it must have been later on because he was considering sending his son to Ampleforth. Thinking of the successful way Frank operated, I asked why he hadn't gone into business, perhaps in the City or something like that, been successful and then played at racing on the side. He looked at me as if I was absolutely crazy. 'What? Do something other than racing? You must be completely mad.'

You ask if we ever did any work at the College of Knowledge. Come on! It was jolly hard work. I mean, trying to file a square cube that fitted exactly through a quarter-inch metal plate … that could take *months*! The fact that Jonathan went off and got his done in a machine shop is beside the point. I still have the set square that I made – that isn't quite square.

As for Goldhawk Road, our lives revolved around that yard. Curiously, I first went down to the yard through no connection with the people there at all. A friend of my mother lived in a nearby flat and he introduced me to Cliff. I walked into the yard and the whole of motor racing life seemed to be popping out of each lock-up. Bubbles was managing a really crazy Formula 1 team, known as Scirocco, for an American called Hugh Powell. It was a bit of a fiasco. The whole of your life was suddenly there. It was an extraordinary place.

I could see that the relationship between Frank and Piers was very important. Piers took Frank's mind slightly off motor racing and into things like music and culture – if I can call it that. But I did notice that there was always a rather strong vanity line with Frank. Even when he was scratching for money, he still had his hair cut at Trumpers in Curzon Street. Which is odd, especially when you haven't got much hair in the first place. Even when he was down and out, he was always well turned out. That would become his hallmark in everything that he did.

LADY SARAH ASPINALL

It was Charlie's flat – I was engaged to him at the time – and he said to come down and have a look. I took a look at the collection of oily guys in there and asked, 'Do they all live here?' And he said, 'Yes!' I've never seen such a bunch. They were all absolutely delightful. They were covered in oil and goodness knows what else. But they were great fun, very sweet. They had these garages at the back containing every bit of broken-down car you'd ever clapped eyes on. There would be someone trying to put them all together. But they were all happy; they loved what they were doing.

Yes, the place was a mess but the point was here was a good group of young men, living their dream. And that was so rare – still is, finding people who can say they're happy doing what they're doing. They were loving every minute of it and talking all the time about motor racing. There would be lots of disappointments and sadness, and tears sometimes. They were always broke, absolutely skint. But that seemed to add to the sense of adventure. Frank was part of the group and he stood out as being a cheeky chappie: very flirtatious, great fun. But I always remember he was quite dapper. I don't know how he managed to afford the clothes.

I broke up with Charlie and I didn't see them for a while because I went away to work in America. I came back and met Piers again. Frank was always around Piers, along with Jonathan. Our house in Pimlico, and then Drayton Gardens, would see them wandering in and out. Bubbles was living with us and people would stop while on the way somewhere – just wander in and say hello. They would have lunch and we had a marvellous housekeeper, Mrs Tee, who would cook and look after them. We always seemed to have about three lodgers at any given time. They would say to Piers they had nowhere to stay and he'd say it was fine, but, 'Go and ask the ol' girl.' That was me, of course. And naturally I'd give in straight away. It was always a pleasure to have them around the place.

JONATHAN WILLIAMS

When Frank and I went racing in Europe, we slept on two lilos between the wheels of the racing car on the back of the Volkswagen. It was pretty brutal, not very comfortable. But we were as happy as could be. Delighted! We didn't feel deprived in the least. It was a great life, and at the end of the week there was a race! It was hugely convivial, and Frank loved every minute of it. Mind you, I did put him to the test in the weeks following an accident in Monte Carlo. I was practising for the support race for the Grand Prix when I crashed and received a knock on the head. It tells you how stupid we were in those days. When two other Merlyn drivers entered for the same race had suffered identical suspension failures, it never occurred to me that the same thing might happen to my car, which was exactly the same as the other two. I simply thought of it as having those two drivers out of the way – two I wouldn't need to worry about in the race. The next thing, I woke up in the Princess Grace Hospital.

Nobody seemed to know much about concussion then. I could remember everything about my life, up to and including the crash. But I couldn't remember what had happened a couple of hours ago. It was so frustrating to find that in the evening you hadn't a clue what you had been doing in the morning. Little by little it caught up, but nobody told me not to go motor racing. And Frank found he had to stop me from wandering off and getting lost. Why he didn't go insane, I don't know. The big thing in our lives would be starting money – usually about a hundred pounds, a hundred and fifty if you were lucky – from the next race.

'Where are we going next, Frank?' I would ask.

'Reims,' he would say.

An hour later: 'Where are we going, Frank?'

'Reims, Jonathan!'

In those days, no one seemed to care about – or notice – concussion. You just got on with it.

THREE

Business is Booming

As poor as a church mouse a few years before, Frank Williams was surprised to find his business buying and selling racing cars turning over £160,000 in 1967. It was hard work and profit margins were small, which meant getting behind the wheel had been out of the question. Meanwhile, Frank could see that Piers Courage was destined for great things even though his 1967 season had been disappointing.

There was one major domestic race meeting left as the October nights closed in. The Guards Motor Show 200 – timed, as the title suggests, to coincide with the London Motor Show in the days when it was a major automotive event in Earls Court – would attract the big names in Formula 3 for a final blast at Brands Hatch before the off season. As a semi-official Brabham agent, Frank had access to their 1968 Formula 3 prototype, and the Motor Show 200 would be the perfect place to showcase the car before prospective purchasers headed home to mull over their plans for the following season. Clearly, he needed someone useful to drive it.

Having moved into Formula 2 and then been entered in three Grands Prix for the privateer Reg Parnell, Courage might have considered a Formula 3 drive a backward step, but times had been so tough – he had not scored a single victory and been involved in several incidents – that Piers did not need much persuading to race the Brabham prototype at Brands Hatch. As Frank unloaded the immaculate two-tone green Brabham BT21B, it was the first of many occasions when his name would be paired with that of Piers Courage in a race programme as entrant and driver. Despite a mere six laps during a damp practice session, Courage qualified third for his heat and then won it at a canter, breaking the Formula 3 lap record in the process. Hopes of repeating that performance in the final took a dive when water got into the electrics of the unproven car, bringing the Brabham to a halt on the warm-up lap, but a point had been made. Several points, in fact.

Although earning only a brief mention within a crowded report in the following Thursday's *Autosport* (the meeting had also staged the final round of the prestigious British Saloon Car Championship and a historic race won by Charles Lucas in a Maserati 250F), enough had been done to show that the Brabham was a potentially good car and that Courage had lost none of his flair. Even more significant in terms of their future together, Frank had enjoyed entering a car and driver that had a chance of winning. This seemed at least as good as struggling to become a successful driver, although Frank continued to harbour ambitions as a racer. Courage and Williams started thinking about a serious Formula 2 campaign for the 1968 season.

Courage spent the winter of 1967/8 racing in the Tasman Series, a championship run in Australia and New Zealand when Grand Prix drivers had nothing to do and were glad of the chance to escape the European winter for the sun. The series attracted top teams such as Lotus, BRM and Ferrari, but the theme was relaxation and fun interrupted by races. Courage, in an attempt to rebuild his reputation, entered a McLaren which he had acquired from John Coombes, the same man from whom Frank had bought the ropey Formula 3 Cooper. While the Formula 2 car was no match for what were in effect scaled-down Formula 1 racers, Courage opted for a consistency that brought podium finishes when the quicker cars ran into problems. He had already done enough to redeem himself when the teams moved to Tasmania for the final round on a terrifyingly fast road circuit at Longford. The track, which crossed railways and traversed a wooden bridge, was considered dangerous in the dry, but the prospect of racing in pouring rain was scary. Courage, though, knew that his nimble McLaren would have an advantage over the more powerful cars, and he was probably one of the few drivers happy to see the race start, albeit with the laps reduced from twenty-eight to fifteen. He drove brilliantly, his spectacular victory making the sports pages of the *Daily Telegraph*. Now it was time to return on the crest of a wave to London and see what his new partner had been up to.

Frank Williams (Racing Cars) Ltd had grown sufficiently to have its owner abandon the practice of spreading its activities around whatever lock-up garages he could find. A small workshop, with a flat overhead, had been found between a bingo hall and a pub at 361 Bath Road, Cippenham, near Slough. As a teetotaller who refused to gamble on anything over which he had absolutely no control, the location was symbolic for Frank in so far as the pub was owned by the Courage brewery – although he might occasionally have felt the need for a drink as he formulated his plans for 1968.

The European Formula 2 Championship was the next best thing to Formula 1 and regularly attracted Grand Prix stars such as Jackie Stewart and Jochen Rindt, who would become world champions in 1969 and 1970 respectively. It would cost Frank £10,000 to set up his team. The one important asset already in his possession was a Brabham Formula 2 car which a customer had decided not to go ahead with. The original purchaser had ordered the Brabham in dark blue and that automatically became the team's official colour.

Williams and Courage made their collective Formula 2 debut on 31 March at Montjuich Park in Barcelona, where Piers finished fourth. Seven days later they were at Hockenheim in Germany. The records show that Courage finished fifth and second in the two heats, but Sunday 7 April 1968 was remembered for something else. The race, run in grey, miserable conditions, claimed the life of Jim Clark, a hero to many and twice world champion, who made it look so easy, took so few risks that he seemed indestructible. It was particularly difficult for Piers, who had got to know Clark well during the Tasman Series. It was also a reminder of the sport's perils, one that would come back to haunt Frank Williams two years later.

For now, though, the show had to go on, particularly with the next round being at home on Easter Monday. Piers finished second in the first heat at Thruxton in Hampshire and led the second before having to retire with a holed radiator after another driver muscled past and showered the Brabham with stones. And so it continued through Europe, Courage temporarily abandoning Formula 2 when his commitment to the Parnell BRM Formula 1 car intervened for eleven Grands Prix. One of them, the Dutch Grand Prix, clashed with a Formula 2 race at Monza, and Frank drafted in Jonathan Williams. Appropriately, his old mate would give Frank his first victory as a team owner.

Piers would win a heat of the Formula 2 race at Zandvoort in Holland, another event tinged with sadness when a young British driver, Chris Lambert, was killed in a collision with another car. Less seriously, a privateer went into a ditch all on his own and badly damaged his Brabham, a sign that Max Mosley was correct in later choosing a career as the head of the sport's governing body, the FIA, rather than pursuing his ambition of becoming a serious racing driver. For Piers Courage and Frank Williams there was no doubt about what they wanted, as they ended the season with a win in a round of the Temporada Series for Formula 2 cars in Argentina. It would be Frank's first major overseas trip. He returned to Britain with plans well in hand for another excursion, this time to the opposite side of the world. Following up Courage's success in the previous Tasman Series, the organisers had offered Williams £6,000 to make the trip. Frank was quick to accept.

He bought a chassis which Brabham had used during the 1968 Formula 1 championship and then ordered two Ford-Cosworth V8s to go with it. These were the engines to have in Grand Prix racing. The trick was that the Ford-Cosworth could be reduced from the three-litre limit required for Formula 1 to the two and a half litres needed to conform to the Tasman regulations, then converted back to three litres. So Frank had the makings of a Grand Prix team sitting in his workshop downstairs – everything he needed, from a couple of Formula 1 engines to a decent car and someone capable of racing it. But at first he did not see it. Not until his secretary asked the obvious question did it dawn on

Frank that he could go into Formula 1. Suddenly, he knew exactly what he was going to do.

FRANK WILLIAMS

I began to realise how good Piers was when we were both taking part in a race at Caserta in Italy. I had managed to finish the race for once and I was on my slowing-down lap when Piers came past on a wildly bumpy section of the track. I realised then what a natural talent he was. That was confirmed a year later when I saw him in the wet at Silverstone. He drove fantastically well. A good driver is always best in the wet and he had the most wonderful reactions. I could see he was very special.

I enjoyed that Motor Show 200 meeting because we had a good car and a chance of winning. I enjoyed it very much. To have someone like Piers in the car, I was very proud, no question about that. Very proud. By that time I must have been becoming a bit of a fan. He was one of us and we had grown up together, our little group. We all wanted to help him in some way or another. He was a lovable character. Certainly he persuaded me to do a Formula 2 programme, although I required no persuasion. I happened to have a Brabham Formula 2 car in stock, or one that a guy didn't want, so we decided to use that.

Piers hadn't acquitted himself well in his first season of Formula 1 in 1967. I was not actually a representative of Brabham but I travelled a great deal abroad and spoke German, French and Italian. In those days, England was the only place where blokes could get their racing cars; it truly was the core of it all. So they'd say, 'Frank, when you're back in England, could you get me four wheels for last year's Brabham?' I'd take a bit of profit. It was literally keeping clothes on my back. I became quite well known. If you want to buy a Brabham, new or used, try Frank. I always knew where I could find a car.

After the Motor Show 200, I made that my own racing team. There was no sponsorship; I was operating hand to mouth, selling as many cars as I could. It wasn't properly capitalised. The Brabham was an easy car to manage and Piers found it very driveable. I got some money from

Dunlop towards the operating costs – quite a few thousand pounds. I was surprised. Then I was offered money to send a car for Piers to the Tasman. I bought an ex-Brabham Formula 1 car from the previous year and Piers did very well out there.

None of this so far was premeditated; it just seemed to happen. I had a lovely Irish secretary, Norma Robb. She was straight to the point and worked very hard. She had a wonderful fighting spirit and it was a tragedy when she died young of cancer. We were sitting upstairs in my little office having lunch one day and Norma said, 'You know, Frank, you could have a Formula 1 car down there. Why don't you do Formula 1?' I didn't know what she was talking about. So Norma said in her Ulster accent, 'I'm only askin', Frank. Yew've got the car, yew've got the engine; why aren't yew doin' Formula 1?' That's how the Formula 1 idea was born; it was thanks to Norma Robb.

JONATHAN WILLIAMS

When I did that Formula 2 race at Monza for Frank, the team consisted of the car, Frank and a Kiwi mechanic called Johnny Muller. Both Frank and Johnny were meticulous. I have never sat in a car like it, before or since. I had been racing for Ferrari the year before and they were junk compared to this. I don't think Muller went to bed; he just guarded and worked on the car twenty-four hours a day! It was beautiful. Anything you wanted done, was done. To drive a car like that was a pleasure. It was an indication of Frank's commitment. He figured out earlier than most that if you polished the wheel rims, it wouldn't make the car go any faster but it would *look* fast. Frank has never fielded a tatty car.

Monza was very quick in the days before the chicanes; a real slip-streaming track which I knew pretty well. Frank was delighted with the win. But he was pretty mean. He gave me half the prize money and bought me dinner that night. That was it! I had to get myself there and pay all my expenses. But it was great fun. Even though Frank was now a team owner, he was no different to the Frank I had known for six years. He wasn't intense and he wasn't critical, particularly after I had a bad practice. But he knew I could win. It was a track I could drive with my eyes shut and it was a hell of a good car.

SHERIDAN THYNNE

There was a defining moment in 1968 that I remember long before I worked for Frank. I went to the Formula 2 race at Albi in France with Piers, who was driving Frank's Brabham. There was another Brabham in virtually the same colour and there was a long pit straight – you could see the cars coming from quite a long way. Frank thought it was necessary to separate, visually, Piers's car from the other dark blue car, so he said to get a white Fablon [stick-on] number 1 and put it on the end of the nose, in the middle, with a third of it tucked into the radiator duct so that we could see this white thing and be able to distinguish Frank's car from the other dark blue one.

So I went and got a number 1 and put it on. When I'd done that, I went to Frank and I was like a cocker spaniel with a wagging tail, waiting for someone to pat my head. Frank was talking to someone, but he saw the job had been done, walked across, bent down, looked at the car and said, 'It's not straight, Sherry. Can you take it off and put another one on?' That was a defining moment in terms of the standards Frank set. I remember that vividly. It implied commitment at every level, which is hugely important. Subsequently, if ever I was trying to wing something when working for Frank, I remembered that bloody 1 and thought, *I'd better do the job properly.*

VIRGINIA WILLIAMS

I can remember going round the back of Frank's place on Bath Road and finding racing cars and a small workshop there. It was very orderly and Frank had a very nice flat above which Sally Courage had decorated; that was very smart. It was a little house, almost the type of house a child paints with the door in the middle and two windows either side above and below with a garage area behind. You can still see it today.

HOWDEN GANLEY

I first got to know Frank in about August 1963. I was a mechanic for Gemini. Frank used to turn up at those Brands Hatch test sessions on Wednesdays with people like Jonathan Williams – we all thought to start off with that he was Jonathan's brother – and Charlie Crichton-Stuart. It seemed to me that Frank and I were the poorest people there. Our net worth was the clothes we stood up in. Little did either of us realise that just ten years later Frank would be a Formula 1 team owner and I would be his number-one driver. elligant

I remember driving the Gemini on the Nürburgring south circuit, and Frank turned up with Jonathan, acting as his mechanic. By the end of the first day of practice Frank had talked his way into some bloke's Lotus 20B, which the previous year had been the car to have. So Frank was in the race – he wasn't a mechanic any more. I remember thinking, *This guy's pretty persuasive.*

When I started off round Europe with my own Formula 3 car in 1967 I discovered that Frank had established himself quite a reputation. Wherever we went, people talked about his speed, his amazing overtaking manoeuvres and, from time to time, his crashes. I was expanding my gearbox rebuild business and in time found myself visiting the famous flat in Harrow Road, where in the words of Charlie Lucas 'Piers [Courage] kept his Merlyn in a pool of oil at the bottom of the garden.'

In late 1968 my gearbox business was expanding and Frank had taken the lease on 361 Bath Road. At one side was a former paint spray shop and I arranged to rent this from him. The business continued to grow and eventually, when Frank moved, I took over the lease on the entire premises, including the flat at the front. This had been very nicely decorated under the supervision of Sally Courage. When Frank moved out, he left me all the furniture, the artwork and even a large photograph of himself in the Formula 3 Cooper hanging on the wall. Many years later, I would return the photograph to him at Didcot.

FOUR

Fast Forward to Formula 1

Frank applied his immaculate methods to everything he did. Full-column adverts in *Autosport* were headed by a distinctive logo, 'Frank Williams' forming the shaft of a winged arrow. A typical advertisement would offer a variety of single-seater and sports racing cars, plus gearboxes and engines. At the end of 1968 a Brabham Formula 3 car would cost you £2,375; a telephone call to Burnham 4646 would ascertain that Frank was offering engines for between £695 and £900, a gearbox for £200. But these would become relatively minor amounts when Frank went into Grand Prix racing in 1969.

Frank had a good relationship with Dunlop and it did not take long to arrange a deal for the supply of tyres and £10,000. A further £2,000 would come from Castrol. This was typical funding at the time. Ken Tyrrell, who would win the World Championship with Jackie Stewart, had started his Formula 1 team at the beginning of 1968 with support from Dunlop and Ford. Apart from the Lotus team, which sported the garish red, white and gold colours of John Player Gold Leaf, commercial sponsorship rarely went beyond the usual trade suppliers, but, typically, Frank was alert to every possibility. When one of his mechanics, Bob Evans, mentioned that he had met a man who knew a man who might be interested in offering support, Frank followed it up and came into contact with Ted Ward, owner of T. W. Ward, a company in the machine-tool business. The connection with racing-car manufacture was obvious but it was Ted Ward's enthusiasm for motorsport that prompted him to support a Grand Prix team travelling and operating outside his UK marketplace. But Ward was no fool. He wanted a return for his company that went beyond having a small sticker on the windscreen of Courage's car. Ward brought important clients and friends to the races, thus boosting the image of the machine-tool business by association with a glamorous sport. Ted Ward would remain a staunch supporter of the team until his death in 1979, and through him Frank would become increasingly aware of the enormous potential of sponsorship. In the meantime, there was racing to be done on the far side of the world.

When Courage won the Tasman race at Teretonga in Invercargill – having scored two seconds, a third and a fourth in previous races – Frank felt he could safely head home to finalise Formula 1 plans while his small team moved on to the Australian sector. However, he was not pleased when Courage became involved in a number of on-track incidents that did not make pleasant reading at a time when Frank was trying to generate interest in his driver and their plans for the season ahead. Exactly a month after Courage dropped out of the final Tasman race with a broken driveshaft after just two laps, the Williams team made its debut.

Frank had chosen to miss the opening round of the championship in South Africa because it followed the Tasman Series too closely. These were more relaxed times, and the 1969 Formula 1 season was typical, the opening Grand Prix being followed by two non-championship races, both in Britain. It was the first of these, the Race of Champions at Brands Hatch, which saw the first appearance of a proper Formula 1 car entered by Frank Williams. And, as ever, thereby hung a tale of wheeling and dealing.

The Brabham BT24 used in the Tasman Series was all very well but Frank wanted the 1969 model, the BT26. Not surprisingly, Jack Brabham and his partner Ron Tauranac were reluctant to sell a BT26, the triple world champion concerned that Courage could become a thorn in his side. Besides, there was a contractual clash since Williams used Dunlop tyres and Brabham was under contract to Goodyear. Then Frank's contacts led to the discovery that Brabham had sold a BT26 to Charles Bridges, an enthusiast and part-time racer in the north of England, on the understanding that he would convert the car for Formula 5000, a domestic series that had nothing to do with Formula 1. Bridges, however, had changed his plans, no longer needed the car, and was persuaded to sell it, meaning Courage now had a competitive car for their first race. The one drawback was that the BT26 had been built around a Repco engine, as raced by Brabham. The conversion to accept a Ford-Cosworth by a couple of mechanics working flat out resulted in the new car arriving at Brands Hatch immaculate – but with virtually no running. It was no surprise when a succession of teething problems forced pit stops in the race to attend to a troublesome gear linkage and finally a fuel leak which brought early retirement.

The second non-championship race, the International Trophy at Silverstone, provided a more accurate indication of potential. Courage gave the works Brabhams a hard time and finished an excellent fifth despite losing fourth gear and sustaining scorched feet thanks to inadequate protection from the radiator mounted at the front of the car. Then, with four weeks to fill until their next Formula 1 outing – this time a Grand Prix proper in Spain – Courage and Williams went Formula 2 racing, Piers picking up a win in a heat at Thruxton. In Spain the promise of the International Trophy evaporated as the starter motor seized on the grid and Courage ended the race at Montjuich Park in the pits after nineteen laps. Next was Monte Carlo.

Frank, Piers and Sally travelled to the south of France in style, courtesy of their former landlord Charlie Crichton-Stuart. Following his marriage to the actress Shirley Ann Field, Charlie had abandoned racing and become the personal pilot for Hugh Fraser, who had just taken over the House of Fraser empire from his father, Lord Fraser of Allander. Crichton-Stuart had a free weekend and used it to ferry the best part of the Williams team to Nice using Fraser's Piper Comanche. It was a good start to a memorable weekend.

Courage qualified in ninth place, but after just four laps his immaculate blue Brabham was sixth and in a points-scoring position. (Points were awarded 9, 6, 4, 3, 2, 1 for the first six places.) A tussle with the works Brabham of Jacky Ickx became a battle for second place when three cars ahead dropped out in quick succession with mechanical trouble, a typical occurrence on this punishing street circuit. Then the Belgian retired with suspension failure after forty-eight laps. With thirty-two remaining and his driver not under pressure from behind, Frank signalled Courage to bring the car home rather than push too hard in pursuit of Graham Hill, twenty-three seconds ahead in the leading Lotus.

The final laps seemed to take an age, Frank scarcely able to believe it when Courage crossed the line and made his way to the podium to meet Prince Rainier and Princess Grace. This was only the second Grand Prix for the Williams team and a tribute to the skill of the driver and the preparation of his car. There was more to follow when Courage finished second again, this time in the United States Grand Prix, the final race of the season and also the richest. Piers earned $20,000 for Frank and the displeasure of Jack Brabham after keeping the works cars behind with the sort of tactics the wily and sometimes ruthless former champion had no right to complain about. Courage was growing up, as was the team.

It had been a very busy year, what with Formula 2 commitments between the Grands Prix. Piers had also won the F2 Mediterranean Grand Prix at Enna in Sicily, beating the cream of the driving establishment in a tough, slipstreaming battle on this very fast track. Courage's performance that day impressed Gianpaolo Dallara, the designer of the neat de Tomaso driven in the same race by Ickx. At the Italian Grand Prix at Monza, where Courage ran with the leading group until sidelined by a fuel problem, Frank had talked to Alessandro de Tomaso about building a car for Formula 1. De Tomaso saw Formula 1 as a way of promoting his exotic road cars, while Frank was tempted by the offer of Dallara's chassis, which was likely to be innovative and, more important, free of charge. In return, Frank would supply engines, the driver and the organisation. Frank was also influenced by the potential of de Tomaso's facilities near Modena, while the Argentinian was impressed when Courage, driving the de Tomaso Formula 2 car, claimed pole position and ran strongly in a race at Vallelunga, to the north of Rome. The deal was done: Williams would enter a de Tomaso powered by a Ford V8 in the 1970 F1 World Championship, and Courage, who had declined an offer from Ferrari, would drive it. The package seemed promising. The reality would be different.

FRANK WILLIAMS

I needed the latest Brabham, but where was I going to find one? Ron [Tauranac] wouldn't sell me one. Then I heard about the Bridges car. I remember leaving at about 5 a.m. on a very foggy morning and driving to Preston in Lancashire. It was a nice detached house in the middle of nowhere and all the rooms were full of racing-car bits. There was no carpet but the place was packed with engines, wheels and tyres. I'd heard about this before, and it was real. There were two Bridges brothers and I don't know which one I met. I paid £3,500 for the car. It was one of the best deals – certainly one of the most important – that I have ever done. I brought the car back and Robin Herd converted that chassis to accept the Ford-Cosworth. Ron wasn't very happy.

LADY SARAH ASPINALL

Frank had this Brabham and it was beautifully turned out. He had wonderful mechanics and everything worked because Piers was able to communicate with them and explain how the car felt. So you had this tiny team and they were absolutely in tune with each other. We had a wonderful year. We'd all go out to dinner together – with the other drivers and teams, I mean. In those days, no one was shut away in motor homes.

I would do my bit by timekeeping but I'm not sure Frank really trusted my lap times. I'd be chatting to Nina [Rindt] and miss the car going by. I'd see what Nina noted down for Jochen and put something similar, sometimes a bit better, for Piers. I don't think it fooled Frank for a minute!

Finishing second at Monaco was wonderful, but we did have trouble getting Piers out of the car. He used to suffer from cramp really badly. He would go rigid and for fifteen minutes we had to put hot water on his legs so that he could get out of the car.

MIKE DOODSON

At the launch of one of BAR's ill-fated Formula 1 devices in 2000 there were more smiling cuties to sign us in than the total payroll at the Tyrrell team in 1969. One of these ladies stopped me to ask a few questions, one of which was to name the best car launch I had ever attended. Having ransacked my memory, I came up with Williams at Silverstone at the beginning of 1969.

She seemed puzzled. 'How many people were there?' she asked.

'Three,' I said: 'Frank Williams, Johnny Muller [his mechanic] and me.'

Because I am partial to a scoop, I had picked a car launch at which I was the only pressman present. Actually I cheated a bit because this appearance at Silverstone was not an official occasion but a test run about which Frank had tipped me off by phoning me at *Motoring News* the previous day. There were still a few things for Johnny to check before Piers arrived for his first run in the car later that afternoon, so Frank invited me to lunch. We found our way to a local pub, where we scoffed a couple of pies. He was extremely smug about the BT26. Ron Tauranac had sold it to Bridges on the understanding that it would be fitted with a Chevy V8 for use in Formula 5000 but had failed to get Bridges to sign anything. It was in fact identical to the works Formula 1 cars to be raced by Jack Brabham and Jacky Ickx in 1969. Jack was understandably furious.

Our lunch didn't take long. There was an awkward moment when the bill arrived, because it became instantly apparent that only one of us had any money (and it wasn't Frank). And that is the story of how your correspondent not only had an important exclusive on the story of Frank Williams's first foray into Formula 1 racing but also ended up footing the bill for sponsoring the launch of the whole project.

SIR JACKIE STEWART

At Silverstone in 1964 I had a Mini for a road car and I ran out of petrol. I was walking along with a can, and who comes along but Frank Williams. He stops, seems to know who I am, which in itself was quite unusual because I hadn't done much at that time. He takes me to the petrol station, I fill my one-gallon can and he brings me back to the car. Of course, he has since turned it around to 'Typical bloody Scotsman, typical Stewart, running out of petrol.'

That was probably my first meeting with Frank. He was selling and buying bits for cars. I never did really know him until he began to enter Piers. Frank carried his clothes well; it didn't matter what he was wearing. He paid attention to how he looked. Eventually we had the same tailor, Doug Hayward. Frank always wore a very smart sports jacket, nicely cut from very good material. Of course, he was in very good shape because of his running. His athletic skills were substantial. I think one of the reasons we've still got Frank today is that he has such an amazing heart with a very low pulse rate, so with all the troubles he's gone through and endured, that old heart is still pumping along.

ROBS LAMPLOUGH

In the early days I raced a Mini Cooper and Frank had an Austin A40. It had a rusty top – I think because he had flipped it somewhere and it had grazed all the paint off and he never bothered to repaint it. He was fast but a bit wild. He seemed to draw a blank when it came to braking distances.

Frank had this ability to be very interested in everybody and an incredible memory. He could recall who'd done what, in what car. He knew which car you'd got; he knew the name of your brother; he knew the name of your mother. He had an incredible ability to assemble and retain information.

When he had the flat in Harrow Road, it's probably unprintable some of the things that went on up there. But it was, let's say, a gathering place for like-minded and enthusiastic young drivers. Frank started making money by having what he called his Volksy transporter, which was a flat-bed Volkswagen. By this stage we'd moved on to Formula 3. I had the Robert Lamplough Racing Organisation and I operated out of Adam and Eve Mews in London W8. Frank used to come down a lot and most nights he could be found in a club on the Cromwell Road, I think it was called the Cromwellian.

He never drank, he never smoked; he was a fitness freak and his big interest was to make money. At the beginning of the season he would order new Brabhams, which were the best cars in those days. The Italians were his main market and on occasions he used to put the Volkswagen on Silver City Airways and fly cars to Basle from Southend. We both sold and dealt in cars and he and I on occasions bought cars together. I can think of a Lotus 32 from a fellow called Jack Maglia, and that had a Cosworth engine. Frank sold the chassis and I took the engine and gearbox, which I used in my F2 car, so we split the deal.

The other thing he did in those days was drive a left-hand-drive Porsche. There were no restrictions on the main roads – there were very few motorways. If you were the chosen one to go in the Porsche with him on a trip, it was flat out. You were put in the suicide seat on the outside. I remember one or two trips with Frank and ending up virtually under the dashboard, which was instinctive to survive the trip.

Cleanliness became the thing. His clothes had to be immaculate; his cars had to be immaculate, and everything he supplied had to be the same. He never liked dealing in anything that was messy. We would meet in the Kings Road and have a meal and discuss trends – who was selling who what. I remember him buying engines and things from me. He was wheeling and dealing right up until the '70s. I remember him being very short of money.

FIVE

End of a Dream

In 1970 Frank reckoned his season with de Tomaso was going to cost £61,000, money he did not have. True, there would be support from Dunlop and Ted Ward, but it was down to Frank to pay his driver, supply engines, gearboxes and mechanics and ship the lot to thirteen races, from South Africa to Mexico. Alessandro de Tomaso had cut himself a good deal by simply supplying a chassis that would carry his name around the globe. That said, de Tomaso had his own problems. The build programme for the Formula 1 car coincided with the debut of his prototype Pantera road car at the New York Motor Show, the biggest in the United States. Meanwhile, de Tomaso had a mere four months in which to build his Formula 1 car.

With time short and Formula 1 experience non-existent, de Tomaso and Dallara took more than a passing interest in the Brabham raced by Frank in 1969. When their Formula 1 car, dubbed the 505, was revealed for the first time outside the factory in Modena, its still unpainted aluminium chassis revealed high-quality de Tomaso workmanship, but it was no coincidence that the suspension and many other parts of the car resembled the BT26. The de Tomaso was also seriously overweight, a major failing that led to handling difficulties and brake problems. The launch took place on 13 February. It was a Friday.

The first Grand Prix, at Kyalami in South Africa, was just three weeks away. It was immediately apparent that Frank and Piers had a struggle on their hands. Courage qualified twentieth in a field of twenty-three, the problems for the Williams–de Tomaso package exacerbated by events at the front of the grid.

South Africa marked the debut of another Formula 1 car, the March-Ford. Like de Tomaso, March had designed a chassis and bolted a Ford-Cosworth engine on to it. The March was not a great car but achieved pole position with another alongside, and it was faster than the de Tomaso to the tune of an embarrassing 2.7 seconds. Courage's misery ended when he locked a brake and hit a kerb to bring retirement after thirty-nine of the eighty laps. He had run no higher than fifteenth. Jack Brabham won, and the March driven by Jackie Stewart finished third. The only good news for Frank was the six-week break until the next race in Spain.

De Tomaso put the time to good use and arrived at Jarama with a modified car. The 505 may have been far from perfect, but the improvements were enough to have Courage set the thirteenth-fastest time. However, he crashed after the skittish car got away from him, the damage to the chassis being so severe that taking part in the race was out of the question.

All was made good in time for Monaco, a race that assumed even greater importance for de Tomaso when he learned that Lee Iacocca, the charismatic head of Ford, would be making a rare appearance at a Grand Prix. With Piers qualifying an excellent ninth, de Tomaso vainly tried to persuade Frank to start the car with less fuel (there were no planned pit stops in those days) and put on a show during the early laps. Clearly he did not understand Frank Williams. Courage had started from the same grid position prior to finishing second twelve months before but everyone knew that the chance of a repeat was slim. Piers worked his way into seventh place before a steering problem meant a lengthy pit stop for repairs.

Their problems were put in perspective a few weeks later when Bruce McLaren was killed while testing his CanAm sports car at Goodwood. McLaren, like Jim Clark, was seen as a safe pair of hands. He was also an immensely likeable man and his loss was keenly felt by Frank and Piers.

With the perils of the sport foremost in everyone's minds, a few days later the Formula 1 teams assembled at Spa-Francorchamps, one of the fastest and arguably most dangerous circuits of them all. The eight miles of public roads used for this track in the Belgian Ardennes meant that a mechanical failure at a lap average of 150 mph could result in a very serious accident. This was a time when safety was only beginning to be taken seriously by certain sections of the motor racing fraternity thanks to the pioneering efforts of Jackie Stewart. To everyone's relief, the Belgian Grand Prix passed off without serious incident, Courage retiring with oil pressure problems after running in ninth place with a car now affectionately known by the British as the Tomato.

The fifth round of the 1970 championship was scheduled for 21 June at Zandvoort in Holland, a popular venue located just outside the seaside town of Haarlem, a short train ride from Amsterdam. The track was fast and challenging, and the surrounding dunes provided perfect vantage points for spectators, many of whom made the short hop across from Britain. De Tomaso had continued to modify and improve the car, Courage qualifying in ninth place, 1.8 seconds off the pole position Lotus driven by his close friend Jochen Rindt. This was progress compared to the start of a season that was now approaching its halfway stage. With not a single classified finish, never mind a championship point to his name, the pressure was building on Courage to produce a result.

Sally Courage set up a folding chair on the roof of the pits with other drivers' wives and girlfriends keeping lap charts for their respective teams. Sally's chart shows Piers holding seventh place for the first four laps before being overtaken by the Matra of Jean-Pierre Beltoise. Courage regained the position on lap twelve when he passed the Lotus of Rindt's teammate John Miles, and set off after the Ferrari driven by Clay Regazzoni. The Swiss driver would win the first Grand Prix for

Williams nine years later, but on this grey overcast day Regazzoni was making his Formula 1 debut. Sally's chart shows Regazzoni in sixth place ahead of Piers and Miles as they completed lap 22 and then stops halfway through the next lap after recording the passing of Regazzoni and the Lotus. Piers was missing.

There was no immediate reason for the disappearance of the car and then a sickening clue as a column of dense black smoke appeared from the sand dunes to the left of the pits.

Having broken free of the midfield group, Courage had been pushing on through the fast sweeps on the back section of the track. The de Tomaso ran wide, possibly unsettled by a bump, crashed into a bank at 140 mph, hit a fence post and overturned. The car caught fire immediately. What firefighting equipment there was proved inadequate as the magnesium alloy used in parts of the chassis was highly inflammable and increased the intensity of the inferno. Piers was trapped in the cockpit but was probably already dead, killed instantly when the impact ripped off the front suspension and catapulted a wheel into the cockpit with such force that Courage's crash helmet had been ripped off.

SHERIDAN THYNNE

I remember that Piers was never, even from the first race, downhearted about the Tomato. He was sure it was going to come good. They were confident they were going to get on top of it. He did say that they were close to moving up a level, and then of course it would be down to him to prove that it was a different level altogether.

PATRICK MCNALLY
(writing as Grand Prix correspondent for *Autosport* in 1970)

Success never changed Piers. I dined recently with him and Jonathan Williams and the conversation between these two was exactly the same as it might have been four years before in a London bistro. His background made some people feel he was a cut above them but he never showed the slightest snobbish tendency and was just as much at home eating in a pub with the boys as he was dining at the Savoy. When we heard of plans to run Formula 1 with Frank Williams there were a good many cynics who reckoned that this had to be a failure. But that was far from the case, for his rapport with Frank made for miracles.

SIR JACKIE STEWART

Frank was very distant from everything going on after the accident; he was enormously affected by it. There had to be an accident report and the police wanted me to help them the following day. Louis Stanley [head of the BRM team and a leading light in Formula 1 at the time] and I drove out to the circuit to reconstruct the accident. Frank did come with us. The crash had set off a complete bank of grass and it was still smouldering in places. There was a horrible, tragic smell in the area and it was absolutely quiet. Only the wind coming off the sea, rustling the dune grass, and the three of us there on that empty road.

The intensity of the fire was overwhelming, so much so that the crews didn't have enough foam to extinguish it and finally had to cover the entire car with a tarpaulin and then bury it in the sand, just to cover it, with Piers still inside. It wasn't until well after the race that they finally got him out and even then, when they took the tarpaulin off, air got in and the fire started again. Both the chassis and the engine were melted.

When you think of what went on then, it illustrates that only professionals should be running sport. There were no professionals then. The errors made and the oversights that occurred were just pathetic. The race wasn't stopped and the fire extinguishers wouldn't put the fire out because it was so intense. The fire went on for lap after lap after lap. I knew it was Piers because his helmet was in the road. But you didn't know whether he was out of the car; you couldn't see anything because of the smoke.

Later the police wanted to know what we planned to do with the wreck. I thought about a scrapyard but then realised people might take bits of it for souvenirs and that sort of thing, so I knew this was out of the question. Frank just said, 'Get rid of it. I don't ever want to see it again. Get it away.'

The funeral was in a small country church in Essex. The organist wasn't very good and the choir was composed of ladies from the village, yet it couldn't be any other way. For Piers, the son of English aristocracy, it had to be in a place where dignity would prevail without public grandeur.

Frank, in times of crisis or pressure, is still the same today as he was then. There was very little reaction physically. If you say to Frank, 'Such and such has happened,' he's not very talkative. In those days the same sort of thing was true. Sally was in a terrible state, and that affected Frank because he thought a lot about Sally. It was his car. Did it break down? Was it a good car? Was it a mechanical failure? All these things go on for every entrant, every designer and every mechanic.

FRANK WILLIAMS

The de Tomaso looked to be a way forward at the beginning of 1970. Suddenly, Piers was dead and de Tomaso lost all interest. Any chance of winning went out the door with a guy as good as Piers. Everybody you've ever heard of in motor racing turned out for the funeral. Nobody ducked it. And there were plenty of red eyes from the hard guys, I can tell you. It was a very moving event. I was heartbroken. I worshipped the guy. He was totally adorable.

Should I have stopped? I don't think I ever properly considered that. I don't remember thinking, *Should I? Shouldn't I?* The question was *how* could I do it? How could I continue? That's all. I was robbing Peter to pay Paul, just keep going somehow.

I tried very hard to get Emerson [Fittipaldi] but [Colin] Chapman beat me to it. That would have perked up the Tomato.

LADY SARAH ASPINALL

Piers was offered a drive by Ferrari. He thought about it. The money was good and it was Ferrari. It was nice to be asked. But there was never any doubt that he would stay with Frank. They could communicate so well. Frank adored him and Piers adored Frank.

The de Tomaso was disappointing. The car was absolutely hopeless. It was really sad. But yet Frank and Piers felt that maybe with a lot of work it could come right; that was the attitude they had.

After Zandvoort, Frank was distraught, devastated. We somehow got home and stayed with my sister and she said that Frank wouldn't leave the house. He was downstairs, lying on the sofa, where he slept. This was just after Bruce had been killed, and then of course there was Jochen's accident a couple of months later. Piers and Jochen were very close and those two deaths really affected that little group. But I knew that Frank would go on because it's what makes him tick. Frank has this total belief in himself, that he will overcome whatever is thrown at him in order to achieve his aim – to the point of almost manic selfishness, in a way. I don't mean that in a derogatory sense. He has a core of steel but he is also very sensitive. Piers would have been *horrified* if Frank had given up.

SIX

The Way You Smile

Virginia Berry had gone to public school before completing her education in Switzerland and Monte Carlo. The last thing she or her parents expected was for her to fall in love with a racing-car salesman running a shoestring operation next door to a pub. This was in 1967, not long after Frank had set up shop at 361 Bath Road. Ginny was engaged to a wealthy amateur driver whose biggest mistake was to have Frank Williams look after his racing car. She fell for his smile on first acquaintance. Despite realising that Frank exercised his considerable charm on almost every woman he met, Ginny's feelings intensified each time she saw him, although encounters at British racetracks became less frequent as Frank's Formula 2 campaign got into its stride, followed by even more time-consuming commitments to Formula 1 in 1969 and 1970. When Courage was killed at Zandvoort, Ginny knew enough about Frank and his relationship with Piers to wonder what he would do next. The answer was not long in coming.

Following events in the newspapers, Virginia discovered that after missing just one race Williams had entered the British Grand Prix at Brands Hatch. The replacement de Tomaso would be driven by Brian Redman, a seasoned campaigner who could be relied on to do a solid job. However, a stub axle broke during practice, ruling Redman out of the race, and when he failed to qualify for the German Grand Prix at

Hockenheim, the team seemed to have lost its impetus. Redman took what would be temporary retirement in South Africa, the deaths in recent months having sapped his motivation. For the next Grand Prix, in Austria, Frank took the sort of gamble that would characterise much of his future decision-making by giving an opportunity to a less-experienced driver. Tim Schenken was twenty-six, no youth by today's standards, but seen as a young charger in 1970 with impressive results in the junior formulae. It was just as much a risk for the Australian, who failed to finish any of his four races thanks to mechanical problems. But he had done enough to earn a place with Brabham for 1971.

Frank's 1970 season ended when the organisers of the final race in Mexico decided to pay travel expenses for just eighteen cars, the de Tomaso not among them. The Zandvoort tragedy had also destroyed Alessandro de Tomaso's enthusiasm. The sole surviving red car was eventually returned to Italy. What next? The one certainty was that Frank would continue. A stocktake revealed two engines, a transporter and sundry equipment. Considerable debts did not deter the search for a suitable chassis to take the Ford-Cosworth V8s, and, typically, Frank had a plan, which he revealed over Christmas lunch with Virginia, who had now become Mrs Charles Sawyer-Hoare.

Despite Ginny's feelings for Frank, she had been committed to a society wedding and lacked the confidence to cancel it. Subsequently, Ginny had answered the telephone one day when Frank called to speak to Charles about his Formula 3 car, and discovered that Frank would be at a loose end over Christmas. Ginny asked him to lunch and Frank accepted with alacrity. It had become a regular date and here they were, in December 1970, discussing the year ahead.

Frank explained that he had been able to attract enough funding to approach March Engineering and buy not just a Formula 1 chassis but also a couple of Formula 2 cars. The clincher had been the signing of Henri Pescarolo as driver. The Frenchman could be fast but was more often erratic, but he had useful contacts with Motul Oil, a French company keen to use motorsport for advertising which saw the

European Formula 2 Championship as a perfect showplace. It did not take much to persuade Motul that it would also be a good idea to have a presence in Formula 1. Pescarolo and Englishman Derek Bell would race for Frank in Formula 2, Henri also being entrusted with the Formula 1 March. Pescarolo won the opening race of the F2 season at Mallory Park in March 1971. It was a freezing cold day at the Leicestershire circuit, a suitable omen for a campaign upon which the sun would refuse to shine.

The Mallory Park result prompted Carlos Pace, a young and promising Brazilian driver, to ask Frank if he could run a third Formula 2 car with support from a Portuguese-Brazilian bank. Frank being Frank, he agreed. The deal helped to settle the debts incurred the previous year but did nothing for the competitiveness of the overstretched team in the current season. The low point came in September when all three cars failed to qualify for a race in France, a disaster that did not sit well with Motul on their home ground. It also exacerbated a dismal Formula 1 effort on the point of collapse.

The March 711 was tricky, so much so that not even the outrageous talent of Ronnie Peterson in the works car could coax a victory, the Swede having to be satisfied with a handful of podium finishes. Pescarolo managed to qualify tenth on two occasions, which was as good as it got during practice. He took fourth place, one lap behind winner Jackie Stewart, at the British Grand Prix and struggled into sixth place in Austria. Otherwise, the absence of points highlighted the lack of technical leadership within Frank's small team. Not that you would have noticed, talking to Frank.

Accepting that he had bitten off more than he could chew in 1971, Frank resolved to focus solely on Formula 1 and then jumped from the frying pan into the fire by deciding to build his own car rather than buy off the shelf. His plans got off to a flying start when the Italian model car company Politoys offered £40,000 towards the project on the understanding that the car would carry their name. The chassis would be conceived by design engineer Len Bailey and made in Woking by

Maurice Gomm, highly regarded for his work in sheet metal. Power would be supplied by the ubiquitous Ford-Cosworth V8.

If Frank thought he was done with March Engineering, then delays in the build programme for the Politoys meant he had to return to the Oxfordshire company for something to start the 1972 season. Unable to afford the £15,000 required for the latest March chassis, Frank had March build a car around a 711 left over from the previous year. Pescarolo would drive this with support worth £40,000 from Motul. A further £10,000 would come from Pace in return for making his Formula 1 debut in Frank's March 711 from 1971. Ted Ward would continue to show his loyalty to the tune of around £15,000. Frank's budget of just over £100,000 would have to cover the manufacture of the car, purchase of engine and transmission and the running and travel costs associated with twelve Grands Prix.

Another small step in the right direction was vacating the now hopelessly inadequate Bath Road premises which had served Frank so well. On 2 February 1972 Frank Williams (Racing Cars) Ltd moved into a 5,000-square-foot industrial unit in Bennet Road, Reading. The move came between the first race of the season in Argentina and the second in South Africa. Pescarolo had finished eighth in Buenos Aires. It would turn out to be his best result of the season.

The Politoys was not merely late; it was almost not worth having. The debut of the new car came at Brands Hatch in July, seven races into the season. Pescarolo qualified the Team Williams Motul entry on the penultimate row of the grid, ran no higher than twenty-second and destroyed the car against one of the substantial grass banks that char-acterised the Kent circuit. With that investment written off in less than half an hour of racing, Pescarolo seemed determined to destroy the remainder of Frank's assets through a series of accidents in subsequent races with the March. Pace, on the other hand, had scored points in two of his first four Grands Prix. Frank's two-year investment in the youngster seemed to be the one redeeming feature of 1972 until the Brazilian took himself off to the Surtees team for 1973. Future Williams drivers would find negotiations with Frank a daunting experience. For now, though, Frank was left with wrecked cars, no drivers and even more debt.

In the meantime Virginia had given in to the inevitable. Frank's flirting had moved a couple of paces beyond eye contact and chat, and Ginny was hopelessly in love even though the sentiment was not being openly reciprocated. Determined to get her man, Ginny moved into a rented flat in Chelsea, while Frank, having lost the accommodation above the workshop on Bath Road, spent his time in England living with the divorced Charlie Crichton-Stuart and his new girlfriend.

VIRGINIA WILLIAMS
(from *A Different Kind of Life*)

The first time I saw Frank Williams, I fell in love with him. Totally. Utterly. Hopelessly. I knew instantly that I wanted him to be the man in my life. Since I was already engaged to be married, this was rather inconvenient.

I was twenty-one years old. My fiancé Charles, who was trying to make it as a racing driver, had taken me to look at his new 'toy', a Formula 3 Titan which was being stabled at a garage in Bath Road. When a smartly dressed, dark-haired man appeared from behind a car in the garage and introduced himself as Frank Williams, he flashed me a private, meaningful and very wicked smile.

I still find it hard to understand why I fell so instantaneously for Frank. He was not tall, dark and handsome. He stood only five foot eight inches high and even in 1967 his hairline was receding rapidly. There was no obvious reason for me to go weak at the knees, which only made it more disturbing. If I'd been looking at Steve McQueen it would have been understandable. But I couldn't get him out of my mind.

FRANK WILLIAMS

Even with Piers it was still very hard because Formula 1 wasn't the attractive item it is today. There was a niche group of people if you like, dirty lunatics with dirty fingers; some people thought we were all mad men. But the next two years after Piers was killed were very, very tough, all hand to mouth. I'd find myself thinking, *Oh God, if I pay for this, how can I pay the mechanics?* Pescarolo didn't help with all those shunts. He had six in a row at one time. Six in a row! I was naïve in those days. I should have said, 'Henri, you're not cut out for this, now fuck off. I'll keep the sponsorship money from Motul.' The Politoys was a baptism of fire.

TIM SCHENKEN

Looking back, I recall Frank as incredibly enthusiastic. He was totally dedicated to succeeding but he had a complete lack of technical knowledge. As a result he was totally reliant on his mechanics at the time – and there were only two of them. When I moved on to Brabham the following year, it was a complete contrast because the guy who designed the cars, Ron Tauranac, was extremely competent technically. Frank's skills were finding the money and putting the programme on the road. I don't think anything could have stopped Frank's determination to succeed. Not even the loss of Piers Courage. In fact I suspect he might have been spurred on by that in a strange sort of way. Certainly he never talked about giving up.

VIV ORRISS

I worked on reception at the British Airways Executive Lounge. Frank was a regular customer flying back and forth to Italy. Everyone adored him. We would get a call from the girl at check-in: 'Frank's on his way,' she would say, and that would have girls dashing to check their hair and make-up. I worked in the lounge for four years and generally you don't remember one passenger from the next. But the two I remember clearly are Frank and David Niven. They were undoubtedly the most charming passengers at the time.

Frank always treated you like an old friend. He always remembered what you had been talking about the last time he came through. I was learning to fly at the time and he was fascinated by flying. If it was quiet and I was on my own, we would sit and chat.

There were no upgrades in those days because there was only First Class and Economy, and the divide between the two was huge. But we helped Frank with his flights, even when we weren't supposed to. He would say, 'I'm booked on the ten o'clock but I really need to be on the nine o'clock. Unfortunately, it's full.' He wouldn't make a fuss or anything like that. But he was so nice about it and he always managed to get his way. He would always look you straight in the eye. But it was his smile which made you melt. It was devastating.

MIKE DOODSON

Back when my overdraft as a journalist was less alarming than his, Frank and I would constantly swap gossip by phone. During one period when the bailiffs were particularly active he actually conducted business from a call box, inspiring an episode of *Minder* in which Arthur Daley was similarly down on his luck. Strangely, when he informed me towards the end of 1971 that he was building a Formula 1 car, Frank's major preoccupation wasn't the money but what name to give it. To call it a Williams, he insisted, would be outrageously pretentious. 'Ken Tyrrell can put his name on his cars because he has achieved so much,' he said. 'I will never be as good as that, so come on, Doods, what are we going to call it?' My suggestion was Wanker-Ford, a moniker our hero had earned for his hapless management and mounting indebtedness.

ALAN HENRY

March 1971, the paddock at Mallory Park. Ignore the fact that there's an unknown Austrian kid called Niki Lauda in one of the works March entries. I'm quaking in my boots as Mike Doodson, who I am just about to succeed as Formula 2 correspondent of *Motoring News*, prepares to introduce me to Frank Williams. For some reason I'm just terrified. Forget Colin Chapman or Ken Tyrrell; I could deal with them. But Frank was the one I was really overawed by. There was a crisply polite yet slightly distant formality about him that I took years to penetrate. Later that same year we were at Mantorp Park in Sweden for a Formula 2 international and Frank buttonholed me in the paddock. 'I expect you'll be coming in early on race day, so if you have a rental car, perhaps I could ride with you,' he said. I was planning on a late start, but I was so terrified that FW might shop me to Dood that I tumbled out of bed early. Only later did the penny drop. FW's team hardly had a pot to piss in, let alone the budget for hire cars. It was an instructive lesson on how confidence is the most important asset in the motor-racing business.

SEVEN

Close to the Edge

Entries for the 1973 Formula 1 World Championship included two Brabhams – for Carlos Reutemann and Wilson Fittipaldi, brother of reigning world champion Emerson. Reutemann would eventually drive for Williams, but for the moment Frank was more interested in the activities of Reutemann's employer, a certain Bernard Charles Ecclestone. Bernie had bought Brabham in 1971, giving him hands-on experience running a Formula 1 team and revealing to the shrewd former motorcycle and car salesman how he could make money for racing teams – and himself.

Ecclestone could see that the teams were laying themselves open to financial abuse by negotiating individually with each race organiser for starting and prize money. The likes of Ferrari usually received preferential terms, and if they were not happy might not turn up, particularly if their season was going badly and championship points were no longer a priority. This was clearly unsatisfactory for all concerned. Ecclestone argued for collective bargaining and the elimination of starting and prize money. In return for an agreed fee, organisers would be guaranteed a set number of cars for their race. Thus the Formula 1 Constructors' Association (F1CA), later the Formula One Constructors' Association (FOCA), was born and everyone was set to become richer.

But for now Frank Williams continued to dislike bank managers and their wholly unreasonable demand that their clients bank with them rather than the other way round. His situation was not helped by the fact that it had been agreed to subsidise travel and freight facilities for races outside Europe – but only for teams manufacturing their own cars. Purchasing another March was therefore out of the question and Frank had to resurrect what was left of the Politoys. The car was just about repairable and acquired a new identity thanks to support from Marlboro cigarettes and Iso-Rivolta, an Italian manufacturer of sports cars. The Iso-Marlboro would also continue to receive (reduced) support from Politoys and be driven by Nanni Galli, an Italian who promised money in return for being able to finally establish his name in Formula 1 after an inauspicious start with March and the small Italian team Tecno. Galli would last five races – best result ninth in Brazil – before Frank had to accept that his promised money might be as doubtful. Even worse, Iso-Rivolta was sliding towards bankruptcy. Had it not been for the money from Marlboro, the Williams operation would not simply have ground to a halt; it would have disappeared without trace.

This was the beginning of what would be a long and fruitful association between Marlboro and Formula 1, but it got off to a shaky start. Marlboro's sponsorship of BRM had been announced with much fanfare but the once-great British team was in rapid decline. Williams may have been the second string to Marlboro's bow but it was a lifeline for Frank as he struggled to build new cars with crash structures, as required by the regulations, in order to give added protection to driver and fuel tanks. Frank was happy to accept Marlboro's nominated drivers. Howden Ganley provided the mainstay as other drivers came and went, the New Zealander finishing sixth and scoring a championship point in Canada. Dutchman Gijs van Lennep scored another point in his home Grand Prix. And that was it for 1973.

Frank's financial position was now even more parlous, and it would get worse. In 1974 Marlboro's continuing support brought with it the demand to replace Ganley with Arturo Merzario. The diminutive

Italian, who enjoyed an addiction to his sponsor's products, possessed what appeared to be an impressive pedigree thanks to making his Formula 1 debut with Ferrari in 1972 and also taking part in a successful season of sports car racing for the Italian team. But fame, such as it was, appeared to have gone to his head. Merzario failed to adjust to moving from the wealthy Ferrari to Frank, who frequently had to borrow the wherewithal to get his motor out of the airport car park when he returned from a race abroad. When Frank arrived back at Heathrow after the first Grand Prix in Argentina in 1974, paying the car park fee was the least of his worries as he contemplated not one but two engine failures caused by Merzario believing the Ford-Cosworth V8 was as free-revving as the twelve-cylinder Ferrari engines he had treated with ferocious Italian abandon.

All was forgiven when Merzario produced a minor miracle by qualifying third for the South African Grand Prix and backed that up with sixth place and a championship point. But it was then mostly downhill as the Iso-Marlboro slipped towards the back of the grid, although Merzario bounced back at his home Grand Prix to finish an excellent fourth at Monza. That was 1974: four points, a mountain of debt and no obvious sign of improvement for the following season.

Marlboro, now heavily committed to McLaren and their champion Emerson Fittipaldi, reduced their backing and added to Frank's difficulties following the inevitable disappearance of Iso Rivolta. The car would now be called a Williams and there was just about enough money from Marlboro and continuing support from the ever-faithful Ted Ward to buy two engines. Merzario, who remained on board for a second season, was joined by the similarly diminutive Jacques Laffite, persuaded by Frank to make his Grand Prix debut. A leading light in European Formula 2, the Frenchman clearly had promise and also backing – from a Swiss company named Ambrozium. Laffite rose to the challenge, but Merzario's enthusiasm seemed to go in the opposite direction. Meanwhile, Frank's attention was focused on an expensive run of engine failures. By mid-season Williams had just one engine and no money for a replacement. When Laffite – Merzario having quit the team six weeks before – retired from the British Grand Prix with a broken gearbox in July, Williams was in dire straits with four more races to go.

The next was on the Nürburgring north circuit. If the Williams had failed to make the finish at the flat and relatively smooth Silverstone circuit, then it would be lucky to complete a single fourteen-mile lap of this twisting, plunging leviathan in Germany. Frank did not hold out a lot of hope, not even when Laffite earned a respectable position in the middle of the grid. However, as the laps ticked slowly by, the Williams not only kept going but gradually moved up the order as others fell victim to the punishing circuit through accidents, punctures or mechanical failure. As he started his fourteenth and final lap Laffite was a minute and a half behind the leading Brabham of Carlos Reutemann, but he was second, more than a mile ahead of Niki Lauda, the driver who would go on to win the 1975 championship for Ferrari. Frank could hardly believe it. But it would be at least seven minutes before he saw his car again. There was nothing for it but to wait. In 1975 there was no way of following a driver, except for occasional bursts of commentary as his car passed landmarks such as Adenau Bridge and the Karussel.

The relief can be imagined when the green and white car finally appeared. A Williams-entered driver was back on the podium for the first time since 1969. More to the point, Frank had won £5,500 in prize money and scored six points, enough to guarantee the all-important FOCA travel subsidies which would be worth £150,000 in 1976. But first he had to get to the end of 1975. The money earned that afternoon would not touch the sides of Frank's bank account as the car received urgently needed bits and pieces to keep it running. Creditors, of which there were a few, would have to wait.

Laffite retired from the next two races, and a succession of rent-a-drivers with financial backing fared little better in the second car. The final race at Watkins Glen, scene of Courage's brilliant second place in 1969, at least held the promise of a decent financial award if Laffite could pull off another finish in the points. However, money would be the topic of conversation at the beautiful New York State circuit for all the wrong reasons.

Frank cringed when Lella Lombardi, driving the second car, raced past the pits during practice with the engine sounding dreadful. The Italian woman's mechanical knowledge did not stretch to noticing that a valve spring had broken. Or perhaps she felt her sponsor's cheque for £10,000 covered such eventualities. Frank and his mechanics knew the truth from the moment they heard the Cosworth V8. But with no pit-to-car radio at the time, there was no way of notifying the driver. By the time she reappeared to see an arrow on the pit board urgently requesting a stop, the damage had been done. The valve in question had made contact with the piston and ripped the engine apart. The rebuild would cost over £9,000 and there was no replacement to allow Lombardi to race. Jacques Laffite may only have managed twenty-first on the grid, but at least he was in the race. Or so Frank thought.

On race morning Jacques was cleaning his helmet visor when he asked his wife Bernadette to put Optrex drops in his eyes, routine before a race. Bernadette mistakenly picked up the visor cleaning fluid and seconds later Jacques was in agony. He was rushed to hospital, where fortunately it was discovered that his eyes had not been damaged, but there was no question of him starting the race. A suggestion that Lombardi take over came to nothing when she could not fit in the cockpit. It was not that Lella was too big, merely that Laffite was incredibly slim. With no cars in the season's richest race, Frank's luck had run out. As had what little money he had left.

VIRGINIA WILLIAMS

I knew what he was like. Frank was always borrowing money, and from me too. I had a little bit of money thanks to my grandfather. During the Second World War he was quite ill and confined to bed with something chronic. He had a house in Newman Street [just off London's Oxford

Street]. He was an inventor. The house was known as Touchbutton House and it could be extremely annoying because no one could get through a door without pressing a button. The maid used to come in and light the fire every morning. He thought that this poor girl shouldn't have to come in and do that, so he began to tinker around with the idea of making a fake fire with red paper. This was called the Berry Magicoal Fire, which he patented. It was a terrible thing when you look at it now, but at the time everyone aspired to one.

My father took over the business because his older brother was killed in the war. So I had a certain amount of money, but most of it went Frank's way. Of course, my father wanted us to be sensible and I didn't tell him where most of my money was going. But I think he had a fairly good idea.

FRANK WILLIAMS

Iso forgot to pay after the first 5,000 lire. They got loads of publicity and I got loads more debt. But Marlboro always paid, thank God. They kept me in business and it was thanks to a guy called Barry Boardman, who pointed Marlboro my way.

BARRY BOARDMAN

I was a motor racing fan and an ex-racer from the 1964/5 era. Frank came up to town on frequent occasions and we all went out to dinner; that's how I got to know him. Sponsors would come across from South America and have dinner with us in that famous restaurant with the big clock face at World's End. It sort of expanded from there.

When I went to live in Paris, Frank was homeless at the time, so he became my lodger in Putney while I was away in France. Then I got a job with Marlboro in Lausanne as second in command to the PR director of Philip Morris. I ended up going to a lot of races and found myself responsible for producing all the Marlboro racing news magazines.

During that time Patrick Duffler looked after Marlboro's sponsorship. I said to Patrick that Marlboro was pouring all this money into BRM and nothing was really coming from it. Wouldn't it be interesting if Marlboro put some money into the bottom end as well and supported a team which had never had major support? He thought this was a reasonable idea and so I introduced Frank to Patrick Duffler. The net result was Iso-Marlboro with Howden Ganley driving the car.

There were obviously times when Frank was down but most of the time he believed he was going to succeed. On one particular occasion he rang up and said, 'Listen, I've got a problem paying the mechanics at a race. Can you help out?' The answer was of course yes. It was all repaid in one way or another. Marlboro felt very good about the fact that they were helping Frank. A lot of the motoring press appreciated that here was the biggest sponsor of them all recognising that there were two ends to the spectrum.

Frank always used to run round the track at night after practice. I remember one particular time at Kyalami when he came back all puffed. We said to Frank, 'Everything all right?' He said, 'Of course. Why not?' I said, 'Don't you realise snakes come out at night and they like the warmth of the road. You've got to be a bit careful when you run after dark.' Frank nearly died. It was only a joke.

BERNIE ECCLESTONE

The thing I remember about Frank when he was starting up was that we were rebuilding engines for him when I was at Brabham. Frank would come down for a chat and he would say, 'Bernie, can you lend me £5,000?' And I would say, 'Sure, Frank. No problem,' and give him a cheque for £5,000. Whatever the day was – two weeks, three weeks – whenever it was time for Frank to repay, he would be there with a cheque for £5,000. He would put it on the table and say, 'Thanks a lot; it's really helped me. Could you do me a favour?' 'Sure, what is it Frank?' 'Could you lend me £7,000?'

So he would get a cheque for £7,000. And this went on for a long time. He would take the cheque and immediately go to Fulham Road and buy himself some cashmere socks or a cashmere sweater or an expensive shirt. That was Frank.

GIANCARLO FALLETTI

I worked for thirty-five years as a journalist and photographer for *Corriere della Serra*, a daily newspaper in Italy. When Frank was racing, you could see he wasn't a Senna or a Mansell. But he was a nice person, working in Italy with many racing people. He imported a few cars and spares, and this worked very well because not many people spoke English and Italian. He found it easy to open the door. He realised he was nothing special as a driver, unlike his good friend Piers Courage, who was also a very nice person. In 1969, when they arrived in Formula 1, you had a nice team with a very well prepared car. You could see that Frank understood the importance of arriving with the car in a good condition to do the race; maybe not so fast – but it was perfect.

I had started to work with sponsors and I introduced Frank to many potential Italian backers, including Iso Rivolta. They had one lunch together at Turin motor show and quickly came to an agreement. Not so much money by today's standards, but good money for Frank at this moment. I found Frank to be a very good man, someone who loves his racing but who also understands about attracting money and working with sponsors. We have remained very good friends ever since.

HOWDEN GANLEY

Big Lou [Louis Stanley, head of BRM] and I had failed to come to an agreement. He offered me the number-one position at Marlboro BRM and then I found out that he had already offered Clay [Regazzoni] the same job. So you never really knew where you were with him. Then Marlboro said they needed a second team. Basically they said we will fund another team and you are part of the package. I remember Jackie Stewart saying at the time that if he wasn't driving for Tyrrell, he would drive for Frank. That seemed a pretty good recommendation to me.

So the deal was put together with Marlboro paying part of Frank's tab. I thought at one point that I was taking Tony Southgate [BRM designer] with me, but unfortunately Tony had a rather better offer from Shadow. I thought with some money now and running his own cars, Frank could really be somebody. But somehow it didn't quite work out; certainly it wasn't Frank's fault.

He had two full-time mechanics, two engine builders, three fabricators – collectively known as the Flowerpot Men – a truckie, a part-time accounts guy, a designer and a couple of other people. He was doing everything right. But I was finding it very frustrating because of the things that were breaking or falling off the car. It was horrendous. At the Nürburgring one of the brake callipers fell off as I went along the straight. I didn't know that had happened until I got to the end of the straight at about 180 mph and found there were no rear brakes. I went flying through the air and down a ravine, finishing up in the bent monocoque with my knees up round my ears. It was a very big shunt and I was seriously ill for quite a while. These things happen and I don't want to slag Frank off because he was doing his absolute best. He was very unhappy about the cause of that crash.

JACQUES LAFFITE

I already knew Piers Courage, but the first time I really met Frank was when I was racing in England. After I won a Formula 2 race at the Salzburgring, Frank called and asked if I wanted to drive his Formula 1 car. I was racing for Martini in Formula 2 and I asked Tico Martini what he thought. I had a really busy season and I wasn't sure if it was the best thing to start racing in Formula 1. My first interest was Formula 2. Tico said it would be a good thing to do, so I went to see Frank in England. But I was still unsure.

I asked Frank if I could drive the car. Arturo Merzario would drive it first and then I would drive it straight after him. This was at Goodwood – not an easy track – and I decided if I was close to Arturo in lap time, I would say yes to Frank. I can't remember my lap time but it was good enough and I said to Frank that I would start with the German Grand Prix at the old Nürburgring in 1974.

I drove the car the best I could. I remember I had dinner with my wife on the Saturday and I could not even open my mouth. It was so difficult with this car to go flat with the throttle. I tried to be as quick as I could and just gritted my teeth. I could speak okay but when I tried to open my mouth to eat, it was, '*Merde*!' It was so painful, like my jaw was broken; I had been pushing so hard. We stayed together during 1974 and 1975. When we went back to the Nürburgring, I finished second. This was the first podium for Frank in a long time and the first championship points for me. It was a big, big moment.

SIR JACKIE STEWART

My last Italian Grand Prix, on the weekend I won my third world championship, there was a running race on the Thursday, which Frank won, hands down. He used to come and stay with us a lot in Switzerland, and he ran there. Where the house was positioned, you turned left out of the gate and there was a hideously steep hill, going up. Everybody who runs will tell you that you walk a little, then you stretch, then you start slowly. It was like an alpine climb up this road. Frank would go out the gate, turn left and start running. He just ran up that hill as if it wasn't there.

DENNIS RUSHEN

I was one of the few mechanics Frank had; there were fewer mechanics than you'd have on a Formula Ford team today. Compared to the likes of Ferrari and Lotus, we had nothing. But it didn't matter because you didn't need an image as such in those days. There was a camaraderie which you don't see nowadays. Everybody would help Frank. We would borrow things all the time – never to be returned. But it wasn't a problem. Frank was very popular. It was the underdog syndrome, but everyone could see that he just tried a lot harder than anyone else.

My memory is of the team having no money. We had to do all sorts of things that you wouldn't get away with now. Little Arturo [Merzario] was so small that we simply put blocks of wood on the pedals! I used to go in the truck with a chap called Simon to the races. We had to drive this great big long rigid thing – it would probably be illegal now. It was a Leyland of some sort, painted red, and I remember at one race having to borrow fifty pounds from Bernie [Ecclestone] to pay for enough diesel to get the thing home. We couldn't afford new tyres most of the time. So I would have to go down to the Goodyear compound and root around among Ferrari's cast-offs, trying to choose a matching set after Regazzoni and Lauda had finished with them.

Despite the hardships, we all liked Frank. I think the thing which kept us there was his enthusiasm. He had a way about him. At the end of every week, we'd ask for our wages. 'Ah,' he'd say. 'It's on the way from Switzerland.' It was always coming from Switzerland, never anywhere else. We used to go for weeks without any money. It always arrived eventually but it was obvious that he had to struggle. He had this belief that everything would sort itself out but I think we worried a lot more than Frank did. But we'd always hang on.

MIKE DOODSON

I sometimes muse about the tenner that Frank charmed out of me as we landed at Heathrow after the 1975 German Grand Prix. He needed the cash to get his Porsche out of the short-term car park, and seeing that his car had fluked second place in the race it seemed a pretty secure loan. I'm still waiting.

WALTER HAYES

(former director of public affairs, Ford Europe)

I used to lend Anglia vans to Frank from time to time, and he would sell them. That was how people like Williams raised money to survive. It was the sport's currency at the time. 'We need money to go motor racing,' they would say, 'and so we get it any way we can.' Now if you had brought in someone from outside and they had seen what was happening, they would have said, 'But you can't let him do that with your property. It's illegal.' But we didn't see it that way.

VIRGINIA WILLIAMS

In the early days Frank and I used to go van driving at night. Frank used to come home at nine o'clock and say something like he had to go and pick up seat belts from somewhere or other, and did I want to come? And I'd say, 'Oh yes please.' People would leave the parcel or whatever outside their premises. It was fun.

EIGHT

For Richer, for Poorer

Virginia was as dogged in pursuit of her man as Frank was in his quest for success on the racetrack. Knowing that he would run a mile – literally – rather than accept a domestic arrangement that might tie him down, Ginny adopted a relaxed attitude to Frank's occasional visits to her apartment in London. She no more discussed the reasons for the break-up of her marriage than he showed signs of wishing to risk a repeat. When her father offered her a loan, Ginny bought a maisonette in Rawlings Street, directly behind Harrods, and took a job as a Girl Friday with a firm of interior designers. There was no set pattern to Frank's visits but Ginny slowly but surely provided a more permanent base by doing his laundry and cooking him meals. Frank would go along with this for a couple of nights in succession – a major break-through – but then seemingly panic and not be seen again in Rawlings Street for a couple of weeks.

If Frank was having financial troubles in 1972, the same was not true of Ginny. A property boom saw the value of her maisonette double in nine months. Ginny reasoned that by moving to a less salubrious area of London she could realise a profit which would not only be useful to Frank but also strengthen the bond between them. The £4,000 she made available was a welcome boost; Frank had already sold his car and other possessions to raise cash. Further loans followed to the point where Ginny found her funds seriously depleted. At the same time Frank was looking for a roof over his head following news that his land-lords Charlie and Jenny Crichton-Stuart were moving on. In a moment of weakness Frank suggested renting a place together. Ginny did not need to be asked twice. At the end of 1972 they moved into a cottage rented from the saloon car driver Gordon Spice at Old Windsor.

Any thoughts of domestic bliss that Ginny might have had evaporated as the hectic 1973 season got under way, and with it the continuing financial pressures of running a racing team. Frank found he did not need the additional obligations – in his mind anyway – of being tied down. A few months after moving into the cottage, he walked out. This was too much for Ginny. Abandoning her softly-softly tactics, she cut the arms off the expensive suits and shirts that Frank had left behind. The remnants were neatly folded and sent off to the factory at Bennet Road. Frank may have been short of cash but he always took great pride in his appearance: the lacerated garments would have made a painful point. Then Ginny changed the locks and made plans to return to London.

Not long after, the evening peace was shattered when Frank and his driver Howden Ganley appeared outside the cottage and tunelessly serenaded its hapless occupant. Admission was granted, if only to bring the crooners' antics to a halt. Ginny stood her ground for a couple of days, and then, to her surprise, Frank suggested they find a house nearer the factory at Reading. A quick scan of *Country Life* – Ginny did not do things by halves – found Drake House, a furnished detached property in Mortimer, a village five miles south of Reading. They moved in at the end of 1973. Ginny's parents were less than delighted. Putting two and two together and definitely getting four, her father realised where the profit from the sale of Rawlings Street had gone, along with, he correctly assumed, Ginny's income from the Berry Trust. The Berry cheques ceased. Now Frank and Ginny were in real financial difficulties.

The bailiffs were frequent visitors to Bennet Road, removing desks and chairs to settle unpaid bills, while the telephone was often cut off at both the house in Mortimer and the factory. When the telephone went dead, Frank would conduct business from a public call box outside the Reading Speedway located at the rutted end of Bennet Road. It scarcely cost him a second thought. As long as they kept racing, that was all that mattered.

While Ginny came to accept this state of affairs, she did not anticipate a proposal of marriage, even though she was expecting their first child. Typically, Frank mentioned it almost in passing as he set off for another Grand Prix. By the time he returned, Ginny had made the necessary arrangements. An appointment had been made at the Reading register office for the following Tuesday, 20 August 1974. Frank did not have a personal bank account and Ginny had no money. David Brodie, a close friend of Frank, lent Ginny the eight pounds necessary for the licence; thirty pounds set aside for the rent was used to buy a wedding ring.

Husbanding their limited resources, Ginny gave a pre-wedding lunch for Brodie and his wife Kath at Drake House. Lacking a dining table, the kitchen table was pressed into service hidden under a cloth to match the white colour scheme, which extended to the napkins, candles and even the cream sauce for the chicken. At one o'clock the phone rang. It was Frank. Fearing he might have had a last-minute change of heart, Ginny was actually relieved to hear that he was only excusing himself from lunch. He had been held up at work and would go direct to the register office. Frank duly appeared in front of the registrar at the appointed hour and said his vows. By 2.30, after kissing the bride and a brief chat, Frank was back at his desk. The only person unsurprised by all this was Mrs Virginia Williams.

Jonathan Piers Williams, named after Frank's two closest friends, was born on 22 February 1975. A few weeks before, his parents had been served with an eviction order. The landlord, unhappy about late rent payments, had seized his chance to claim breach of contract when

WILLIAMS

he discovered the presence of Sam, a black Labrador, and an impending child, neither of which were permitted. Ginny negotiated a six-week extension to the eviction order while she set about finding a new home.

Turning once more to *Country Life*, Ginny discovered the Laundry House on the estate of the Colman family, of mustard fame. The agents explained that about £8,000 worth of renovations were needed to make the house habitable, improvements which the tenants would be expected to undertake. In return, they would pay a peppercorn rent of twelve pounds a week for a seven-year lease. Taking a deep breath, Frank and Ginny presented themselves for interview, along with several other candidates. Surveying the well-heeled competition, Ginny doubted they would be found suitable. She was sure of it when Frank told Sir Michael and Lady Colman that he ran a Formula 1 racing team and that he had no money – but hoped to have some soon. Ginny was appalled, but Frank had hit the right note. The Laundry House was theirs. They would worry about the renovations later.

HOWDEN GANLEY

Frank was having this romance with Ginny but she was having trouble tying him down and he didn't want to fall out with her. She was really good for him at that time – she still is, of course – and he realised that only too well. I think he just wanted some moral support that evening when we ended up outside the house but, in the end, as ever, his winning smile helped do the job.

VIRGINIA WILLIAMS

We got married on the twentieth, which was a Tuesday, and he was going to some Grand Prix or other on the Thursday before. Just as he was leaving, he asked me to marry him and said, 'Why don't you arrange it whilst I'm away?' I remember thinking that I had better arrange it quickly in case he changed his mind. When he came back on the Sunday he asked if I'd done anything, so I said yes and that it was going to be the following week. You could see him blanch! And it's quite true that Brode had to lend us the money for the special licence. I bought a ring. Sadly, when I was attacked in London ten years ago, it went.

My girlfriend helped me with the wedding preparations – white food, white soup, white chicken, white flowers on the table – and he didn't come home. He was only five miles away. He at least turned up for the ceremony and then had to go back to the office. I wasn't disappointed. It was actually quite funny. I went off with Brode and Kath and we had tea at the Old Rope Walk in Henley. Extraordinary, really. I have to say that, if I'm honest, Frank was a bit quiet for about two weeks after that. He wasn't quite himself after we got married. I asked him what was the matter and he said, 'To be honest, I'm shit scared of being married.'

It was a big step for him. I was very surprised because I didn't think he would ask me to marry him but I think one of the reasons that I was able to cope with all those early problems was that I was so determined about Frank. I was really passionate about him and it never really ended. I didn't mind what he did to me, I really didn't mind. No problem was insurmountable.

We were evicted from Drake House. We hadn't paid the rent. In fact it was very naughty of us because we took the house under false pretences really. It was thirty pounds a month and we hadn't really got any way of paying it and the poor landlord got ever so upset with us and gave us notice to quit when I was heavily pregnant. I can remember sitting in bed and crying and Frank saying, 'Whatever is the matter with you?' I reminded him that the baby was due in two weeks and that we'd been given notice to quit and he just looked at me as if I was mad.

Frank has always done things like that. I can remember Dave Brodie asking how Frank could sleep at night. He slept like a baby – out like a light. I don't think he ever worried about things. He will think about a problem and, if he hasn't thought it through, he can just dispose of it until he thinks it through again. He's an optimist rather than a pessimist; he doesn't stress and he doesn't worry.

Michael and Judy Colman remain good friends of ours. I have always said that the Colmans letting us have that house was our turning point. I was amazed that we were considered suitable tenants. We had to go through an initial interview process with Knight, Frank and Rutley, the agents handling all the Colmans' rental business. I had phoned up and said I'd like the house, and they said they were very sorry but you have to have an appointment with the Colmans – *if* we think you're suitable.

So Frank and I turned up and we had Jonathan in the back of the car. There was quite a smart car driving out as we arrived, and it was clear that this was another would-be tenant. I was quite depressed because Michael Colman was asking Frank about his business and he asked if Frank would be bringing the racing cars to drive around the estate! Frank obviously said he wouldn't, but I thought that we wouldn't be their sort of people at all: they were into horses, shooting, fishing and so on. Judith later said to me that Michael had decided straight away, from the moment he met Frank. He just saw something in Frank and decided there and then that he was going to give him a chance. He even said to me, at his eightieth birthday party recently, that he saw something very, very special in Frank.

The day we moved in, we told the most terrible whoppers to keep the house, but Judith knew, and she said she used to laugh. We were supposed to do the carpets and curtains, put in a kitchen and two bathrooms – that sort of thing. Structurally, the house was pretty sound but the walls and plaster needed completely redecorating. We lived in pretty bleak conditions while the builders – who came and went because we couldn't afford to pay them – worked around us. There was no washing machine, for example. I had to take all our clothes to a laundrette in Reading.

I could hardly believe it when Frank came home one day and said he needed a secretary. Prospective candidates started arriving at the front door for interviews. I couldn't help but wonder if they knew what they were letting themselves in for. That's when I first met Alison

Morris, a tall blonde lady with an infectious giggle. She didn't have any children and wanted something to do. Frank appointed her on the spot. I remember him telling Alison that she would be working from our house while the office was being redecorated! That was another way of saying there would probably be no desk or chair for her if she went to Bennet Road. Alison was no fool. She worked out what was going on and didn't seem to mind in the least. In fact, she loved it. The wonderful thing about Alison was that she *always* laughed. She found everything terribly funny. Her husband Bobby worked for British Leyland and had quite a good salary. They lived in a very nice house up the road and they used to invite Frank and me so that she could feed us! I don't think Frank could pay her on many occasions and she didn't mind at all. She just used to laugh. She was wonderful, Alison. That was exactly what we needed.

Frank used to go off for quite long periods, to Grands Prix and the like, and Alison was *very* supportive of me. I think she adored Frank and she really loved the job. Sometimes it was like she didn't care if she didn't get her twelve pounds at the end of the week. She seemed to relish confrontations with the bailiffs. One day they arrived for another attempt at removing furniture and Alison simply refused to get off her chair, saying it would be ungentlemanly of them to expect her to work on the floor. She kept the chair. She would sit for hours if necessary in the bank in order to borrow money. There was one time when she and I had to go to Barclays to try and get thity-six pounds because the bailiffs were coming; she was not going to leave until she got it. Frank and I were always *terrified* of bank managers. But we thought that might change when Walter Wolf came on the scene. It was the first time that Frank would have any sort of salary. We thought our troubles were over.

NINE

Bleeding Wolf

In the spring of 1975, during a chance conversation with Frank, Gianpaolo Dallara had mentioned Walter Wolf, an Austro-Canadian who had made millions in the oil equipment business. Wolf had been talking to Dallara about the possibility of running an exotic sports car at Le Mans. Dallara had noted that money did not seem to be a problem for Wolf, who was passionate about cars but had never been to a Grand Prix. Frank called him and Wolf needed little persuasion to accept an invitation to the non-championship International Trophy Formula 1 race at Silverstone. When Merzario suffered two engine failures and failed to start on a cold and wet April afternoon, Frank must have wondered at the success of his introduction, but Wolf was captivated by the urgency and atmosphere of Formula 1, so much so that he offered to pay for the engine rebuilds.

Wolf's stocky figure became a familiar sight at subsequent Grands Prix. Each visit fed his ambition to have a team of his own and led to the suggestion, in late 1975, that he become a shareholder in Frank's company. Frank refused, but Wolf was persistent and offered to settle the team's debts, estimated at £140,000. The catch would be a 60 per cent interest in the team for Wolf. Frank declined once more. Wolf then switched his attention to Hesketh Racing, a colourful collection of individuals led by Lord Alexander Hesketh. This small team, based on the

Hesketh estate in Northamptonshire, had its day when James Hunt scored his first Formula 1 win in that year's Dutch Grand Prix, but his lordship's champagne was drying up and they needed an outside backer. Hunt was about to be snapped up by McLaren – with whom he would win a dramatic world title a year later – and Hesketh then went into liquidation. Wolf was offered the team's assets, including an apparently promising new car, for £450,000, and since he had no experience in the field, asked Frank to join him.

Frank discussed this latest development with Ginny, who felt, after sharing all the hardships, that she had at least a non-executive stake in Frank Williams (Racing Cars) Ltd. The thought that the name would be changed to Wolf-Williams did little to weaken her objections. Why should Frank give up everything he had worked so hard for? Marlboro were offering Williams £100,000 to give a drive to Jacky Ickx, a former Ferrari driver and Grand Prix winner. There were also the FOCA travel benefits to consider. On the other hand, there was the offer of a brand-new car and enough funds to allow Frank to choose a driver. No more wannabes whose bank balances exceeded their talents, and no debts. Finally, Frank would get to run a team as he had always wished.

Since moving into Drake House and then the Laundry House, Frank's penchant for an occasional run had evolved to the point where he was not happy unless he did at least five miles after work each evening. Running helped him keep extremely fit and gave him time to think. One night towards the end of November 1975, his mind spinning with the pros and cons of Wolf's proposal, Frank went for a long run. He returned to the Laundry House, called Walter Wolf and accepted his offer. Frank Williams (Racing Cars) Ltd ceased to exist.

Shortly before that phone call Frank had had arguably the most important meeting of his life. Given the rundown state of the Bennet Road factory and the tatty condition of the Laundry House, Frank preferred to put on one of his smart suits and conduct interviews in the Carlton Towers Hotel in London. The irony was that the interviewee would have been completely at home in the more relaxed surround-ings of either property in Berkshire.

Patrick Head had come directly from a boatyard to talk to Frank about engineering racing cars. Patrick had graduated as a mechanical engineer in 1970 and worked for Lola Cars before briefly setting up his own business, preparing engines for SuperVee cars. He had designed and built a Formula 2 car, the Scott single-seater, which earned admir-ing looks although lack of money denied any opportunity to prove its worth. After a period working for a racing-car company known as Trojan, Head turned from automotive to maritime pursuits, spending 1975 and '76 building his own boat. Frank, acting on advice from Ian Phillips, a journalist, had contacted Head with a view to persuading him to join Williams.

One of Frank's first jobs once Patrick had come on board was to explain that he no longer owned the company and the chief designer would be Harvey Postlethwaite, the man responsible for James Hunt's car. The team had moved from Towcester to Reading; the pity was, they had also brought their latest car, the Hesketh 308C. Whereas Hunt's car had been notable for its efficient simplicity, the 308C was complex and presented Jacky Ickx with handling difficulties.

Frank also had problems coming to terms with his new role. Walter Wolf expected results and was less than impressed when his guests were shipped into Brands Hatch only to see Ickx fail to qualify the Wolf-Williams for the British Grand Prix. Things went from bad to worse when the season ended and Frank had overspent his budget. Wolf hired Peter Warr, the former Lotus team manager. However, Frank's salary was doubled and he was also given the role of sponsorship seeker and personal assistant – whatever that meant. It turned out to mean he became a glorified gofer, fetching and carrying and moving Wolf's expensive road cars around Europe at the behest of their owner. Mean-while, Postlethwaite had designed a relatively simple car for 1977 and Wolf had hired Jody Scheckter, a hard-charging South African destined for greater things. The package looked promising, but for Frank the tragedy was that he was not in Argentina to see Scheckter score a sensational victory in the first race of the season; he had been told to remain in England. His team in previous years may have lurched from crisis to crisis but at least Frank had been in charge of its destiny. Wolf-Williams was now a slick well-funded operation but Frank was no longer directly involved with the actual racing.

As for Virginia, she had quickly become accustomed to helping Frank spend his £25,000 annual salary. Her first act had been to visit Conran and lavish fifty pounds on what would be their first proper kitchen table. The phone was reconnected and the renovations to the Laundry House were completed. The timing was right because Jonathan now had a sister, Claire, born on 22 July in the middle of a scorching summer. Money, though, was not everything, and Ginny had watched with growing unease as the team reached a point where they were hard pressed to find drivers willing to take on the difficult Wolf-Williams. There was likely to be just one scapegoat at the end of all this. Her concern mounted at the news of Frank's sideways promotion. That concern turned to quiet outrage when Ginny discovered that Walter Wolf's wife had telephoned and asked Frank to advertise for and select a married couple to live in one of their many houses. The time had come to move on.

Fortunately, Patrick Head had chosen not to do the same when presented with either walking away after one week or staying on to work under Harvey Postlethwaite. Head was in South Africa when he received a call from Frank asking if he would care to join him in starting afresh with a new team. It would be a gamble. He was with a team that was clearly going places and Frank's track record was not impressive. But there was something about Frank that struck a chord. He was the antithesis of Wolf, whose leather jackets and expensive jewellery did not appeal to the son of Colonel Michael Head. Patrick accepted Frank's offer. It would be fun in the short term. By no means did Patrick think he would still be there thirty-two years later.

PATRICK HEAD

I suppose I must have had some awareness of Frank's existence but I really wasn't that heavily into Formula 1. It's been documented before that I was doing race cars up at Lola and various odd projects, and then I ran out of money. I was told that this chap Frank Williams had called me.

He asked for a meeting and I went to see him. I was unbelievably scruffy because I was building a boat in the Surrey Docks and Frank was trim, dapper and fit – everything that I wasn't. We met in the ground floor of the Carlton Towers. He was actually negotiating with Walter Wolf for the sale of his team, so I don't think Frank ever envisaged having more than one designer. He took me on thinking that if the thing with Wolf turned sour, then this guy will have to be my designer. And if it doesn't turn to shit then Harvey Postlethwaite would be his designer. When the deal with Walter went through, literally a week after I joined, I got called up to the front office, where I discovered that Harvey had said to Frank that they needed to keep me on. I think I was offered £500 or something if I wanted to go, but I was completely and utterly broke at the time.

Deciding to stay was the best decision I made. I had a whole year of being able to observe very much how *not* to do it because the car was awful. Harvey was a lovely bloke but he liked to pontificate about how race cars should be. Actually getting in and drawing them with a pencil was not what he wanted to do. But I learned a lot because nothing we did to the car, *nothing*, made it any faster.

I stayed there for all of 1976. Frank stood down as team manager and was replaced by Peter Warr. Frank was told that he was going to be a 'sponsor getter'. In truth, it seemed that Walter would just ring up and say do this, do that, pick me up at the airport. Frank was feeling like the bottle washer so he decided that, quite rightly, that was not for him. He did tell me he was going to leave and set up a new team and asked if I would be interested. I don't think I made much comment. Then, when I was in South Africa at a test, Frank rang me up and said, 'I've moved, do you want to join me?' I asked if he had any money and he said that he was putting together £100,000 and the driver was bringing £100,000 – and that would do us. In those days you could run with one car and get away with not doing all the races. So the expensive ones, like Japan, we didn't do.

Wolf were potentially going to do well in 1977, so my feeling must have been, *What the hell am I doing?* Frank was very enthusiastic and I really didn't have any argument with Wolf in any way. Peter Warr clearly was a much better team manager than Frank. To be fair, though, if you've got a brilliant car, then it makes everyone look good. The fact is, if you have a bad car it doesn't matter how good the team is because the result is crap and thus it makes you look like you have a crap team.

FRANK WILLIAMS

Patrick joined me and then woke up one morning and found he was working for Walter Wolf. Anyway, he understood. Unfortunately, the Hesketh which became the Wolf-Williams was the biggest load of crap. We got to the end of 1976. In the meantime Peter Warr was in charge and I was a second-class citizen. Patrick said, 'This is not for you. Let's eff off.' That's what happened, so we started again. The deal had been that every debt had been paid off by Walter in return for 60 per cent of the company. In February the following year I sold the remaining 40 per cent, and that second tranche of money opened the way for Williams, the company you know now.

VIRGINIA WILLIAMS

I think at the time when Walter Wolf came along the debt we had was £140,000. That was a lot of money for those days. I don't think it ever occurred to me in a million years that it would end up the way it did. I was, for once, thinking, *Hurray!* But it ended very quickly. I think Walter told Frank that he was going to move him into a different position. He asked Frank to go down to Stuttgart and pick up his wife's car and drive it to the south of France. It was at that point that it started to feel a bit worrying. He then employed Peter Warr, and that was quite hard to swallow.

PATRICK HEAD

At the end of 1976, when Frank was still with Wolf, a chassis had been written off at Mosport. We had a spare in England and that was flown out for the next race, the United States Grand Prix at Watkins Glen. Frank rang around to try and get a driver for the Wolf-Williams and we couldn't find one. As soon as they knew what car it was, they all said, 'No bloody way.' Eventually, Frank got this guy, Warwick Brown, an Australian who was living in LA doing the American Formula 5000 series.

That weekend, the rains descended and the place was absolutely flooded. Warwick Brown arrived at the track very late on Thursday night. He was in his LA gear, a white see-through shirt and a tight pair of jeans. He had a couple of big suitcases. We got him in the car and found a seat for him but he had 'Lola limp' as he'd been driving this Lola and eighteen months before he'd broken his leg in a Lola. His right leg went off at an angle, so when his leg was up against the inside of the monocoque, his accelerator foot was where the brake pedal was, so we had to bend the pedals across.

Warwick was sitting in the car saying, 'God, this car is a thing of beauty. It's unbelievable. I've never sat in such an exotic machine.' The mechanics were pissing themselves. It was very unfair. We didn't finish until about two in the morning. I had a hire car and said to Warwick, 'Do you want to drive?' He was happy to do so. The rain was still coming down, the wipers were going flat out.

Frank had us staying in a holiday camp on the side of what they call the Finger Lakes, a glacial area where the hills around the lakes are very steep. Frank had persuaded this holiday camp – it was November and it had closed down – to open up and take five dollars a night. There were these little chalet rooms and a cooker, but otherwise nothing. I had bought coffee, bread and sugar and it was all in a box on the back seat.

We set off and Warwick was saying, 'Goodness me, it's the greatest achievement of my career to be driving a Formula 1 car.' I thought he was driving a bit too quickly. As we started coming down a long hill towards the lakes, I said, 'Warwick, it's very steep here and there's a tight bend at the bottom.' He said, 'Ah, yeah right, no problem.' I said, 'Warwick, it's bloody tight at the bottom!'

Suddenly the headlights picked up this Armco barrier, which was the right-hand bit at the bottom. He said, 'Jesus!' He put the car sideways to try and slow it down, couldn't, clipped the barrier with the back of the car, and the next thing I knew we were flying through the air, the headlights pointing up at all this rain. I was looking at the dashboard, thinking, *Shit, that thing is going to come back and crush me. What a stupid way to die with this idiot alongside me.* There was total silence and then all of a sudden there was a great crashing, thumping, a huge compression and then silence. The interior light was on and the whole of the inside of the car seemed to be sliding down with crap running down the interior. What had happened was that all the coffee and milk and sugar from the back had hit the roof and exploded on the inside. The windows were coated with this mess.

We had descended through a load of birch trees, dropped eighty to a hundred feet, I would think, but our landing had been taken by the trees, and fortunately none of them had come up through the bottom of the car. Bloody lucky. It was not a small drop. As we landed and came to a sticky halt, Warwick said, 'Shit, what a way to start my Grand Prix career.'

As I said, he had these two enormous suitcases and I refused to carry either of them. We got them out of the boot. The car, a great big American hire car, had literally broken its back. It was a big accident. We had to walk about a mile along the road to this place. Then Warwick drove a very ordinary race and finished eleventh. But we were lucky to be there at all.

VIRGINIA WILLIAMS

We had originally been down to stay at the Glen Motor Inn, a motel by the side of a lake. They only used to allocate three rooms per team, and the owners, the Franzese family, were rather selective and liked only the drivers and the team owners to have the rooms. Frank and I had a room but Walter turned up with an entourage and more or less said, 'You've gotta go; we're staying here.' So we had nowhere to stay. Frank went out and found this holiday camp. It was terrible. Absolutely shocking. There was no food; it wasn't even a B&B. Patrick had gone off to get supplies and he came back, very late at night, with Warwick Brown. The first we knew of the accident was when they arrived at the door, completely drenched and covered in milk, coffee and cereal! It was quite a sight. But not a great start to a bad weekend.

TEN

Back to the Beginning

For someone accustomed to the threat of eviction, there was a delightful irony in Frank Williams having to break into his new headquarters. Due to a mix-up, there was no key available on the day the new venture was raring to get started in a 5,000-square-foot unit on an industrial estate in Oxfordshire. Formerly used for storing carpets, the premises on Station Road in Didcot were as down to earth as the company name. Having tried, and failed, to secure every combination of 'Williams' and 'Racing' – Wolf held the rights to Frank Williams (Racing Cars) Ltd and there was a startling number of bookmakers named Frank Williams – Frank settled on Williams Grand Prix Engineering, a wordy title that nevertheless left no doubt about this company's priority and intent.

Frank had forfeited more than his company title when he sold out. Most significant was the loss of FOCA membership and its all-important financial benefits. Williams could not gain immediate re-admission because the team did not plan to compete in all of the 1977 races and, more fundamentally, there was no question at this stage of designing and building his own car. A stop-gap was required and Frank trod the familiar path to Bicester and his old friends at March Engineering. March just happened to have a chassis based on the previous year's design available for what seemed a reasonable £14,000. It would later become apparent why.

Ford-Cosworth engines were picked up from an Italian privateer and from stock Bernie Ecclestone had available at Brabham. There was also a damaged V8 from Penske, the American team having abandoned a brief foray into Formula 1. Frank picked this up for a mere £1,500. The engine was returned from Cosworth in mint condition with the cost of a new block, worth at least £2,000, omitted from the bill. Many years later, after having become one of Cosworth's most valued customers, Frank revealed the engine company's inadvertent but valuable contribution to the cause.

The £100,000 funding mentioned by Frank to Patrick came from Patrick Neve, a personable young Belgian driver with support from the Belle Vue brewery. A further £30,000 was made available courtesy of Barclays Bank, the last place on earth Frank would have considered. His aversion to bankers as strong as ever, Frank had hidden in his office when Alison Morris announced that the manager of the Didcot branch was at the front door of Unit 10. John Makepeace, just transferred from the north-east, was drumming up new business. Once they met, Makepeace, a motor-racing fan, quickly and correctly assessed the potential of the company and offered a generous overdraft.

Despite the turnaround in his fiscal affairs Frank's credit rating elsewhere remained rock bottom. Ginny recalled their previous debt of £140,000 and worried that the bank loan might lead to the same slippery slope. This time, however, Frank's friend Dave Brodie became a director of the company for a short while. As the owner of a successful metal-plating business with a solid reputation, Brodie was able to secure loans for the purchase of machine tools and a truck to transport the racing car. The indefatigable Ted Ward provided a brand-new capstan lathe and the services of a joinery crew to make workbenches and partitions for the factory.

The workforce had doubled in size and contained several employees who would go on to make their names in motorsport. A new name on the payroll was Ross Brawn, starting off as a mechanic and general all-rounder at the bottom of a long ladder that would take him to technical director at Ferrari in the golden era of Michael Schumacher and, later, the boss of his own race-winning team. Johnny Dumfries, later Johnny Bute when he inherited the marquisate of Bute, would make a humble start as a van driver before becoming a Formula 3 champion and Formula 1 driver for Lotus. And Neil Oatley, not long out of college, would go on to become responsible for some of the most successful Formula 1 cars ever made by McLaren.

Frank meanwhile continued to seek prospective sponsors. One of his contacts, John Harris, worked for the London advertising agency that had the account for Saudia, the airline of the Kingdom of Saudi Arabia. Saudia were looking for something out of the ordinary to sponsor and Harris immediately thought of Frank. An introduction was arranged between Williams and Muhammad Al Fawzan, the airline's sales manager in Jeddah. Following a visit to a Formula 2 meeting at Silverstone, Mr Al Fawzan appreciated the value of being associated with a glamorous global sport, and Williams got the go-ahead to display the 'Fly Saudia' emblem on the rear wing of the March in return for £30,000. Things were looking promising as the small team of six prepared for their first race, the Spanish Grand Prix on 8 May 1977.

It was not an auspicious team debut, particularly as the driver of the truck managed to back into a much larger and smarter transporter belonging to none other than Walter Wolf. It was the only mark Williams Grand Prix Engineering made that weekend, as Neve qualified twenty-second and finished twelfth. His best result would be seventh, just outside the points, at the Italian Grand Prix at Monza. Elsewhere, he failed to qualify three times, which was perhaps no surprise since the car was actually older than was originally thought – at least by Williams, if not by the slick salesman at March. As Head and Williams planned for 1978, it was clear that Neve was not the best driver for the brand-new Williams designed by Patrick and now under construction. On the other hand, what ambitious young driver in his right mind would drive for Williams when Frank had just spent another season trailing around at the back of the field?

Not that it bothered him, judging by his outrageous ambition. Frank approached no less than Ronnie Peterson, one of the fastest and most spectacular drivers of the day. The Swede had just spent an unproductive year with the six-wheeled Tyrrell but would return to Lotus, with whom he had scored seven of his eight Formula 1 victories. Discussions were also held with Riccardo Patrese, among other middle-ranking candidates, some of whom did not even bother to return Frank's calls.

The Austrian Grand Prix had provided a maiden win for Alan Jones and the only first place for the Shadow team, the tenacious Australian producing a daring drive on changing track conditions. Almost as an afterthought, Frank invited Jones to Station Road. It was an inspired move. There was an instant rapport between Head, Williams and Jones, three motivated men of roughly the same age, and when Jones saw the beginnings of the Williams FW06, a straightforward but neat little car, he was impressed. The deal was clinched on the spot when Frank offered Jones £40,000 to drive it.

FRANK WILLIAMS

Patrick and I got on very well as blokes; he loved his racing. I have to confess that I was not astute enough at that time to think, *Phwoar, this guy's really good.* I thought he was a good engineer, someone we had always needed. A good, solid man who knew his stuff from the ground up, proper engineering stuff.

When it came to choosing a driver, I remembered watching Alan Jones coming through a right-hander before the pits at Mosport. This was when he was driving the Shadow in the 1977 Canadian Grand Prix. Every lap, he would come through that corner with the same amount of beautiful oversteer, about twenty degrees of lock. I loved what I saw and told Patrick about it. Jonesy was perfect for us. He had massive self-confidence, aggressive as they come. He and Patrick got on very well; they understood each other.

VIRGINIA WILLIAMS

It was no surprise when Frank decided to go it alone again, but I can remember a feeling of *Oh no, not again!* He'd had a salary for six months and now we were going to go back to none. But it moved quite quickly from then on. I'd met Patrick a couple of times. Frank had gone through quite a lot of different engineers who had been brought in as the 'great hope' but they never really turned out that way. I didn't necessarily think that Patrick was going to be any different. But then you could see the relationship developing between Frank and Patrick very early on. I might be wrong but if Patrick hadn't been on board, then Frank may not have been able to put it together. It had to be the two of them.

Saying that, I had no reason to think it would work. If anything, I probably felt quite negative about it all, but just kept quiet. I knew that Frank wasn't going to follow any other path, so there was nothing I could do. I supported it, but I didn't have any positive vibes that this was going to turn into anything.

PATRICK HEAD

I can't remember what happened exactly on the day we moved into Unit 10 at Station Road, but for some reason we didn't have a key, so we forced an entry. We just couldn't wait to get started. The place was absolutely filthy inside, so we had to sort that out even though, at that stage, we had nothing to put in it. We really were starting from scratch.

Patrick Neve drove our March in 1977 and he was okay. The car was nothing special but Patrick usually managed to qualify better than the works March cars. We went to a test at Zolder in Belgium for what should have been Patrick's home Grand Prix. He had quite a big accident and wrote off the monocoque. March said they would re-skin it for us. Max Mosley had sold it to Frank as a 1976 ex-Brambilla March. I went up there when the fabricators were working on it and they said,

'This is one of Vittorio's old cars that he used through all of 1975.' I said, 'No, no. It must be 1976.' They said, 'No. Look, here's the orange paint [for Brambilla's sponsor Beta Tools]; it's a 1975 car.' Max had sold it to Frank as a '76. He's not changed!

ROSS BRAWN

I worked for Frank for a year when he was with Walter Wolf. That was when Hesketh kept the good car and sold the rubbish one to Frank. It was a sizeable team then, probably a hundred to a hundred and fifty people. I stayed with Wolf until they won that first race in 1977 with Jody in Argentina, then I went off and did Formula 3 for a year. Frank was in the throes of leaving when I left. Frank and Patrick called me and said that they were re-forming the team in Didcot, and would I come back and work with them? I remember walking into the canteen and looked around, and there were eleven of us including Frank and Patrick.

We had wonderful times. I went from being a machinist in the first year at Wolf and then I became a mechanic in Formula 3. When I rejoined Frank, I came back and did a bit of everything: mechanic, making the pieces and fitting them to the car; I even remember driving the truck even though I didn't have a proper licence. It was a fantastic experience and it's a shame that that sort of thing is not available any more. I was to stay there for seven years.

NEIL OATLEY

In my childhood I lived quite near Brands Hatch, so I used to go down fairly regularly in the mid- to late '60s. I remember seeing what seemed to be loads and loads of cars with Frank Williams Racing Cars stickers on their nose. It gave the impression that he was running them but I think they were just cars that had actually been through his hands.

Even though I didn't know Frank, he had a passion which came through. To me, it was a great opportunity. I saw an ad in *Autosport* but most of my friends and my parents thought I was barking mad for not only going into motor racing but also with someone who had a history of struggling for money. But I was in my early twenties and I thought it wouldn't matter if it all went wrong in a year or so. Fortunately, it went very rapidly from strength to strength.

I had heard these stories about Frank being unable to pay the wages. It certainly didn't happen in my time. But in previous incarnations when the pay cheques arrived on a Friday afternoon everyone downed tools and ran off to the bank. It's true in the early days of Williams Grand Prix Engineering that a lot of people wouldn't deal with us unless we handed over pound notes. You couldn't rely on credit so you literally had to turn up with a paper bag full of money to pay for all your bits and pieces. We were buying one race's gear ratios at a time. Fortunately that disappeared fairly rapidly, and by the end of 1978 things were pretty sound.

When I joined as a junior draughtsman in September 1977 there was just one factory unit. It was tiny, no bigger than a couple of tennis courts strung together. Patrick was the only engineer there so I joined him just after he had started work on the FW06. That first car was drawn by the two of us. He was a fantastic guy to learn from. I wasn't that long out of college and hadn't really been in real engineering work for very long. I was very unsure, made lots of mistakes, but Patrick was very patient and hopefully I was reasonably enthusiastic, so it all worked out quite well. Cars in those days were the standard Cosworth engine, Hewland gearbox, the radiators came off a VW Golf, so the number of parts necessary was tiny compared to a modern racing car. It was a fabulous way to learn and something that people in the sport nowadays just can't appreciate.

BOB TORRIE

I was one of the first employees at Station Road. I knew all about Frank because I had seen him at the circuits while I was a mechanic with Lotus.

He was ambitious and you could tell he was going places. When I went to Station Road on the first day, I have to admit I had my doubts when we eventually got inside. It really was in a dreadful state. It looked enormous: 5,000 square feet and nothing to put in it. We had absolutely nothing. Then a grotty little lathe arrived, and then a small drill. That's all we had for quite a few weeks. One of my first jobs was to paint the dark green walls white and my first technical question to Patrick Head was 'One coat or two?'

JOHNNY BUTE

I'd left school and started working in London. Charlie [Crichton-Stuart, a close relative] had said that his friend Frank Williams was starting a new team and he was looking for someone. At that stage I knew practically nothing about Frank because, although I was a motor racing fan, I didn't have the detailed knowledge about who was who in the sport.

Charlie arranged a meeting with Frank in early 1977. I was rather surprised when Frank said he would visit me rather than me going to have an interview with him. He was going to be in London on that day and he arranged to come and see me in the flat. It was my mum's flat and I was sharing it with my two sisters. It was a pretty wild place! It was on the seventh floor of a block of flats opposite Battersea Park and most people arrived at the top gasping for air. Frank rang the entryphone and I let him in and then wandered off to do something else, expecting him to be quite a long time. He sprinted up the stairs in about twenty seconds and rang the bell. He wasn't even breathing heavily! He was in this immaculately pressed shirt; he always had those fantastic shirts.

I didn't have ambitions to be a racing driver at that stage; I had such a lack of knowledge. I'd been working from the day I left school. I was very motivated by being my own person and the offer of a job with a race team sounded like a fantastic opportunity. I had no qualifications. What I wanted to do was learn how to be a mechanic but going into a Formula 1 team as a van driver and gofer seemed as good an offer as I was going to get. There was a really small core of people and they were all fantastic. I walked in there knowing absolutely eff all and they all treated me really well; it was excellent. The van was a Morris Marina, an awful thing. I hammered the hell out of it and forgot to check the oil. I was out on a run one day when the engine started to make a massive knocking noise. I pulled into a travellers' camp by the side of the road. A guy came out, took a look and said, 'You've blown the engine up, mate. There's no oil in it.' I had to ring the factory and tell them what had happened. They came to collect me. I wasn't very far away. Frank was surprisingly okay about it. Needless to say, I felt like a complete dick.

I was there till the beginning of 1978. I was saying more and more, 'I want to work on the cars. I want to learn'. But because I was unqualified there was no way that could happen. It came to the point when Frank had to say to me, 'Unless you want to carry on doing what you're doing, which you clearly don't, you've got to go away and get some qualifications if you want to work on Formula 1 cars.' He wasn't going to have unqualified people working on the cars. So I went off to work for a very small team and learn a bit more before I started racing in 1980.

ELEVEN

Jousting at Giants

The handful of reporters had come to Didcot for two reasons: curiosity over the first car from Williams Grand Prix Engineering and affection for the man in charge. There did not appear to be much of a story. This, after all, was likely to be the next inconsequential chapter in the racing life of Frank Williams. We had seen his cars before, the Politoys springing to mind. Why should this one be different?

But this time there was a noticeable change. From the moment you walked into the cramped reception area, to be ushered a few paces into the workshop, there was an unmistakable sense of purpose. The place was spotless – something of a novelty for small racing teams in the 1970s – and dominating the floor area was an equally immaculate white car with a green flash on each side. Even to the untrained eye, the Williams FW06 had a workmanlike quality. This was no off-the-shelf item from a production line or the hand-made product of talented amateurs. The car, with Saudia logos front and back, looked the part, as did its stocky, dark-haired driver Alan Jones in his new shiny white overalls.

Frank mingled with the writers, most of whom he regarded as mates. Tea and coffee were on a small table to the side, along with press releases consisting of ten typed pages in binders from WH Smith. Getting his priorities right, Frank paid homage to Saudia on page one and to his secondary sponsors on page two: Fruit of the Loom, introduced to

Williams by Nanni Galli, who had since become a distributor for the American clothing company; Personal, a steering-wheel manufacturer with whom Williams had been involved since 1969; ABMTM, the Association of British Machine Tool Makers, introduced to Williams through his connection with Ward; and trade sponsors Goodyear and Champion.

Throughout the morning Frank seemed even more hyper than usual. Certainly, this was a major moment, but everyone began to realise just how potentially important it was when the beat of a helicopter rotor was heard. Throwing open the back door, Frank watched a helicopter land on a football pitch at the back of the industrial estate, then, straightening his striped tie and buttoning his suit, he walked briskly towards the temporary landing pad – but not before pausing briefly and turning to the assembled company. 'Don't let me down, lads,' he said, and then winked and flashed the familiar smile. His four airborne guests from Saudia included Al Fawzan and the airline's director general, Sheikh Kamal Sindhi. This was a new experience for the Saudis and Frank knew he was bringing them into a nest of potential vipers capable of doing serious damage with humorous tales of past exploits. The car was pushed into the sunshine and everyone watched as Jones posed for photographs with the sponsors, Frank standing slightly to one side but beaming from ear to ear.

Watching from a distance, the staff, now numbering twenty-one, knew the next step was discovering whether or not the FW06 was any good. A test run in bitterly cold weather at Brands Hatch revealed very little other than that the wheels went round and there were no major glitches or leaks. The first two races of the 1978 season in South America would tell a different story.

The heat of Argentina contributed to a vapour lock which starved the engine of fuel. Jones had qualified in the middle of the grid, which was more or less where the team had expected to be. Two weeks later in Brazil Jones was eighth fastest. This was new territory in every sense. Having lifted themselves into serious reckoning, Williams now had the full attention of Goodyear in their fierce tyre war with Michelin and were offered softer and faster rubber of the type normally reserved for the usual pacesetters Lotus (winner in Argentina) and McLaren. This was exciting and augured well for the rest of the season, although as ever Frank did not let enthusiasm get the better of him. Sure enough, a wheel-bearing problem during the race caused difficulties with the brakes and handling, prompting three unscheduled pit stops for tyres. Jones finished eleventh, but was the fastest Goodyear runner. A crash during practice caused a setback in South Africa and Jones qualified eighteenth, but ignoring his poor grid position and a severe cold, Jones sliced through the field to claim fourth place and the first championship points for Williams Grand Prix Engineering. And there was even better to follow on the streets of Long Beach in California. For a while, at least.

After qualifying eighth – ahead of Scheckter's Wolf for the second time this season – Jones drove a storming race and got into second place. The Williams was closing on the leading Ferrari of Carlos Reutemann when the front wing began to collapse. An engine misfire then contributed to a slide back to seventh place. A new lap record did not prevent Patrick kicking himself for the nose wing problem. The concept had come from the March raced the previous season, and this particular wing, from the March, had been brought along as a spare. It should never have been put on without strengthening the internal ribs, but in the race to get things done the modifications had not been carried out. It was another lesson learned the hard way. And there would be more to come as the team found its feet.

There would be mechanical trouble at the next race at Monaco, where the Ford-Cosworth began to emit telltale blue smoke not long after the race started. A stud had come adrift from the oil tank and it was only a matter of time before the oil ran out, with obvious disastrous consequences. This placed Frank on the horns of a dilemma. Under normal circumstances Jones would have been called into the pits and retired before expensive damage was done to the engine, but Frank allowed Jones to continue because he knew his progress was being keenly watched by a group of influential Saudis. If Frank played his cards right, their visit could mark the successful culmination of several months of patient work.

Saudia had increased its support to £100,000, a vote of confidence from a country that knew next to nothing about motor racing. Now Frank urgently needed to tap further into this rich seam courtesy of a very old friend and former landlord. Charles Crichton-Stuart had moved from flying to selling expensive cars for H. R. Owen in Kensington. Still in close contact with the team, Charlie had brought a potentially important guest to Monaco. This would be the first Grand Prix Mansour Ojjeh had ever seen. The Franco-Saudi, whose family owned Techniques d'Avant Garde, would be swept away by the moment and eventually become an important supporter of the team.

This had come about because one of Charlie's customers, Prince Sultan, had not only bought a Ferrari but also Charlie's overtures about investigating motor racing sponsorship. When the prince moved out of London's Dorchester Hotel and on to the United States to study at Denver University, Charlie had made a flying visit to Colorado with Frank. Their proposal had been impressive enough to persuade Prince Sultan to bring it to the attention of his family in Riyadh. Such was the massive potential of this deal that Frank had actually missed the opening race in Argentina in order to fly to Saudi Arabia, where Prince Sultan introduced him to his cousin Prince Muhammad bin Fahd, eldest son of King Fahd. Frank returned home uncertain where this might lead. Next came a call from Jonathan Aitken, Conservative MP for Thanet, who looked after the British interests of Albilad, an international trading company operated by Prince Muhammad. Aitken asked Frank for background to his team. Nothing more was said until Frank received a call saying Prince Muhammad was in the country and a visit might be appropriate.

Seizing his opportunity, Frank had loaded the FW06 into the truck and parked it in Park Lane right outside the Dorchester. Undeterred by the inconvenience to rush-hour traffic, Frank unloaded the car and used his powers of persuasion to have Prince Muhammad come downstairs. One look at the FW06 with the Albilad name prominently displayed had been enough to do the trick. Frank had secured the blessing of the Saudi royal family, which had prompted the visit to Monaco.

Although Jones was to retire before half distance, astute enough to switch off the engine before the internals were destroyed, the Saudis had liked what they had seen. Subsequent results did not make impressive reading – including four retirements in a row – but when he finished Jones was consistently in the top six and frequently in the first three. Indeed, he might even have won the British Grand Prix had it not been for a mixture of bad luck and the sort of mechanical failures that hit any new team. The learning curve was steep, and at the penultimate race of the season in Watkins Glen, Frank and Patrick went through every emotion in the book.

Practice had not been going long when Jones crashed. He walked back to the pits and without a word tossed a broken bolt in Head's direction. Patrick quickly established that it was not a manufacturing problem. The bolt, which had held one of the wheels in place, had sheared because it was not up to the job. The obvious conclusion was that the same applied to the remaining three bolts on the race car and the four on the spare chassis. There was no way Jones could be allowed to continue practice. Unless he found a solution, Patrick would have to tell Frank to withdraw their car from the race.

They needed to find a heat-treatment company, and quickly. This was a job for Crichton-Stuart, who had now joined the team full time in charge of sponsorship liaison and acquisitions. Charlie located a firm whose owner had no interest in working all night and none in parts for a racing car about which he knew very little except that it was a risky area given the product liability laws which dominate commercial life in the United States. But the engineer had reckoned without Charlie's powers of persuasion: before he knew it, Patrick was beginning a lengthy series of tests in his hot and dirty workshop. By morning the job was done and the four bolts were rushed to the racetrack. Frank's admiration for Patrick's skill and resolve was matched by his respect for Jones, who stepped straight into the car and put it third on the grid. Jones went on to finish second in the race. The FW06 did not miss a beat.

Williams Grand Prix Engineering won eleven championship points in 1978, one short of the total achieved since Frank had started to build his own cars six years before. There was the feeling, however, that Williams had the potential to double that figure. With ease. Having designed a solid, straightforward racing car in 1978, Patrick was about to produce the FW07, an absolute classic.

ALAN HENRY

I had been asked to write the press kit for the FW06, something of a novelty for Frank at the time. It was even more novel to be paid for doing it. I remember a man travelled down from Didcot to London, giving me fifty pounds in cash and taking away the typed pages.

ANDREW MARRIOTT

I worked for CSS Promotions and we handled the press coverage of the launch of the FW06. I gathered material for the press release in association with Patrick. I remember noting that the oil tank was a very neat and novel arrangement located between the engine and the gearbox. Aerodynamics were coming at the time and there was some surprise that Patrick had not been influenced by that. In fact the FW06 was typical of Patrick. It was very neat and straightforward. Just what the team needed at that stage. It looked good and everyone present seemed to be aware that, at long last, maybe Frank was going places. Certainly, we were aware that this was the start of a new era.

FRANK WILLIAMS

I was almost speechless when Jonesy qualified eighth for the second race. It was a completely new world for me. I had difficulty coping with the enormity of it. Alan was among the quick boys. For years I had become accustomed just to hanging in there hoping to qualify and now we were showing signs of becoming truly competitive once again.

MANSOUR OJJEH

I went to Monaco as a guest of Charlie Crichton-Stuart. I was with a couple of members of the royal family who were friends of mine. This was the first time I met Frank and it was the first time that I went to a race.

I really didn't know that much about Formula 1. People ask me, how did I get into Formula 1? I've been in it almost thirty years, and I say 'by accident': that's exactly what happened. I became part of the Saudi connection.

I was absolutely overawed by it. I think this is the reaction of anybody who comes for the first time to a Formula 1 race. You might watch it on TV, but when you feel it, when you see it, it's different. And of course it was a lot different thirty years ago to what it is now. It was really the old grunt and dirt and grease in your hands. We didn't have all these communication centres and the motor homes. We had the wives and the girlfriends making the sandwiches; it's come a long way.

I didn't think about becoming involved at that point. TAG didn't have any products. We didn't have TAG Heuer at that time. We just had a name, but we were not into any kind of consumer goods. What made us come in was a political decision really. A lot of the sponsors that Frank had at the time also had other companies, not only from royal families but from big businessmen. We just wanted to be associated with Formula 1 to show that we're a Saudi group and we are consolidated. They said, 'Come on, Mansour. Come and give us a hand.' We couldn't really say no. That's how we started.

ALAN JONES

That accident when the bolt broke could have been a bloody big one. It was through a real quick left-hander, and at the time Watkins Glen did not have a particularly good record when it came to crash barriers. It could have been a nasty shunt. But I got away with it. When I came in the next day, Patrick assured me that the problem had been dealt with. And once Patrick said that, then that was it. I had absolute blind faith in Patrick's ability, and still do. I dismissed it immediately. I mean, if a racing driver is going to dwell on that, then he may as well dwell on every other bloody thing that the designer has done.

NEIL OATLEY

I went to a few races in the middle of the 1978 season and it was pretty much a hand-to-mouth existence. We had just two cars but we only had two tiny trucks. I can't remember where Frank had got one of them from but when we went to load the car for the first time on the rising ramps, as soon as we started to crank the car up, the struts supporting the ramp began to bend.

Each car had its own truck; they were too small to carry two cars. The second truck broke down on the way to Austria and some of the parts needed for the first car were on the second truck. The night before practice began we didn't have exhausts for the car and we tried to borrow them from other teams in the hope that the tail pipes would be in the right position. The truck eventually arrived during the night and we just about had the car ready for practice. That was fairly typical of the operation at the time.

I'm guessing a little bit, but by the end of 1978 we must have grown to about fifty or sixty people. We'd just taken over the next-door unit, so the floor size had doubled. Even so, at tea break the whole team would sit in this communal room around a big table. It was very good to foster camaraderie. It was a relatively young team so there were a lot of people like myself who were single in their early twenties, which meant that socially it was good for everybody.

IAN ANDERSON

I joined as a mechanic in April 1978. Originally I had been going to join Wolf in the days when Frank was there. At that time I was buying a house. When I mentioned Frank's name as a prospective employer to the people we were getting a mortgage from, the guy said he didn't think that was a good idea because from what he'd heard I might not get paid! So, I didn't go to Wolf-Williams.

Later on, when I realised Frank was going on his own and Patrick was with him, it looked like it could be a good little set-up. I applied and got a job. They had just finished the FW06 and done about three races when I joined. Then the chief mechanic decided he didn't want to continue and Frank and Patrick asked if I would do it.

VIRGINIA WILLIAMS

Frank deserved every penny he got from Saudi sponsorship because of the work he put in. He would drive into London in the evenings and wait for hours and hours because the Saudis were always on completely different timetables. He would end up not seeing him even though Prince Muhammad had said he would see him at some point. The next night he'd be back there still waiting. Then he'd go to Saudi Arabia for two days and come back two *weeks* later.

PATRICK HEAD

The FW06 wasn't bad. Our biggest fault in 1978 was reliability. A lot of it was bad engineering from me, such as that front hub failure at Watkins Glen. Otherwise it was things like quality control in manufacture, throttle cables that broke, electrical connections and so on.

The Lotus 79 was the outstanding car at that time. They were supremely quick but often almost walking wounded. Alan was the next one hovering around to pick up the pieces. We moved into first place once or twice and should have won races, but through our reliability problems failed to do so. We could have had a much better year. It wasn't a great car, but it was very driveable. Alan said it was a fantastic car to throw around.

During 1978. I went from thinking, *Well, this is a bit of fun and maybe I'll go and do something else next year*, to thinking, *Actually, this is quite good and, if we put our heads down, we could maybe achieve something and perhaps win a Grand Prix*. In 1977 we had been just jousting at giants. But in 1978 we were actually starting to annoy a few people.

JONATHAN WILLIAMS

I can remember Zandvoort in 1978. Because the race fell in the summer and the circuit was near to the beach, it was always the race my father had to take the family to for a summer holiday. The motor homes in the paddock backed up to the track. My mother held me up as a three-year-old by the fence when a Williams came by and the noise just terrified me.

My second memory from the following year is a little clearer. My mother decided that we would watch from a grandstand. She expected to pay on the gate to get in and she was told, quite rudely, that this grandstand was reserved for Renault VIPs. We went back to the paddock. This was in the days when everyone knew everyone, unlike today. My mother went to Jean Sage, the Renault team manager, and said I was four years old and couldn't be in the pits and it would be nice to be in the grandstand. Jean didn't hesitate to give her two tickets. I clearly remember her explaining to Alan Jones that this would be my first race which I would probably watch from beginning to end. She pointed out the grandstand where we would be, easily recognised by all the yellow Renault signs, and was there any chance he could wave on the warm-up lap? Alan said, 'Yeah, okay.' Sure enough, as he came by, there was a hand waving from the cockpit – as if he didn't have enough to think about. Quite what the Renault guests must have thought about a Williams driver waving to them, particularly as their drivers, Jean-Pierre Jabouille and René Arnoux, went by without a single sideways glance, I really don't know.

TWELVE
Nearly, but Not Quite

The world of motorsport aerodynamics was turned upside down by the car that won the 1978 world championship. Colin Chapman's Lotus 79 introduced the term 'ground effect' to Formula 1. By enclosing inverted wings on either side of the Lotus and trapping the air by sealing the gap between the side pod and the ground with a sliding skirt, an effect like the reverse of an aircraft wing was achieved and the car was pulled towards the track, increasing tyre grip and allowing the car to corner as if on rails. Mario Andretti, the 1978 champion, was in a league of his own. There was no doubt in the mind of every designer that this was the route to follow, but it was not that straightforward. Chapman, perhaps carried away by his success, took the theory further. The resulting Lotus 80 was unmanageable, as was the 1979 McLaren, an exaggerated copy of the Lotus 79.

Patrick Head did not fall into the trap, the Williams FW07 being relatively conservative, but efficient. He was helped in his quest for a competitive car by the arrival of Frank Dernie, who would pay special attention to the aerodynamics, an area about to assume massive importance. Patrick, armed with the latest knowledge, was shocked to discover how inefficient the FW06 had been when for the first time he made use of a wind tunnel.

Now that Frank Williams had earned the right to be readmitted to FOCA with its attendant financial benefits, it was necessary to think about running a second car. Jones had been astute enough to agree terms for 1979 as long ago as the previous July, so it was a question of finding a teammate who would be quick without rocking the boat. Clay Regazzoni fitted the bill perfectly. Experienced, fast, totally without pretensions and a man who loved racing as much as Frank and Patrick, the genial Swiss was happy to accept the role of number-two driver. Ferrari had dismissed Regazzoni at the end of 1976 for no other apparent reason than that he had been around for too long. Two indifferent years with middle-order teams had brought the right mix of circumspection and the need to re-establish himself.

After the first three races Regazzoni could have been forgiven for thinking that perhaps his had not been such a wise move. The team had believed that the FW06 would see them through until such time as the FW07 was ready, but such was the rapid pace of development elsewhere that Jones and Regazzoni struggled to finish in the top ten, never mind the point-scoring positions at the front. The French Ligier team – with former Williams man Jacques Laffite as one of its drivers – was leading the championship as the teams assembled in California for the fourth round at Long Beach. The FW07 had been finished in time for display in the pit lane at Long Beach before initial testing. Jones, finding the FW06 with its lack of aerodynamic finesse at less of a disadvantage on the street circuit, finished third. The Australian's stock was continuing to rise, his name appearing increasingly on the wish lists of rival teams. Obviously aware of his rising status, Jones pointed to the FW07 and said half-jokingly, 'This car had better be fucking good.'

As far as Frank was concerned, that was Patrick's responsibility. Frank was focused on raising money to pay for the car and a team consuming a budget in excess of £500,000. Frank was commuting regularly between England and Saudi Arabia, where Prince Muhammad had used his influence to bring on board Dallah Avco, an airport maintenance company, Bin Laden, a road builder, and Baroom, a steel and cement merchant. It was almost irrelevant that these companies would gain little from having their names on the sides of a Formula 1 car racing everywhere in the world but within their markets in the Middle East. If Williams was good enough for Prince Muhammad then it was good enough for them. The team's income rose accordingly but it took a lot of work from Frank in an alien business culture. Moreover the bottom line was results on the racetrack. Much depended on the FW07 and its debut now that the European sector of the season was under way.

In Spain both FW07s retired with various technical problems, but not before Jones laid down an important marker by setting the second-fastest lap. Potential was almost realised at the next race in Belgium, where Jones and Regazzoni qualified on the second and fourth rows. Clay got himself involved in an accident on the second lap but Jones settled down in third place before gradually moving forward. Lap twenty-four was another milestone – for the first time since 1969 a Williams-entered car led a Grand Prix – but with thirty laps to go an electrical problem caused the engine to cut out.

Jones was not slow to vent his frustration but received a reminder two weeks later that these things work both ways when he crashed during practice at Monaco and then made another uncharacteristic mistake by touching a barrier and damaging the suspension and steering while lying third in the race. The day was saved by Regazzoni, who despite the absence of second gear, a major handicap on the tight street circuit, slashed thirteen seconds off the leader, Jody Scheckter, and chased his Ferrari across the line. Clay had brought the race alive, much to the relief of Williams and the delight of the Saudi sponsors, again in Monaco to watch their cars race.

Meanwhile, on the technical front things were moving with alarming speed in another direction. Ever since the three-litre formula had been introduced in 1966, allowance had been made for turbocharging, should an engine manufacturer choose to go down that route. This alternative had been written into the rules purely as a sop to engine makers who wished to continue using their now-redundant 1.5-litre engines left over from the previous formula. The theory was that by turbocharging the smaller engine its performance would roughly be on a par with a three-litre motor – although no one knew for sure, or cared. That was about to change.

This option had not been taken seriously until 1977, when Renault entered Formula 1 with a car powered by a 1.5-litre turbocharged engine. There were smirks when the V6, beset with throttle lag problems, droned round at the back of the field before retiring early from its maiden race at Silverstone. In the two years since that inauspicious debut Renault had been working diligently. Their day was to come at Dijon-Prenois on 1 July 1979, when Jean-Pierre Jabouille not only won for the first time but did so on Renault's home territory.

Frank was worried. The writing was on the wall and it was in French. The next race was the British Grand Prix, and he fully expected the Renaults to wipe the floor with the opposition on the fast sweeps of Silverstone. If only he had known how the boot was going to slip with remarkable ease on to the other foot, courtesy of a little aerodynamic tweak that no one could see deep down inside the FW07.

PATRICK HEAD

I didn't go to the last races of 1978. We really were one man and his dog at that time. Neil Oatley had joined us in the design office and it was quite clear that the Lotus 79 had huge amounts of grip. Alan was saying that it just made him feel silly when a Lotus was ahead of him. In a slow corner he could generally keep up, or actually close up, but in the fast corners he said it was just unbelievable. It was as if the Lotus had tyres five compounds softer than he had. It had to be downforce.

I'd heard somewhere that Lotus used a wind tunnel in Imperial College, so I rang a chap called John Harvey, who ran the department of aerodynamics at Imperial, and asked if we could book a week. He said, 'Yes, no problem.' So I drew out what I thought the Lotus 79 was like underneath and had a think about it. Our fibreglass man, Nigel Buckingham, made the models, and in October 1978 he and I spent five days in the Donald Campbell Tunnel at Imperial, which was a 25 per cent model scale size. When we saw what was possible with a skirted car I was somewhat flabbergasted. We only had five days, but I was able to do pressure tapping on the underside, and when we took the front wings off, all of a sudden the pressures on the underside became hugely better. It was quite clear it would be preferable if you could have literally no front wings, or front wings which were almost neutral to the flow trimmers on the car. So it was a very useful time in the tunnel.

In January 1979 Frank Dernie joined us and did the skirt system. He was a clever guy and we had a very good skirt system as a result. We didn't get the car ready for the start of the season so we took two FW06s, which I thought should be good enough for the middle of the grid for the first few races. But any sort of ground-effect car was going to be quicker than a non-ground-effect car and we were really blown away. The only place we did reasonably was the last race with the 06 at Long Beach, where the corners were all quite slow.

We had one FW07 out there for some of our Arab sponsors to look at. Ian Anderson was our chief mechanic. He'd worked for John Wyer doing the Porsche 917. He was brilliant in a way that you don't see now. It's not the mechanics' fault. Unfortunately they're all fitters now; they get given a complete assembly and bolt it together. They're very good at it, very meticulous. But Ian understood modality, heat treatment, geometry and so on. A lovely man and a very clever guy.

The paddock at Long Beach was in the convention centre – a massive hall. Ian turned up one morning to find a pair of feet sticking out from under the tarpaulin covering the FW07. Ian was quite a fearsome-looking fellow with wild hair. He got hold of these feet and pulled them out. It was Morris Nunn [owner of the small Ensign team] just having a look. Ian told me what had happened when I arrived, so I went round to see Morris. He said, 'I was only having a little look, you know, and this bloody madman, a *wild* man, came and attacked me!' He looked quite shocked. It was very funny.

After the race we took the FW07 up to what was Ontario Motor Speedway, now a housing estate. Alan did about three laps, came in, pulled up, switched off and said, 'Now I know why those bloody Lotuses had such an advantage. I cannot slide this car, whatever I do. It's got *so* much grip.' Needless to say, another fifty laps and he was sliding the car as he stepped up to the new level of grip.

The FW07 was good right from the start. We missed out on its first few races through not really understanding the car in terms of the electrics, for example. But Alan gave them a bit of a fright later on.

STEVE FOWLER

I'm a fabricator and I've been with the team for more than thirty years. When I first arrived, it was only intended to be a temporary job. I had worked for Wolf Racing, with Jody Scheckter and Peter Warr. Peter and I didn't agree on certain things. One day I threw the toolbox in the back of the car and said, 'That's it. I'm going.' Within about a day, Frank phoned me up. Ian Anderson, who I had worked with before, had spoken to Frank and said, 'We need someone like Steve here.' I'd had aircraft experience, testing the Olympus engines for Concorde.

Frank asked if I could start work. I said, 'It's a long bloody long way; I live in Camberley.' I said I didn't mind helping out. One of the guys in the fabrication shop used to sand-bend the aluminium water pipes. There was no machine. You filled the pipes full of sand, heated the aluminium and gradually put bends in the pipes; the sand would keep them uniform. The guy who usually did the job had gone on holiday to Australia for six weeks and they asked if I could cover for him. I had no work so I said I would do it for that time. The guy came back and they asked me to stay another couple of weeks. Then another couple of weeks. In the end, I said, 'I've got to go; it's costing me too much money.' Patrick asked if I'd start on the race team. On the race team you're away most of the time, not travelling backwards and forwards to home. I thought I could see the world for nothing; this was fantastic. So I joined the team.

The first race was Jarama in Spain, which was where the 07 raced for the first time. We were working out of the back of a Bedford truck, which would only take one car. At the time we had to take the other car on a low-loader with these wagon train-like hoops which held the canvas over the top. Halfway through Spain it collapsed on top of the car and we had to mend all the bits and pieces when it arrived at the track. In the hotel room that night, my first night, about one in the morning, I'm lying on the bed and thinking, *Shit, do I need all this? What have I let myself in for?* But it's like a disease: you want to do it again.

JOHN CADD

I was a car mechanic. A friend of mine was working for the racing team and one evening he asked if I fancied working for Williams. I said I'd give it a go even though I'd never been in motor racing. I came down for an interview in November 1979 and they took me on. I started in one of the sub-assembly departments, mainly for the uprights, gearboxes and that sort of stuff. There were three of us: myself, Bob Torrie, who used to be the main man, and a guy called Peter Digby. It was great. I'll always remember my first day. Bob introduced me to Frank and I said, 'Good morning, Mr Williams,' and he said, 'First thing, it's Frank.' That's always stood with me from day one. I think I was number thirty-one or thirty-two, but there was a great family atmosphere.

Eventually I fancied doing racing. I tried to get on the race team, but I wasn't accepted at first. Ian Anderson said, 'I can't understand why you're not on the race team because they could do with someone with your experience.' Not that the other guys on the race team weren't good, but they needed mechanics. I had a word with Frank and he sorted it out. I was put on the test team, which to me was a lot more interesting than racing. You're more involved with the car in testing, trying newer things on the car. I still did a load of races, maybe five or six. You would go testing, come back, get some clean clothes and go off racing.

FRANK DERNIE

I got to know Frank through Harvey Postlethwaite when it was Frank Williams (Racing Cars) Ltd in Bennet Road. At that time I was doing some analysis for Harvey: I wrote a computer program to analyse suspension geometry and I also analysed wind-tunnel results.

Bennet Road was a relatively small place – all teams were pretty small then. There was a Portakabin in the car park, where Harvey had his office. He introduced me to their two designer/draughtsmen, Patrick Head and Gary Thomas. Harvey didn't have a drawing board. I knew that Harvey didn't design anything; he was a sort of engineering manager, a Mr Fixit. He used to do the odd sketch. Whereas Patrick and myself used to draw everything, do the calculations. The difference between Patrick and Harvey was … profound, shall we say.

Frank started up Williams Grand Prix Engineering and asked me to join him. Hesketh was going nowhere and Frank was telling me it was going to be great, which is what Frank does. He can be very, very convincing. But to put it into perspective, I worked for Frank for three years before I moved house into that area because in those days Formula 1 teams were not very stable. You didn't know if they'd be able to pay you from one month to another, or buy the air tickets. I'm not being critical; that's the way Formula 1 was. Apart from two or three well-funded teams, the rest of them were pretty much hand to mouth.

Patrick can be quite physical and intimidating. He'd made it clear to Frank that his role was keeping morale going and raising the funding. If he was to interfere with the engineering, he'd be strongly criticised. It stayed that way as Williams got bigger and bigger.

Just as I was joining, the team had got an extra unit on the trading estate in Station Road to expand the machine shop. I was doing wind-tunnel stuff. Patrick isn't that interested in aerodynamics; he'd rather it would go away, to be honest. In fact, I think he'd ban air if it wasn't for the fact the engine wouldn't run! He obviously knows the physics of it very well but he always rather resented the fact that it gets in the way of the nice bits from his perspective, so the aero fell to me, among other things.

Whenever we went to the Imperial College wind tunnel, we used to get a huge gain and the car was massively quicker. I suggested that Williams should get their own wind tunnel. Patrick said he had heard where there might be one available at a company called Specialised Mouldings. Frank took a look at the tunnel and bought it for cash. Patrick and I installed it at Station Road. The working section was five feet by four and it was suitable for a quarter-scale model. It worked reasonably well, but it didn't have a moving ground and in some ways was inappropriate for what we wanted to do. We installed a moving ground. All of the electronics and computing were done by Ross Brawn and myself. Ross was my technician at the time and he put it together. I designed bits. I soldered every connector on, every bit of electronics. I wrote every word of every bit of software. Ross tightened every bolt, moved everything and he actually drew a lot of the bits. We would borrow a couple of race mechanics when they were free in the winter, but basically it was a two-man job building that wind tunnel.

NEIL OATLEY

Brian Henton had shaken down the FW07 for us at Donington before we took it to Long Beach. Alan [Jones] couldn't understand why we weren't racing it. But Frank and Patrick stood firm and said, 'We've got to do a proper test before we race it.' Even so, there would be the usual teething problems when we got to the first races in Europe.

MAURICE HAMILTON

I was covering F1 races for the *Guardian* newspaper. I'll never forget coming back from having watched Jones lead the Belgian Grand Prix only to lose a certain win with electrical trouble. The race had been held at Zolder, a pretty tacky place but a good circuit none the less.

Being not far from the coast, my colleague and mentor Eoin Young and I had travelled by car. Boarding the return ferry to Dover with us on the Monday was none other than Alan Jones in his brand-new Mercedes-Benz 6.9. Being Jonesy, eating in the restaurant on his own was of no interest and he joined us in the cafeteria. I have to say it made an incongruous sight: Jonesy with an expensive leather briefcase, which were all the rage at the time, and a gold Rolex watch above a large hand carrying a tray of fish and chips and a mug of tea. It didn't bother him in the slightest. He was a great character, a journalist's dream, as I was about to find out.

I had my notebook on hand while trying to construct a follow-up story for the following day's edition of the *Guardian*. I had been struggling to think of an interesting angle but Jones was about to deliver one into my lap. In words of one syllable he said what he thought about the succession of reliability problems, which, if they continued, would stop the team from succeeding as much as they deserved to do.

Jones knew exactly what he was doing, and the fact that he was prepared to have his team criticised in print actually said much for a working relationship which he knew would respond in the correct manner without taking mortal offence. The headline the following day, RELIABILITY WEAK POINT AT WILLIAMS, probably told Williams what they already knew and, typically, they soon had it sorted without the driver–team relationship being in the least affected. You wouldn't get such honesty from the politically correct drivers of today, most of whom are terrified to tell you their name.

THIRTEEN
Win One

'You had no need of a stopwatch. Five minutes of watching at the entry to Copse or Stowe – or anywhere else on the circuit where the road turned – told the story far more graphically. The Williams was measurably, demonstrably, visibly quicker into, through and out of the turns than anything else in the place, its particular strength being its turning-in ability. The sheer adhesion of the car was breathtaking.' Simon Taylor, writing in *Autosport* on practice for the British Grand Prix, summed up in words the sight that everyone in Formula 1, including Williams, had difficulty believing. The FW07 was not simply quick, it was utterly dominant.

Tidying up of the flow of air around the base of the engine had had an effect disproportionate to the simplicity of the modification. Fairings are commonplace on even the most humble racing car today but in 1979 this was virgin territory and the Williams team had arrived before anyone else. Run for the first time in a pre-Grand Prix test session at Silverstone a few days before, the fairing improved the handling to such an extent that at first Frank could not believe what his stopwatch was telling him. When practice began for the Grand Prix itself Jones rattled off lap times six seconds under the three-year-old lap record. Pole position was a mere formality – another first for Frank – as a British underdog came good. A dream maiden victory had to be on the cards.

Frank and Patrick were not so sure, and neither were Cosworth, their engine manufacturers. The long straights and fast corners of Silverstone were playing havoc with oil consumption, so much so that Cosworth advised an engine change for the race. Wayne Eckersley and John Jackson carried out the swap, finishing at 11.30 p.m. the night before the race. As a matter of routine, they fired up the engine to check for leaks, only to discover that the fuel pump was not working. There was nothing for it but to take the engine out and start all over again. By the time they finished at 5.30 a.m. it was not worth going to bed.

Regazzoni, his car now also fitted with the demon aerodynamic tweak, had qualified fourth to line up directly behind the Renault of Jabouille – with Jones on the front row. Knowing that the turbocharged Renault would be sluggish away from the line, Regazzoni shot past the yellow and white car at the start but also overtook Jones. Regazzoni's lead lasted as far as Hangar Straight, where Jones dived past both cars on the way into Stowe. Jabouille moved into second and hung on for a couple of laps but the pace was too much for his Michelin tyres, allowing Regazzoni to close in.

For more than half of the scheduled sixty-eight laps, there was no hint of the oil pressure problem as Jones dominated the race. His lead of twenty-five seconds was comfortable enough to allow a reduction in engine revs. Then, as Jones passed the pits at the end of lap thirty-seven, Frank noticed a white mist swirling from the back of the car. There was a leak and the engine was overheating. Frank gave it two more laps. Sure enough, at the end of the thirty-ninth Jones came slowly down the pit lane, the engine coolant having drained away through a crack in the neck of the water pump. The mechanics dived on the car but there was nothing they could do. Jones was already wriggling free of the cockpit. There was no need to ask how he felt. He changed out of his overalls, said his goodbyes and quietly slipped away with his wife Beverley.

Frank, with an absence of emotion that had become his trademark, continued filling in his lap chart – which showed his other car was leading. Almost unnoticed, Regazzoni had overtaken Jabouille when the

Renault stopped for fresh tyres. For a brief moment at the end of lap thirty-nine the two Williamses had been side by side, one entering the pit lane, the other inheriting the lead on the track. To mark the occasion, Regazzoni then set the fastest lap of the race, a full three seconds under the record, but given Jones's problems, would the second Williams survive the remaining twenty-nine laps?

Williams had become the story. Camera crews abandoned Renault, Brabham, Lotus and the rest and headed towards the figure sitting by the pit wall on his fold-up chair, his eyes flicking from track to stopwatch to lap chart, his face expressionless. Frank counted down five laps to go. Regazzoni continued to lead. Then three laps. Then one. As car number 28 swept through Woodcote Corner for the final time, the grandstand lining the long pit straight stood as one. Regazzoni, with his moustache and bandit smile, was hugely popular, but the applause was also for Frank Williams. Everyone, from race fans to rivals in the pit lane, knew just what he had been through.

Frank had difficulty finding the right words when besieged by the media. At the back of his mind was the niggling thought that he had let down Jones. He would make amends at the next race, but meanwhile Saturday 14 July 1979 would go down as one of the best days of his life.

FRANK WILLIAMS

When we turned up with that car at Silverstone, it was a case of, 'Goodbye, everybody.' The mods put on the car looked like a reasonable step, but nothing more. But suddenly the car was going a bit quicker and a bit quicker. Then Alan came in and said, 'You can't believe what's going on out there. It's just unreal how quick it is'. Suddenly life was 100 per cent in another direction. I'll never forget that feeling. I was checking the opposition to make sure they weren't doing those times. Loads of people were looking at their stopwatches; I'll never forget the despair on their faces. It was like God had given us a miracle, except it wasn't; it was something they had found in the wind tunnel.

PATRICK HEAD

The so-called trick was just sealing off the low-pressure area where the undersides of the car came up and sort of wandered around close to the engine. There was a big air gap in an area where there was low pressure, which meant there was a lot of air leaking through this gap. It had always been intended to panel that bit in, but we didn't get round to it. Those bits were made by Bernie Jones in metal. My memory is getting underneath and saying to Bernie, 'Can you make some panels to fill that in?' I've heard Frank [Dernie] saying over a cup of tea that he did it. It doesn't matter who did it; I don't really care.

The point is we got the job done by simply sealing off this low-pressure area. There was no trick to it. I don't think we realised how important it was going to be. We went to the test at Silverstone and Alan lopped about 1.2 seconds off his time. He said, 'I've just got to learn to persuade my mind to go into Copse and Stowe. I go in there and I'm halfway round the corner, thinking, *Fucking hell, Alan, why are you going so slowly?* It's a question of persuading my foot not to come off.'

Practice for the Grand Prix itself was very interesting. Being a Saturday race, Thursday afternoon and Friday counted for qualifying. Alan did his grid time on the Thursday. He started his lap and lost it at Copse. He came in with the rear wing hanging off the car and we put another one on and sent him out with a new set of tyres. First lap, bang! One minute, 11.8 seconds. Everyone else was doing fourteens. He'd done a 13.6 beforehand; he'd completely missed out the twelves! Literally, the whole pit lane went silent. The place was stunned. Nobody was going to get near Alan's pole-position time. It was pretty obvious we were in good shape for the race, provided we didn't have any reliability problems.

When Alan came down the pit lane with steam coming from the car, we didn't know what it was. The Cosworth had a water pump entry which stuck out sideways, wider than the chassis. So, we had to modify the water pump to put an entry that went down. We took the pump off the engine, ground away the normal entry and welded on a bit of tubing bent round and sticking downwards. Keith Duckworth [designer of the Ford-Cosworth V8] would have had kittens if he'd seen it! The weld on Alan's car got a bit thin and it cracked, whereas on Clay's car the same modification had done less mileage and hadn't been polished away.

So yes, we were pretty sick when Alan retired. It's not that we were against Clay; he was such a lovely guy. But it was very much Alan's team. He was such an indomitable character that even if he qualified on the third row of the grid, all the guys in the team knew he was going to win the race; knew he'd be second coming out of the first corner. He would have barged Nelson Piquet off the track, pushed him into the boonies. He projected confidence, in himself and in the team, and that was wonderful really.

Clay drove a good race. I've never really been a great one for celebrating when we win. My attitude has always been that we go to a race to win. It really feels like job done. Don't get me wrong: I've never been grumpy about winning! But that's what we went there to do.

FRANK DERNIE

Three of us, for different reasons, wanted to tidy up the floor round the engine. I did a fairing based on trying to keep the flow attached and it was the biggest single improvement I think I've ever seen in the wind tunnel. It was so big I came back early from the wind tunnel – still at Imperial then – [and] drew it. I think the wind-tunnel test was the week of the Grand Prix, so Monday it looked good, Tuesday I drew it and Thursday we were making it in the factory. We were all chuffed. That was a big step. I was told by one of the Brabham guys that they never resolved that problem on the BT49.

Patrick and I at that time used to split the races fifty-fifty because we had our own work to do at the factory and there weren't many engineers. Patrick and I split running Jonesy, depending on what we were

Above: Frank Williams and Gianpaolo Dallara (centre) discuss the De Tomaso with Piers Courage during practice for the ill-fated 1970 Dutch Grand Prix at Zandvoort.

Right: Piers Courage and Frank's immaculate Brabham-Ford BT26 on their way to a magnificent second place in the 1969 Monaco Grand Prix.

Below: Ready to roll. Patrick Head (left) and Frank Williams pose outside the team's headquarters in Station Road, Didcot, with their first car, FW06.

Left: Alan Jones leads the field into the first corner of the 1979 Dutch Grand Prix. Clay Regazzoni's Williams follows with a front wheel missing after a collision at the start.

Above: Speaking the same language. Alan Jones and Frank Williams enjoyed a close working relationship.

Right: Job done. Frank and the team welcome home Alan Jones in Austria 1979 for the team's third win in succession.

Left: One champion to another. Jackie Stewart interviews Alan Jones after winning the world championship in Montreal, 1980.

Right: Carlos Reutemann narrowly missed winning the 1981 championship.

Left: Clay Regazzoni, the popular and perfect number 2 driver for Williams in 1979, scored the team's first win in the British Grand Prix.

Below: Jacques Laffite gave Williams a huge boost by finishing second in the 1975 German Grand Prix and returned to the team in 1983.

Above: Keke Rosberg, in typical pose.

Right: Nelson Piquet, champion in 1987, but never particularly happy during his two years at Williams.

Above: Tension mounts. Frank Dernie, Patrick Head and Frank Williams were on hand to see Alan Jones win their first championship in Montreal 1980.

Left: Neil Oatley (right) keeps an eye on progress as John Westwood signals Alan Jones as he leads the 1981 Las Vegas Grand Prix.

Below: Alan Challis (centre) and Ryuchi Nakaya, a Honda technician, prepare to help Keke Rosberg push his Williams-Honda into the pit lane at Monaco in 1984.

Above: Mutual respect. Nigel Mansell and Patrick Head discuss the Williams-Honda in 1985, the driver and technical chief making a strong working partnership.

Right: Frank Williams, proud owner of the pair of FW10s in Austria, 1985.

Below: Murray Walker sits in the hot seat in Portugal 1986, the BBC TV commentator flanked on his right by Nelson Piquet and, to his left, Nigel Mansell and Frank Williams.

Above: Nigel Mansell (left) celebrates his first Grand Prix win at Brands Hatch, October 1985. McLaren's Alain Prost (right) has just become world champion.

Below: One in the ear for the champion-elect. Nelson Piquet (right) in a frisky mood as the 1986 championship contenders pose on the pit wall at Estoril in Portugal. Ayrton Senna (left) would be eliminated at the next race in Mexico, leaving Alain Prost (second left) to fight Nigel Mansell and Piquet at the final round in Australia.

Below: Nigel Mansell waits in the Williams-Judd for a tyre check at the end of the Paul Ricard pit lane during practice for the 1988 French Grand Prix.

doing. Patrick did the detail design and I did the concept stuff so it tended to be the first four races Patrick would do while I fixed all the problems like overheating, in the wind tunnel if necessary.

The British Grand Prix wasn't my race, so I didn't go until Saturday. I was there doing corner times and the debrief, but I wasn't running the car. Jonesy just disappeared into the distance and I was so disappointed when his car stopped, but Clay came through and we won. I don't really think at the time that you appreciate the magnitude of the first win; it had been such a long time in coming. We celebrated but, typical Silverstone, you can't stay long otherwise you would never get home because of the traffic.

IAN ANDERSON

I was chief mechanic and in those days there were two mechanics per car. I was responsible for getting the cars built. We had a small sub-assembly unit but generally the mechanics built all their own cars. I oversaw that, did a bit of research and development, and that was more or less it.

The biggest disappointment at Silverstone was obviously with Alan when the water pump broke. The car came down the pit lane and went straight into the pits. Everyone was running around like headless chickens. I could see what had happened, and I was wondering if the same thing was going to happen to Clay's car. Then Biggles [Ken Sagar, ex-RAF, the team's truckie and spares man] decided he would shut the roller door. He overreacted a bit and shut it on my head! I had a headache from that point onwards.

STEVE FOWLER

We thought before Silverstone that with a bit of reliability we were going to win races with this car – it was so quick. A water-pipe modification was needed for the pump on both cars, but I could only make one pipe because I was busy doing the skirts as well. They had another company make the second pipe. The one on Jonesy's car cracked. Of course, I thought, *Shit! That's mine.* But it wasn't. Mine was on Regazzoni's car. Whenever the car breaks down, you always think, *Is it my bit?* It's a natural instinct. In this case they made it with the wrong gauge material. I don't know why that happened because it would have been specified. It might have been because the part was very complicated to fabricate and they found it easier to do in a thinner gauge.

The feeling after the race was absolutely fantastic. Absolutely incredible. Everyone was jumping around, grins from ear to ear. Most of the factory were there. In those days Frank really encouraged everybody to come to the track. If Frank didn't see all the people in the workshop at the track, he'd ask them why they weren't supporting us! He was very into that. He wanted everybody to be part of the team in every respect. Before his accident he'd say cheerio to every single person in the factory before leaving for a race. I don't know whether it was some kind of superstition thing, but he did that without fail.

NIGEL ROEBUCK

I was reporting for *Autosport*. Back in 1979 journalists didn't have post-race press conferences in Formula 1, but sometimes there would be an informal ceremony, and they had one at Silverstone in a marquee near the paddock. The atmosphere was unusually emotional, for Frank Williams had become a winner at last, and everyone wanted to share his joy. At first he could barely speak. Then someone gave him a whisky and another lit a cigar, and Williams, a lifelong teetotaller and non-smoker, gamely sipped the one, puffed on the other. 'Thank you, thank you so much,' he murmured to well-wishers, and there were tears in his eyes. After a few minutes his driver came in, dabbing at his face with a towel, for the afternoon was warm. On the podium, in deference to the team's Saudi Arabian sponsors, he had toasted his victory with orange juice; now he looked ready for a swig of his boss's Scotch. He shook Williams's hand. 'Bravo, Frank,' he quietly said. That was the essential modesty of a man who had class to throw away. Clay Regazzoni had won a Grand Prix for the first time in three years, but uppermost in his mind – in all our minds – was that this was Frank Williams's day. Unforgettable.

NEIL OATLEY

I was Clay's engineer that year, so it was obviously fantastic that my driver won. Understandably, there were some mixed emotions in the team because of Alan's rapport with Frank and Patrick and the fact that he'd contributed a lot to how we had developed as a team. It was a shame that he didn't have the first win, but on a purely personal selfish level it was a fantastic day.

If there was a celebration, I didn't go to it. Frank's not one for big celebrations. The race was on a Saturday, so you had Sunday off as well. I had a load of motor-racing mates camping on the infield. After the race was over, I just went and joined them for a few beers. It was obviously a very nice feeling. In a relatively short period of time I had come into motor racing, and here I was, working on the car which had won the British Grand Prix.

RON DENNIS

I remember Saturday 14 July 1979 very well indeed. I wasn't yet running the McLaren Formula 1 team but I'd already been involved in motorsport professionally for thirteen years, having spent time with both Cooper and Brabham in the late 1960s. In the 1970s I began running my own race outfits – mainly in Formula 2 – and by 1979 my team, Project Four, was a successful Formula 2 operation sponsored by Marlboro.

On that weekend there was the Formula 1 race at Silverstone and a Formula 2 race at Zandvoort, and Project Four was fielding two March-BMW 792s in the Dutch event: one for Steven South and one for Derek

Daly. I was at Silverstone that weekend. Project Four were running a BMW M1 for Niki Lauda in the Procar series, which supported most European Grands Prix in 1979 and 1980. Niki won the Procar championship with us that first year, and he won the Silverstone round too, so mid-July 1979 was a good time for me as well as for Frank.

Despite the fact that I had no formal connection with Frank, I really did cheer Clay home. I did so because I recognised, as I think most motor-racing people did who were there that day, that good old Frank had finally broken through to the big time, after years and years of struggling with poor cars and little money. It felt good to see his face light up as Clay powered his Williams across the line to take the chequered flag.

TONY DODGINS

In 1979 I decided to enter the Sir William Lyons Award for aspiring young motoring journalists. I wrote to a number of people in Formula 1, and ended up being granted interviews with Frank Williams, Ken Tyrrell and Colin Chapman at the British Grand Prix. Lotus, having dominated the previous year with Mario Andretti and the Lotus 79, were having a bad time with the Lotus 80. Carlos Reutemann had signed to partner Andretti after leaving Ferrari when Jody Scheckter arrived. I remember Chapman gritting his teeth and trying to retain a sense of humour while this young kid with a huge tape recorder asked him questions like, 'Why doesn't the 80 work?' The look in his eye said, 'Well, if I knew that ...'

Ken Tyrrell was great, really helpful and very encouraging, but it was Frank who provided me with the interview that allowed me to win the award and get a foot in the journalism door. Maybe because he, like me, was born in South Shields, or maybe just because he's a good fellow, he'd responded to my request personally and immediately, fixing up a time early that Silverstone weekend.

Formula 1 paddock hospitality in those days generally consisted of a small motorhome or caravan, and I'm pretty sure it was the latter that I entered, turned left and sat down on a brown sofa for my interview with Frank. Moments after I arrived, so did Carlos Reutemann. Frank ushered him in and asked him to sit down while he did his interview with me.

The season had been an exciting one for Williams with the FW07 emerging as the class of the field, and my first impression of Frank was this live-wire guy with enthusiasm that you could almost reach out and touch. Being young I'd approached these interviews with a bit of trepidation but Frank was tremendous, took my questions seriously and really made an effort. The only concern I had at one stage was whether he'd said, 'My, you do ask pertinent questions,' or else 'My, you do ask impertinent questions.' I couldn't hear because Carlos coughed at the same time. He was doubtless getting fed up waiting for the kid with the enormous tape recorder.

Funny thing was, I was so focused on my questions and intoxicated by the moment that I didn't start to think outside the box. What was Reutemann, the Lotus driver, doing having a coffee with Frank in the middle of July? I just figured that these Formula 1 folks were a sociable old bunch! And so my first scoop eluded me. I remember Frank shaking my hand, wishing me good luck and giving me a smile and a wink as I left. On reflection it probably meant keep your mouth shut about Carlos.

VIRGINIA WILLIAMS

It was after the Saudi involvement that things started to accelerate. I think a lot of people felt that Frank's success had come overnight, but it hadn't. Frank had spent ten years building up to it. But it did seem that one went from also-ran to suddenly being in front. I mean, everybody was surprised. When Jonesy suddenly put in a time at Silverstone, all of them – Frank, Charlie, Patrick – were sitting on the pit wall looking at their watches and thinking, *Hang on a minute* ...

I'm a bit vague about some of the results the team has achieved but I don't remember anything quite as clearly as that first win with Clay.

It was quite difficult for us because Alan was so much a friend as well as being a driver, and Beverley was a friend and a very nervous girl. My job, if I was at a race – because I went to a few more in those days – was always to take the drivers' wives who did not want to watch the start. Most of them never watched the start, and Beverley most certainly wouldn't. We did have a little white caravan at Silverstone, and I can remember going there with Beverley; she was absolutely shaking with worry and fear. When Alan retired, Beverley was so upset. I can remember her walking through the garage and crying, 'I wanted Alan to win the first race.' I knew Clay was winning and I remember thinking, *I don't know quite what to do here*. Anyway, Beverley said that I should go because Frank was going to win his first race. So I did. It was lovely to see Clay winning, but I did feel for Beverley and Alan.

Frank and I didn't want the day to end. The two of us sat there in this little caravan and watched the sun go down, people drifted away and Frank just did not want to leave the circuit. There was that overwhelming feeling of 'we've won a Grand Prix!' It was absolutely extraordinary. Unforgettable.

FOURTEEN

Champions of the World

Frank and Virginia's journey home from Silverstone took them to the village of Aston Tirrold and an old rectory which had been bought at auction twelve months before. At the time Ginny had been startled by Frank's cavalier attitude to money he did not have, but in July 1979 she could breathe easily as the way ahead seemed more financially secure. The rectory was a Grade II listed building in need of repair, and funds would now be available to bring it up to scratch. Better than that from Frank's point of view, Aston Tirrold was only a few miles from Didcot, thus avoiding what had been an eighty-mile round trip from the Laundry House to work and back.

On the Monday after the British Grand Prix Frank dropped Jonathan at school before arriving at the factory shortly after nine. Waiting upstairs were messages of congratulations, including a telex from no less a person than Enzo Ferrari, whose driver Jody Scheckter was heading for the drivers' championship. The South African would claim his only world title by winning three races. Gilles Villeneuve, his teammate, would be runner-up with just two victories. Alan Jones, on the other hand, would round off the season with wins in Germany, Austria, Holland and Canada but would have to be satisfied with third on the points table. Williams had lost too much ground waiting for the FW07 to appear and then frittered away points while sorting it out. Ferrari had won through consistency from the start.

Plans for the next car had been put in place long before the first win at Silverstone and Frank was already deep in discussion about the sponsorship he would need. Mansour Ojjeh, following his first visit to a Grand Prix at Monaco in 1978, was taking increasing interest in the team and literally taking them to new heights. Following Jones's win in Germany, Ojjeh had flown the entire team to the next race in Austria in TAG's Boeing 707. But while Ojjeh played a significant role in attracting support from the Middle East, Frank was aware that the team needed other sponsors who could work with the Saudis. By September 1979 he had travelled a long way down that road – by truck and bus.

This was courtesy of Steve Herrick, the astute overseas sales director of Leyland Vehicles. By a stroke of good fortune, Herrick had taken time out from a sales visit to a bus operator in Los Angeles to nip down the coast and watch practice for the 1979 United States Grand Prix West at Long Beach. When he saw a Williams flash past with Albilad and Saudia decals on its flanks, his business brain latched on to the idea of using a Grand Prix car as a calling card for the Arab marketplace. Five months later the deal was done. The Williams entry for 1980 would be known as the Albilad-Williams Racing Team with cars referred to as Saudia-Leyland Williams. A bit of a mouthful perhaps, but when it secured half of Frank's £2 million budget, who cared?

Frank and Patrick realised that they would need to up their game in every department, and that included drivers. While Clay was popular with everyone, he was not considered fast enough. Winning was now expected, rather than hoped for. If one driver failed, the other had to be able to take over at the front. Carlos Reutemann stood out as the strongest contender on Frank's list of candidates. After winning races with Brabham and Ferrari, he was keen to get back on track following a miserable year with Lotus. And where better to do that than with the team touted as championship favourites for 1980?

So the Argentinian took over from the Swiss. Reutemann and Jones would each have at his disposal a Williams-Cosworth FW07B, the updated FW07. Jones used his to good effect at the first race in Argentina, where he won more through persistence on a track crumbling in the searing heat. By the time Williams reached Long Beach for the fourth round, Jones was second in the championship, five points behind René Arnoux, winner for Renault in Brazil and South Africa. But Reutemann was languishing near the bottom of the table with just two points – thanks, in part, to his car failing twice.

If Williams thought Renault would be the main opposition that season, a new name emerged at Long Beach. Nelson Piquet led from start to finish in a Brabham-Cosworth to score his first Grand Prix win. Williams did not score a single point that day. Jones, running second, collided with Bruno Giacomelli while trying to lap the Alfa Romeo. Reutemann, having earlier been forced into a spin at exactly the same spot by the same driver, snapped a drive shaft on the Williams.

Jones slipped to third place in the title race after retiring from Monaco with a broken differential while lying second, but Reutemann's season finally seemed to be taking off as he drove a beautifully measured race in Monte Carlo, biding his time and scoring his first win for Frank. That would put Williams back on top of the constructors' championship, where they would stay for the remaining ten races, gradually building an unassailable lead. The drivers' title was not so straightforward, thanks to Piquet.

A driver needs a certain amount of luck, and Jones thought he had more than his fair share in Spain. Things had started badly when a potential overheating problem forced circumspection and a drop to fifth place away from the action at the front. But then Reutemann lost the lead he had held for twenty-eight laps following a collision with the second-place car due to a mix-up with a backmarker. Then Piquet retired his leading Brabham with gearbox trouble, allowing Jones to move into second. He thought that would be the height of it and could scarcely believe his good fortune when a front wheel fell off the leading Ligier of Didier Pironi.

Jones's lead in the championship was to be short-lived. Jarama, scene of the race, had been the site of one of bloodiest battles in the

Spanish Civil War. Forty-four years on Formula 1's governing body FISA was fighting for control of the sport with FOCA, the constructors' association. Flexing its muscles, FISA outlawed the Spanish race. At a stroke of a pen, Jones had dropped back to third in the championship. Revenge would come in France. Ligier were the favourites to win at home when Laffite and Pironi took first and third on the grid, national expectations being raised further by the presence of Arnoux's Renault between the blue cars. Jones qualified fourth, Reutemann fifth. Williams seemed poised for a possible podium finish.

As ever, the team had gone about its business in a workmanlike manner, trying various tyre compounds and wheel sizes, running with a full load of fuel and when half empty – there was at this time no refuelling during races. With so much work to do, the drivers had shared the load, one checking tyre wear by running laps, the other working on chassis set-up. The information was pooled and considerable time spent deciding which technical route to take. Meanwhile, the Ligier pit had descended to farce as the team's prime sponsor, Gitanes cigarettes, conducted a film shoot so chaotic that at one stage a gantry carrying an air line had been knocked on to the neatly coiffured head of Gerard Ducarouge, the team's svelte but increasingly harassed technical director.

The massive crowd that had flocked to the Paul Ricard track in expectation of a French victory were not initially disappointed as the Ligiers and Arnoux shot into the lead. It was a gloriously hot midsummer day in the south of France, and as the laps ticked by the ferocious pace of the Ligiers began to play havoc with their front tyres, particularly through Courbe de Signes, the 170-mph right-hander at the end of the long back straight. Jones, using front wheels larger than those on the Ligiers, was in good shape. With Arnoux having succumbed early on, the Australian bided his time, picking off one Ligier and then the other. By lap thirty-five of fifty-four, the Williams was in the lead. And there was nothing the Ligiers could do about it.

Spanish Grand Prix points or not, Jones was back at the top of the championship, the victory made sweeter by its location. With mechanic Wayne Eckersley having placed 'MBE' beneath his driver's name on the engine cover in recognition of Jones's recent award, the British victory was rubbed in by crew chief Ian Anderson, who thrust a large Union Jack into the driver's willing hand. With the other, Jones raised a finger briefly at the FISA dignitaries watching unhappily from the side. Naturally, the French wanted to return the favour, and the next race happened to be on British soil. But it was not to be. Despite initially running away with the race, both Ligiers succumbed to problems with cracked front wheel rims. Step forward Alan Stanley Jones MBE to make up for his disappointment in the same race twelve months before, by winning at Brands Hatch and extending his lead to six points over Piquet, who finished second.

This marked the team's ninth win but Frank was not happy. Jones had blistered a front tyre, and had it not been for Ligier confounding themselves yet again, victory would not have gone to Williams. Frank vowed to do better during the remaining six races. In Germany the fast Renaults made the most of Hockenheim but retired on successive laps; Jones took the lead, only to lose it when he picked up a puncture thirteen laps later. He finished third; the good news, Piquet could do no better than fourth. It was even better in Austria, where Jones took second place to the Renault of Jean-Pierre Jabouille, with Piquet struggling home fifth. Jones 47, Piquet 36.

There seemed no reason why that lead should not lengthen at Zandvoort, a fast sweeping track just right for the Williams, and Jones duly shot past the Renaults on the front row for a two-second lead by the end of the first lap. This was too good to be true. Unable to believe that the Renaults had disappeared so soon and assuming there had been an accident, Jones glanced in his mirror a fraction too long when emerging from the left-hand hairpin at the back of the pits. The Williams drifted across the concrete kerb – and over it. The right-hand wheels dropped off the edge, destroying the skirt running the length of the side pod on the right.

Given the importance of the downforce created within the pod, having an ineffective side skirt was as crippling as a punctured tyre. Jones had no choice but to make a pit stop. It took three laps for the mechanics, working flat out, to fit a replacement. Jones drove his heart out but was too far behind to improve on eleventh place. To make matters worse, the race had been won by Piquet. Jones 47, Piquet 45. And three races to run.

The pressure showed briefly when Jones spun more than once during practice for the Italian Grand Prix at Imola, where he finished second to Piquet to put the Brazilian at the top of the championship for the first time, a position which he found uncomfortable judging by his preoccupied look alongside the smiling Jones on the podium. Piquet had become the quarry instead of the hunter as the teams headed to North America for the final two races. Piquet 54, Jones 53.

Tension in Canada was high as the championship contenders lined up side by side on the front row, but with Piquet on pole by a considerable margin. Williams had been staggered by Piquet's speed and the suspicion was that Brabham had installed – quite legally – a special engine high on power but short on endurance. The first corner, a few hundred metres from the start line on the Circuit Ile Notre-Dame, swung right, then left, then right again, lined on either side by menacing concrete walls. As they came under starter's orders, Piquet was on the right, Jones on the left. Jones made a slightly better start and was on the racing line for the right-hander. Believing he was far enough ahead, he began moving right towards the apex and the left-front wheel of the Brabham made contact amidships with the Williams. Piquet spun, hitting the wall and scattering the pursuing pack. Such was the chaos, cars strewn across the track, that the officials had no alternative but to stop the race.

Damage to the Williams was slight but Piquet's car was beyond immediate repair. He prepared to take the restart in the spare Brabham, the one with which he had claimed pole position. Incredibly for such an important race Brabham had not made contingency plans, and the special engine remained bolted into the spare car, so it was no surprise to see Piquet move into the lead. Equally, it was no surprise to Brabham to see their car parked by the side of the track with a blown engine after twenty-four laps. Jones was leading, and by Frank's reckoning if he stayed there the championship was his. But it was not over yet. The Williams was under heavy pressure from Pironi's Ligier. Jones could deal with that but was flummoxed when he had a pit signal saying that

Pironi had been penalised one minute for jumping the start. He signalled for confirmation, and the following lap there was the same message on the pit board, with Frank himself hanging over the pit wall nodding for all he was worth. Jones let Pironi through and finished second on the road, but he was the winner of the Canadian Grand Prix and the 1980 Formula 1 World Championship.

SHERIDAN THYNNE

In 1979 I had lunch with Frank shortly before the French Grand Prix. We were chatting about this and that, and he said he had somebody from the commercial side of Leyland Vehicles who wanted to discuss sponsorship. I asked who was going to look after this man. Frank said, 'No one. He's a grown-up so he'll look after himself, I suppose.' So I said, as a joke really, 'Tell you what, Frank: I'll come to the French Grand Prix. You don't have to pay me or anything, and I'll persuade him to be a sponsor. And when he does, I'll come and work for you. Ho ho.' And Frank said, 'Ho ho. Okay.' And that's what happened.

It was about five years later that Steve Herrick admitted to me that he'd already decided to sponsor Frank before he even came to the French Grand Prix. As a result of that I was working with Williams from November 1979. I had a desk in reception. I was lucky in that such sponsorship support Frank already had came from Charlie and his work with the Saudis. We didn't cross over with each other; we had different skills. Charlie was brilliant when it came to things like finding a parking space in Monaco harbour for a Saudi prince's yacht. But I was better equipped to look after Leyland and subsequently Denim, ICI, Mobil and people like that.

VIRGINIA WILLIAMS

We were living at the Laundry House and wanted to get on the property ladder. I had been to see an old rectory at Aston Tirrold two or three times with Frank and we were keen to own a home now that we had two kids. I went to my father and said that we would like to actually buy a house. I thought that the two grandchildren would help my case. The rectory needed doing up and was at auction with an estimated price of £30,000. My father said he would provide £10,000 and I thought this was going to work. We could raise the other £20,000 with a mortgage.

Frank, Dave Brodie and I went to the auction. When the property went up to about £35,000 I thought, *Ohhh, we've lost it.* When it reached a final figure of £52,000 I was certain we had lost it. Then the auction-eer, looking at the final bidder, said, 'Is that Mr Williams?' I thought I was going to faint. Brode said, 'Frank, you've bought the house!' Frank then said to me, 'Do you want to drive past your new house?' and I said, 'No!' I was furious because, when you buy a house at auction, you have to put down the deposit straight away. And here was Frank writing a cheque for over £5,000. I had no idea how he was going to find that, never mind the balance in twenty-eight days. He just gave me one of his wicked grins. Somehow we found the money and within a year we had settled into our first house.

ALAN JONES

The Dutch Grand Prix was a complete disaster for me. I had been a bit twitchy because everyone was going around saying, 'Hello, champ!' and stuff like that. I kept telling them not to say anything; it was too early. I said anything could happen. It did. I had quite a nasty accident during practice when my throttle stuck open. And then I threw away nine bloody points in the race. I couldn't believe it.

PATRICK HEAD

In truth, Nelson definitely had a quicker car that year, mostly to do with the differential they were running, which meant the Brabham was mighty in and out of very tight corners. But Alan knew he had a quicker car in Montreal. I'm not saying he pushed Nelson into the wall on the first lap, but he certainly took no prisoners.

I didn't actually go to the final race in Watkins Glen, where Alan drove one of his most outstanding races. He qualified on the third row, went off at the first corner, damaged the skirt, got back on the track in about twelfth place and literally, one by one, picked off the pack. The only person he didn't catch was Bruno Giacomelli, but then the Alfa retired from the lead with electrical failure. Alan may well have beaten him anyway, but he just drove through everybody else. It was nice to see the new world champion go into the next race and blitz it.

IAN ANDERSON

I well remember the French Grand Prix and giving the flag to Jonesy. It really upset Ligier. Afterwards, Jacques Laffite went back to the Ligier motorhome and punched one of the doors. It was a great race, that one. It should have been the same in Holland, except for Jonesy running wide and taking out that skirt. They were a real bugger, those skirts; I don't think we have ever changed one so fast.

One of the things I remember about Canada was something that happened when preparing the cars for the race. We initiated the lifing of components. That was the sort of thing they did on aircraft, and Patrick was keen on doing it in Formula 1. He set up a system that gave us a very good idea about how long components would last. When exhausts were brand-new, if they were going to crack, it would happen within the first hundred miles. But once the crack was welded up, they would be fine for maybe another 500 miles or so. We were preparing Alan's car for the race, and obviously Frank and Patrick were very twitchy about everything being checked and nothing going wrong just at the point when we had the potential to win the world championship. They said they wanted everything new on Alan's car. That included new exhausts.

I said, 'No, don't do that. It's a known fact: they will be good for the race. This set has been run. They've cracked; they've been repaired; they'll be fine.' They asked me if I was sure and I said I was absolutely positive. Frank thought about it for a bit and then said we would put the new exhausts on Reutemann's car. They did that, and in the race the exhaust cracked on Carlos's car. Otherwise it would have been on Alan's car.

It was one of those things where Patrick weighed everything up, reckoned I knew what I was talking about and trusted me. He didn't override me; he was extremely good like that. If he believed you were correct, he would let you get on with it. Everyone makes mistakes. If you made one, you went to Patrick and told him. He would sort it out. He was brilliant to work with.

STEVE FOWLER

I was working on both cars in Canada. We'd all spoken about Piquet and I reckoned Jonesy was going to have him off on the first corner in Montreal, and sure enough he did. The one thing that has stuck in my mind since winning the championship was the way you feel. I would watch people win something like the Olympics and they would break down. I used to think, *What are they crying for? I can't believe the emotion is that bad.* But, you know, we were all in tears. I couldn't believe how emotional I became. When all of a sudden it's there, it hits you – bang! I was crying like a baby. You don't realise how much work you've been putting in until that happens.

NEIL OATLEY

We had a fairly lucky escape in Germany in 1979 because when we went into *parc fermé* after the race one of the rear tyres on Alan's winning car was completely flat. And when we got the car back to the factory, the fuel cell breather had jammed. The fuel cell had literally sucked itself almost inside out. How the thing kept going, I don't know.

In 1980 Brabham caught up with us. There wasn't really a huge difference in speed between the two cars. If anything, the Brabham had started to creep ahead. It came down to whoever made the error, the other guy was going to win. It did get very tense. When Nelson had an engine problem at one particular race, I remember Frank getting very upset because the natural reaction from our guys was to start cheering. In Frank's mind that wasn't the done thing. He went and apologised to Brabham.

Alan used to have a pair of lucky underpants, which I think he wore when he won the Austrian Grand Prix in the Shadow back in 1977. He wore them in every single race after that and, you can imagine, by 1980 they'd got pretty tatty. At the British Grand Prix he lost them: gone, nowhere to be seen. We then had a spate of really bad races. We were sitting in the motorhome in Montreal when this package arrived from England. Alan opens it, and there's the underpants. I think at Brands Hatch Alan had rented his own motorhome. He must have got changed in there and they got kicked under the table or somewhere. The motorhome hadn't been used since and they were found just before Montreal. The owner of the motorhome, a friend of Alan's, knew the story and airmailed the underpants off to Montreal, and he won the championship. It was his first win since last wearing the underpants at Brands Hatch.

VIRGINIA WILLIAMS

Mansour Ojjeh had a suite in Montreal's Bonaventure Hotel and we went to a lovely party after winning the championship. About an hour after we went to bed, the phone rang. It was Jonesy, who said to Frank that he'd had a big offer from Ferrari. I can't remember if it was a wind-up but it was a funny way to pour a bucket of cold water over the end of the day. Frank looked most concerned. I can remember that phone ringing. It is the one thing that doesn't happen any more, the phone ringing at all hours.

MANSOUR OJJEH

We had a small party. Compared to today it was nothing. There were about twenty of us in this small suite with a cake and champagne. It was a really nice feeling, just this small group celebrating such a huge achievement. Then I went out with Alan and had a couple of beers – and that was it.

FIFTEEN
Giving It All Away

During the 1980 season Frank and Virginia had moved again, this time to Battle House, a nineteenth-century six-bedroom house standing in splendid gardens on a prime site near Goring-on-Thames. Beverley Jones would go there on the weekends Alan raced to avoid the stress of watching her husband.

Alan had not been joking when he called Frank in Montreal to tell him he had received a lucrative offer from Ferrari. He had no intention of leaving but it was a useful way to keep Frank on his toes. Jones's understanding was that he would remain number-one driver in 1981, with Reutemann in support. That agreement, as far as Jones was concerned, was broken during the closing stages of the Brazilian Grand Prix. The arrangement was that if Reutemann was leading Jones by fewer than seven seconds, then he should let his teammate through. Carlos had agreed because he felt he could beat Alan in a straight fight. Jones had won the opening race at Long Beach, but in the teeming rain in Rio de Janeiro Reutemann was in front and had every intention of staying there despite pit boards bearing the stark message JONES-REUT. It was a Williams one-two and would have been the perfect result if the right man had been leading. Frank knew he had trouble on his hands when Reutemann crossed the line with Jones less than seven seconds behind.

The relationship between the two drivers, formal at the best of times, was now ice-cold. They would continue to exchange technical information since it was to their mutual benefit, but Jones made little effort to hide his dislike of his teammate. The season rolled on until, two-thirds done, with a win in Belgium and consistent finishes else-where, Reutemann led the championship by seventeen points after yet another podium finish at Silverstone. Jones knew his championship chances were slim, nineteen points behind, but that did not mean he would end the year without having his say.

By the time they reached the final race in Europe – at Monza in September – Reutemann's points advantage had evaporated, Piquet holding the lead jointly with him on forty-five points. Jones then announced that he was retiring two races hence at the end of the season. The reigning world champion was also sporting two bandaged fingers on his left hand, the result of an altercation with a van driver and his mates on London's Chiswick High Road. It was scant consolation for Frank when Jones overcame his broken little finger – he chopped the fingers off his driving glove – by finishing second with Reutemann third, Piquet collecting just one point for sixth place.

The gap closed again in Montreal after an indifferent drive by Reute-mann, finishing tenth in appalling conditions. The tenacious Piquet got fifth, while Jones blew his slim chance of retaining the championship by spinning off in the lead. The surviving title contender from Williams went to Las Vegas with a one-point advantage. Reutemann might walk it; on the other hand he might not. With Carlos you never knew.

At first it looked good, brilliant in fact. Reutemann had arrived early in Nevada in order to wind down and acclimatise himself. He was relaxed and confident, which he proved with a truly mesmeric qualify-ing lap of the sort which had become his trademark when everything was right. By race morning, however, circumstances had changed. Pole position had been secured on the first day of qualifying. On the second, Reutemann had collided with Piquet, and the damage was such that he had to switch to his back-up car. Somehow the car did not feel right, and this feeling increased when he drove to the grid. Jones, starting from the outside of the front row in his last race for Williams, knew his teammate was beaten before they had so much as turned a wheel.

Sure enough, the Australian powered into a lead he would never lose. Reutemann travelled in the opposite direction, completing the opening lap in fifth place. Which became sixth. Then seventh. Piquet, ill at ease on the flat and bland temporary track zigzagging through a hotel car park, was initially behind Reutemann but caught and overtook the Williams after sixteen laps. Despite vomiting in his helmet and on the point of collapse as the seventy-five laps neared completion, Piquet eventually drove on automatic pilot into fifth place and the necessary two points to become 1981 world champion.

At Williams feelings were mixed. Jones had signed off a spectacular four years on a high note with his eleventh win for a team which was celebrating the constructors' championship for the second year in succession. On the other hand, there was disappointment over the failure to take the drivers' title.

PATRICK HEAD

Alan did project phenomenal confidence in himself and the team around him, and it really worked. He was very much of the same generation as Frank and I, but I'm not sure that was the only thing. The three of us were proving ourselves capable at the same time. There was a very good relationship all round.

As for Brazil, I thought that was fairly straightforward. According to Carlos's contract, if he was first and Alan was in second and there was no threat from behind, then he had to give way to Alan. Whether Carlos should have signed a contract like that is neither here nor there. It was something Frank put in the contract. Maybe Alan had insisted on it; I've no idea. But Carlos had put his name to that.

Carlos was in the lead, Alan was second and whoever was third was thirty seconds behind. When the sign was put out, Carlos did the

I-see-no-ships routine. If I was Carlos, I probably would have done the same. But the contract was very clear. I think Alan reckoned, *If that's the name of the game, fuck you. I'll never speak to you again.* Alan wasn't childish enough to be small-time about it, but I don't think he ever said another word to Carlos in the whole season. But it didn't really affect the atmosphere in the team. This sort of thing happens. If you allow yourself to get sucked into drivers' little vendettas, you're in real trouble. I don't think that happens quite so much these days, or I'm not aware of it. It only happens when you have two guys who can take positions from each other.

Carlos was a wonderful guy, completely obsessive about his racing. He could remember, and probably still can, exactly what gear ratios he had in every car, and every engine number. He had a wonderful relationship with Neil Oatley, who's never one to say a word if he can spare it. At Monaco in 1980 Alan was doing fastest laps in practice but Carlos didn't set a decent time. He was about six seconds slower than Alan and he seemed to be cruising round. I went down to Neil and said, 'You've got to throw a few fucks into your guy. What the hell is he doing?' Neil looked at me in one of his no-statement, questioning looks. It turned out that Carlos would go out and do about three or four laps hard, but at different places on the track, then come in and change the car a bit. He never put a complete lap together. So we all thought Carlos was in trouble. Come Saturday afternoon, however, he hung about on the pit wall for twenty minutes or so. Then he got in the car and – bang! Pole position. One lap, that's all he did. That was Carlos. He was a remarkable person.

He did the same thing in Las Vegas. He had incredible mental control during practice. He was probably too intense: he wanted everything to be perfect. He wanted the car to be perfect – the gearbox, the brakes. If something wasn't perfect, it physically upset him. But I've never really understood what happened during the race. Peter Windsor, who was very close to Carlos, kept saying that Nelson Piquet's physio had told him that Nelson was absolutely rooted. He told Carlos so many times that Piquet was finished that I think Carlos began to believe it. When Piquet was snapping at his heels in the race, Carlos just couldn't believe it and gave way. He said that the gearbox had been baulky, but when the mechanics took the gearbox apart, there was no damage at all – it was immaculate. We did have a clutch drag problem and I can imagine the gearbox was a bit gratey, but I think he just let it get to his head. There has been mention since of Carlos having a tyre vibration. I have to say I really don't remember that being raised after the race in any shape or form. He had a remarkable empathy with the car. If he felt that everything was perfect, he would be like a god: he was unstoppable. But if it wasn't perfect, he'd be awful.

PETER WINDSOR

Frank always loved the idea of having Carlos in the car. He was a Carlos fan back in 1973/4. That's when I got to know Carlos really well. I remember chatting to Frank and asking what he thought of Carlos. Frank said, 'If a driver can win four Grands Prix in one year, he is a serious player. He's a wonderful man; I'd love to have him drive one of my cars one day.' Carlos was Frank's sort of guy – exotic, difficult, charismatic, impossible to understand – and Frank always loved having drivers with whom he could speak in their native tongue because it would annoy the engineers and mechanics. Carlos fitted the bill perfectly.

It had been a torturous road for Carlos to join Williams. It was a shame because he would have been ready to join Williams at any point if Frank had given him a serious offer. Carlos's career was in disarray in the latter stages with Brabham and Ferrari. He was obsessed with Lotus. He wanted to get away from Ferrari; he wanted a Cosworth engine and he wanted ground effect. He went to Lotus and quickly realised he was never going to gel with Colin [Chapman]. Whatever way Frank and Patrick looked at it, Carlos was a better driver than Clay Regazzoni. Carlos actually had to buy himself out of the Lotus contract. He took the opportunity with Williams and signed away his status and all sorts of things.

Patrick was probably the first engineer, backed by Frank, to be so obsessed with having the two best drivers he could possibly get. It is much better to have a happy team in which there is harmony rather than have two guys who are quick enough to annoy one another. Ultimately, Carlos was quicker than Alan but he wasn't as good in some ways.

Williams was Alan's team in the sense that if he walked into the motorhome at 7 p.m. and Tim and Mo, who ran the motorhome, were ready to go and all Alan wanted was a cup of tea or a beer, Mo would stop everything, get the beer and they would have a laugh. But if Carlos wanted to do the same thing, then no way. Those are the little details that mattered.

The one thing Frank liked was that Carlos wasn't very good at going to debriefs and talking openly in front of people, partly because he is very shy and partly because his engineer was Neil Oatley, who is just as shy. So neither of them were very outgoing. Carlos very easily got into the habit of phoning Frank at night, which Frank loves and which he encouraged. Frank also loved Carlos's attention to detail – things like engine numbers and tyre compounds and the specific matches of Goodyear tyres. Carlos could persuade Frank – as he did before the German Grand Prix in 1981 – that he wanted a particular engine with such-and-such a number. When Alan found out about it, he would go to Patrick, who would tell Frank that Alan should have that particular engine. Frank would be powerless to overrule Patrick. That's where the Williams team was quite dysfunctional. It should never have got to that point, and that's where all the Alan–Carlos stuff came from, I think. Carlos was simply trying to do the best job for himself.

He felt he had been let down by Alan at Long Beach. Carlos felt he had let Alan win, but afterwards Alan didn't thank him; he didn't say anything. So after Long Beach Carlos said, 'Right, I don't care about this contract. All bets are off now. If the guy doesn't have the courtesy to thank me, then I'm not going to bother any more.'

I don't think Carlos went into Brazil thinking he was going to screw Alan Jones. It was a bit like Lewis [Hamilton] in Hungary 2007. He suddenly found himself leading by seven seconds, reading the conditions extremely well and, at that point I think he said, 'Stuff it; why should I?' He also felt he had helped Alan throughout 1980 with set-up [on the car] and also giving him places occasionally. Therefore, Alan had won it in 1980. So what was the problem if Carlos was quicker? He had a good chance of winning it in 1981.

No one can blame Alan for not being more courteous to Carlos at Long Beach, because he was a race driver. He only cared about himself and he won the race. It was Frank's fault as much as anyone else, to be honest. It should never have got to that point. After Long Beach Frank should have sussed out the situation and got it under control because I suppose he had this rather naïve belief that the contract would be adhered to by both drivers. Then again, no team has ever really got on top of that situation. Ferrari basically allowed their drivers to take points from one another as recently as 2008. McLaren have done the same thing over the years.

In 1979 Carlos had a long talk with Gilles Villeneuve before Monza. He told Gilles [to] never play around with the world championship. 'If you have a chance to win it, take it. You're not going to have many opportunities. Why would you want to give this race to Jody? Don't even think about it.' But that's what Gilles did. And then he was killed in 1982. It upset Carlos a lot that Gilles gave the 1979 championship to Jody and then lost his life. At that point, in 1981, Gilles was still in the shit and I think Carlos thought, *Well, I'm never going to let that happen to me. If I have a chance of winning the world championship, I'm going to take it.* He knew 1981 was his big chance.

Las Vegas hit him hard metaphorically and realistically because he had a horrendous tyre vibration throughout the race. With the absolutely rigid suspension, if you did have a mismatched set of tyres, it was like driving with square wheels. It is very easy to use clichés and platitudes to say Reutemann was off form, but I'll never buy that. Carlos was on brilliant form at Vegas, as we saw during qualifying.

One of the biggest problems was that Williams were going to bring one spare car as usual to Las Vegas, the race in which Carlos was trying to win the championship. Alan insisted the spare car had always got to be ready for him. If they wanted a spare car for Carlos, then make it a four-car team. Williams went to North America very overstretched in terms of how they operated; they had never operated four cars before and suddenly they had four in Vegas.

It annoyed Carlos that Frank had given in on that point. It became a problem on Sunday morning. Instead of going through three or four tyres, which you always had to do on race morning to make sure you had all the diameters correct, Carlos had to bed in new brakes for about eight laps; so he had no tyre bedding-in at all. The spare-car system had not worked correctly. Normally you'd bed them in on the spare car. None of that had happened so he had to bed in his own race brakes on Sunday morning, which was ridiculous. He never did any tyre testing [and] started the race with a mismatched set of tyres, which all stemmed from running four cars.

ALAN JONES

I can honestly say that I can never remember having a stand-up row with Frank. There was one occasion – I think it was Spain – when I spun my wheels leaving the pits and took the jack with me. I can't remember what that was all about but we did have a bit of a verbal to-do afterwards. And that was it. We had our say and the whole thing was forgotten immediately. We had our little blues every now and again – as anyone does in any working relationship – but none of them were really serious.

I know this sounds like a mutual admiration society, but to be perfectly honest Frank is the best bloke I've ever driven for. I used to say that at the time, and I still believe it. Frank worked on the basis that if he was paying you that sort of money and he didn't believe what you were saying, or he didn't have any faith in your ability, then he was the bloody idiot for paying you the money in the first place. The trust between us was absolute. If I said to Frank that I thought the engine was down on power, or something like that, he would always give me the benefit of the doubt because I was the guy with my bum in the car.

We had a really special rapport and I certainly had a fantastic working relationship with Patrick. It got to the stage where we could almost communicate without talking. Patrick would say he was going to try something on the car and I would say, 'Yeah, that feels better,' and we'd just get on with it. Nine times out of ten, his ideas would work. Our understanding was such that we even changed things on the grid. We reached the point where we didn't have to verbal very much because we knew what we needed to get to the source of the problem.

FRANK DERNIE

Alan Jones couldn't have been better. Most drivers have left school quite early and haven't done much in the way of maths or physics and generally speaking don't understand how the car works anywhere near as well as they think they do. If there were as many amateur doctors in hospitals as there are amateur engineers in motor racing, there would be dead people everywhere. Jones didn't try to understand how the car worked; he just had the gift of understanding exactly where he was losing the most time. Jonesy and Patrick were like brothers and even looked like brothers: they were just so close.

PETE FOSTEKEW

I had spent seventeen years in aviation. Williams were advertising for a person for sub-assembly with aircraft experience. Coming from aviation to to motor racing, especially Formula 1, is like chalk and cheese. In aviation you're taking your time while, in Formula 1, you're rushing around so quickly you forget where you are half the time.

I'd only been here a few months when there was a bit of a misunderstanding. Frank knew all about engines: their output, their numbers and so on. He knew exactly which engine he wanted in which car for each race. We had about twenty-two engines and one of them was supposed to go back for a rebuild, but it was still sitting in the workshop. He asked me why the engine was still there and I said I didn't know. He stomped off. He thumped his way upstairs to the buying office. After a couple of minutes he came out, stood at the top of the stairs and ripped into me. I wasn't even sure he was talking to me at first. I thought, *Christ, what have I done?* About two hours later he discovered what had gone wrong and that it had nothing to do with me. He came straight back and apologised. I thought, *Any boss that can do that, goes way up in my estimation.* I've stuck with him ever since.

ALAN CHALLIS

I joined on 3 November 1980, just after Williams won the championship first time. I'd been with other Formula 1 teams before, virtually done nothing else since I'd left school.

I saw an advert in *Autosport* for chief mechanic. Ian Anderson didn't want to go racing any more and I took over from him. So I more or less walked straight into the Jones–Reutemann business in Brazil. I couldn't believe that. I was on the pit wall, hanging out that board. But Carlos wouldn't budge. You knew there was an atmosphere between them, but I didn't think there would ever be anything different because of who they were – two quite different characters. I think Carlos was one of the most underrated drivers that ever drove a Grand Prix car, but he sometimes got a blockage in his head. Carlos had his foibles about the chassis and the engine. When he arrived at a racetrack, the first thing he would want to know was which engines he would have. If it wasn't a certain engine, you could see that he would worry about that. Which was a pity because he was an incredible driver.

NEIL OATLEY

Because I was running Carlos's car, I controlled his pit board. In Brazil I kept getting messages from Frank: 'Jones-Reut'. Our two guys were way ahead of the field and there's no doubt this contract business was playing on his mind. At the previous race at Long Beach Carlos was ahead of Alan when Carlos misjudged one of the chicanes and took a wheel off. This contract thing was eating into his head. When he found himself in a similar position at the next race, he thought, *I will cease to be a racing driver if I stick to that and obey that signal*. That was his view, and obviously Alan took a fairly dim view of it. They barely spoke after that.

It wasn't that big a problem. I was left to run the number-two car by myself. Frank and Patrick always stayed with Alan, so during practice and the races there wasn't much interplay. By that time Carlos was a good number two, but he wasn't going to be someone who would push Alan for the whole season. He was regarded as very much the second driver and not an equal number one. I couldn't say if it really affected much of what we were doing. In Las Vegas I think you could say that Carlos had convinced himself that he wasn't going to win. And, sure enough, it came true. I honestly don't recall any complaints from Carlos about a tyre vibration in the race.

He was an emotional driver. He was pretty upset when we switched from Michelin to Goodyear tyres in mid-season. I think Silverstone, the British Grand Prix, was the first race when we changed. He was convinced that was the wrong thing to do, and if you compare the points he won before and after that, the two halves of the season bear no resemblance to one another. I still love the bloke and still see him occasionally now. He was a unique character. When it became obvious that Alan couldn't really win the 1981 championship, it didn't really change the dynamic of how Patrick and Frank operated. As a result, Carlos didn't feel they were on his side. He seemed to think, *They don't really care if I win or not*. Alan knew when he was going to win; Carlos seemed to know when he was going to lose. But, whenever it was all lined up for Carlos, he was absolutely phenomenal.

NIKI LAUDA

I had retired from Formula 1 in 1979 and started Lauda Air. I had zero interest in Formula 1 after that until Ron [Dennis] called me and invited me to my home Grand Prix at Zelteg. I liked what I saw, went to the next race at Monza and found all the emotions coming back. On the Tuesday after Monza, Ron, reading my mind perfectly, called and asked if I would like to test a McLaren at Donington. We told no one, not even my wife Marlena. We flew to London, and when Marlena went shopping in Harrods, I said I had some business to do and went to Donington. I was out of breath after about three laps, but after a full day I was faster than [John] Watson and I liked it. I went back to the hotel in London to talk to Marlena – who wasn't happy about this – and have a think about a comeback.

The phone rang. It was Frank. 'How you doing? I hear you are in England.' I said I was and that I had been testing a McLaren. 'Yes, I know,' said Frank. 'Come and see me first.' How the hell did he know? I would have tested for Frank but it was too late because I was now so far ahead with talking to Ron. But I would have liked to have driven for Williams; at the time it was a very good team.

SIXTEEN
Job Done. Next?

It says much about Williams at the end of 1981 that neither Patrick nor Frank was present at the test that decided the identity of the driver who would win them the world championship the following year. Following Las Vegas, Reutemann had disappeared back to Argentina saying he was going to retire, but then changed his mind and returned, while Frank appeared to hope that he could tempt Jones to reverse *his* decision to quit. With the first race of 1982 scheduled for South Africa on 23 January, time was running out and there were very few top drivers available. Almost as an afterthought, Keke Rosberg was invited to Paul Ricard to drive the Williams. Thinking Formula 1 had written him off, Rosberg jumped at the opportunity. He had been with Wolf since 1979 but Walter Wolf's interest was declining and a merger with the Fittipaldi team had not been a success.

Rosberg was snapped up. When the cocky little Finn then qualified ahead of Reutemann at the first two races, the already tricky atmosphere between two disparate characters deteriorated and Reutemann retired for good.

Williams had a problem. From fielding two top-line racers in 1981, they had gone to someone whose best result had been a win in a non-championship Formula 1 race plus one third place and a fifth in thirty-six F1 races in a variety of admittedly hopeless teams. They managed to persuade the vastly experienced Mario Andretti to stand in for the third race at Long Beach, but for the rest of the season hired Derek Daly, an Irishman with roughly the same level of experience as Rosberg. Having driven briefly for Hesketh and then Ensign, Daly had learned a great deal during a season with Tyrrell, even though the former champions were beginning their long decline. But Daly was best remembered for a first-corner accident at Monaco where he misjudged his braking, slammed into the car in front, shot into the air and landed on his Tyrrell teammate. Neither driver was injured, and perhaps it was just as well that the Williams drivers were ahead and clear of the carnage, otherwise Frank's view of the Dubliner might have been tainted. As it was, Frank and Patrick would have their hands full dealing with arguably one of the most extraordinary seasons on record.

The South African Grand Prix, the first race of the season, set the tone. Here there was a drivers' strike. Thirty professional racers locked themselves in the function room of a Johannesburg hotel and refused to come out. They were angry about the wording of the contract they had been asked to sign by FISA. Agreement was reached in time for one practice session and the drivers produced a superb race – Reutemann finishing second, Rosberg fifth – only for the drivers to be fined for the lock-in.

Fines and threats of suspension were mild compared to the disqualifications handed out in Brazil. Nelson Piquet and Rosberg were excluded from first and second places in Rio because their cars were alleged to have been underweight – it was claimed that the topping-up of the large water tanks on the cars prior to post-race scrutineering was illegal.

Sanity and sport returned briefly in California, where Niki Lauda, having retired in 1979 from the sport that had almost killed him three years before, made a comeback and won the Long Beach Grand Prix. But the Brazilian disqualifications were then upheld on appeal, closing a technical loophole which had allowed non-turbo teams, the majority of whom were British, to keep pace with Ferrari and Renault. The

British teams sulked and stayed away from the San Marino Grand Prix. Fortunately, the spectators did not.

There were a mere fourteen cars present, two of them Ferraris. A tedious race was in prospect but the Ferrari drivers, Gilles Villeneuve and Didier Pironi, fought each other for the lead. Pironi won, but Villeneuve felt so strongly that this had broken a pre-race agreement that he swore never to speak to his teammate again. Two weeks later in Belgium, going for a fast lap, Villeneuve clipped the back of a slow-moving car as the driver inadvertently moved across at the last second. Villeneuve died of his injuries after being flung from the cockpit of his cartwheeling car. Italy and Ferrari were grief-stricken; Pironi was distraught.

Having raised Ferrari morale by securing pole position in Canada, Pironi stalled at the start. The rest of the grid squeezed past with the exception of Ricardo Paletti, a novice making his first start in a Grand Prix from the back of the grid. The Italian slammed into the back of the stationary Ferrari, the impact killing him instantly. The race was won by Piquet seven days after he had actually failed to qualify for the previous race in Detroit.

If you wanted some desperately needed humour, there had been plenty of that during the final laps at Monaco. Alain Prost hit the barrier with his leading Renault when a few spots of rain threatened chaos; Riccardo Patrese assumed the lead, only to spin and stall his Brabham; Pironi, now in charge, ground to a halt with an electrical problem on the last lap; Andrea de Cesaris should have been on course to win his first Grand Prix but was found weeping by the guard rail, his Alfa Romeo having stopped with fuel starvation; Daly should have inherited a victory no one seemed to want but wiped the back of the Williams against a guard rail; a furious Patrese, meanwhile, restarted his car and crossed the finish line completely unaware that he had just won his first Grand Prix.

There was an argument between the Renault drivers over who should have won their home Grand Prix at Paul Ricard. René Arnoux took valuable championship points off Prost and said he couldn't care less because he was leaving at the end of the season, which helped Pironi into a healthy lead in the championship. But, powering through the mist and rain on race morning at Hockenheim, Pironi failed to see a slower car. The Frenchman's right leg and foot were badly crushed in the ensuing accident. Meanwhile, Piquet crashed his leading Brabham while lapping a backmarker and proceeded to lay into the hapless driver with his fists and feet, all of which was captured on television. The race was won by Villeneuve's stand-in, an emotional Patrick Tambay.

Grand Prix racing returned to sanity in Austria when Rosberg and the Lotus of Elio de Angelis crossed the line separated by half a car's length in a thrilling finish. That made it nine different winners so far, three of whom had stood on the top of the podium for the first time.

Although Rosberg's name was not among them, he was second in the championship, six points behind the injured Pironi. But finally, despite starting from eighth on the grid, clever tyre choices inspired by Frank gave the Finn his first victory – in the Swiss Grand Prix which, of course, was held in France. By the time the team returned to Las Vegas for the final race, Rosberg led John Watson, winner in Belgium and Detroit, by nine points. All Rosberg had to do was finish sixth or higher and the championship would be his, regardless of Watson's result.

This may have seemed simple but motorsport is never that straight-forward. The car was as immaculately prepared as ever, with attention being paid to the fact that the driver would be completing seventy-five laps in searing heat. A supply of drinking water – something of a novelty in a racing car at the time – was on board, with an electric pump which, at the flick of a switch, squirted the liquid through a tube into the driver's mouth. Far from reviving Rosberg, it would almost cause his downfall.

The Williams held seventh place for the first twenty laps. Watson, driving brilliantly, was in second place. Two retirements then moved Rosberg into fifth place, good enough for two points and the championship. That was put in sudden jeopardy when Rosberg pressed his drink switch and was scalded by boiling water just as he was changing into fifth gear. Somehow he kept his composure at 160 mph between the concrete walls while stemming the flow of searing liquid. Twelve months on from their disappointment at this most artificial of race-tracks, Williams welcomed home their second world champion.

KEKE ROSBERG

I had arrived the night before the test at Paul Ricard. Charlie (Crichton-Stuart) and I drank Beaujolais nouveau in the evening, and then at eight o'clock the next morning they put qualifying tyres on the car and, without warming it up, they said get in and see what you can do! Frank sometimes made strange decisions and this was one of them. I came from nowhere, did this test, and he signed me up more or less straight away.

PATRICK HEAD

At the end of 1981 we had some bits we wanted to test and we were wondering who we could get to drive the car. I don't really think we thought, *Let's give Keke Rosberg a run and we'll decide whether he can race for us.* We thought, *He's the best Formula 1 driver we can get to test for us.* I think Frank still thought he could get Carlos back and then he could ease Alan out of retirement.

I was working on the FW08, so Charlie Crichton-Stuart and Frank Dernie went to Ricard. They rang up saying, 'This guy's really good. He's not just your average; he's something pretty special.' So more or less on the say of Frank Dernie and Charlie, we signed up Keke for 1982.

Frank rang Carlos in Argentina and said, 'We've run Keke Rosberg. He's actually gone quite well. What do you think of him, Carlos?' And Carlos said, 'I don't know, Frank. The big gold watch, the big gold rings, the briefcase. I don't know, Frank.'

Carlos would go through the grid and say, 'The old boy, the young lion, old boy, old boy, young lion.' He was very aware of the new brigade coming through and he'd seen in South Africa that Keke was going to be aggravation as a teammate. I'm not saying for one moment Carlos was frightened of aggravation. He was seriously quick but he would have registered by then that it was not going to be a walk in the park. He's a very clever man. It wouldn't surprise me if, in about five years' time, Carlos is president of Argentina. In the meantime the Falklands War had started and it gave Carlos a wonderful excuse for him to say to Frank, 'I stop.' So we lost Carlos.

One way or another, 1982 was a remarkable season. The championship should have been won by Villeneuve, then by Pironi. The Ferrari was by far the best car and it did win the constructors' championship. Although I may have been unflattering about Harvey's work rate in 1976, Harvey taught Ferrari how to make a decent chassis, and all credit to him.

Keke was a fighter. He got on well with Frank Dernie. I'm not saying that I didn't get on with Keke, but I was probably a little bit less touchy-feely-carey than Frank was over Keke. Frank Dernie was the person who said to Frank that this guy was seriously good, so he always had a very good relationship with him.

Keke and I worked together on a test and then he finished second in Austria and almost won it. He did win the next race at Dijon. Now it wasn't directly because of those tests, but we definitely got to grips with some of the problems. The FW08 was a very critical car and you had to run it as stiff as a brick with its skirt system. It was all about finding where the sweet spot was. I put quite a bit into that with Keke in those tests. But Frank Dernie did a very good job with Keke.

PETER WINDSOR

It took a lot of persuading by Frank to get Carlos back into the car in 1982. Carlos basically asked for too much money in the hope that Frank wouldn't pay it, but eventually Frank did pay the money. Carlos drove brilliantly in the South African Grand Prix. There was quite a bit of testing going on before Rio – a lot of sitting around, debriefing and chatting to people. Carlos could see that Keke was building the same relationship Alan had with the team. He just thought, *I can't do it any more.* Here was a driver in the other car who drove in completely the opposite way. I think he just thought it all too much. The Falklands thing was just an excuse for him to get out. There was no issue there at all.

BERNIE JONES

Williams won the Queen's Award for Export Achievement. Frank chose Bob Torrie and I to go along with him to the reception at Buckingham Palace because we had been with the team more or less from the start. It was typical of Frank to think of us. It was a brilliant day; I'll never forget it. And you could see Frank was really thrilled by the award and getting to meet the Queen.

NEIL OATLEY

Frank tended not to get involved in the technical side of things at the factory; that was left to Patrick. But at the races he had a passion for tyres. This was at the height of a war between Goodyear, who had returned to Formula 1, and Michelin. We were running Goodyear and there was a huge selection of different compounds to choose from. Frank loved that. He had a tremendous feel for it and the tyre choice was generally left to Frank after consultation with Patrick and the drivers. Purely technical decisions were almost entirely Patrick's, but when it came to tyres, Frank really got involved.

At Dijon we discussed the tyre situation at length. Because of the nature of the circuit, Frank decided on three different compounds spread around the car. Then, just about five minutes before the car was due to go to the starting grid, he decided to go for a harder compound than originally chosen for the left-rear tyre. A lot of people had tyre trouble that afternoon but that harder tyre probably helped us win the race.

ALAN CHALLIS

At Brands Hatch Keke was on pole. There had been a vaporisation problem but we'd done nothing about it. You knew damn well that if you poured cold water on the pump, it would work. But we didn't have a watering can on the grid. By the time somebody had rushed back to the pits to fetch one, Patrick and I had decided we were going to push the car and get it started that way. Everybody else ran away. God, I've never been so knackered in all my life because of course, that grid is uphill. It didn't actually start until we got the watering can, but by then we'd pushed it a bloody long way. It was something that we never did again.

MAURICE HAMILTON

In those days following the race was a bit of a haphazard affair for journalists. You could not rely on television pictures – such as they were – being broadcast in the media centre. There were a few monitors from Longines giving lap times and positions, but that wasn't much use without pictures. The best solution was stand trackside and keep a lap chart.

Frank always kept the lap chart for his team just in case the Longines monitor on the pit wall crashed, which it did quite frequently at the time. But in Las Vegas, with so much riding on the result, he wanted to maintain a general overview of events on the track and in his pit area. I was asked if I would watch the race from the Williams pit and keep a lap chart. On the one hand, I welcomed the opportunity since the Williams pit was normally out of bounds to the media; I would be right in the heart of the championship story. On the other hand, I was terrified of screwing up on such an important occasion.

On race morning, as I walked by the Williams motorhome, Frank called me inside. 'Will you be all right?' he asked anxiously. When I replied in the affirmative and showed him my prepared lap chart, he handed me a sheet of A4 paper. 'I find this useful,' he said. 'You'll need it for scribbling down the numbers when they come past in a tight bunch at the end of the first lap. Then you can transfer them neatly to your lap chart before they come round for a second time.' It was something I did as a matter of course but I said thanks and reassured Frank everything would be okay. He nodded and ticked 'Maurice – lap chart' off a long list. On such fine details are championships won.

KEKE ROSBERG

The atmosphere at Williams that afternoon in Las Vegas was typical. I had won the championship. The attitude was, 'Okay, well done. The next problem is next week.' It was business. I think Frank and I both thought the same way. But it was also a lot of fun. There was a gang of nice people around Frank in 1982: Patrick and Charlie, and Alan Jones was around quite a lot. We used to take the piss out of Frank. We would say something every day, maybe about his running or something else he was very serious about. It was good fun. But it was businesslike too. No bullshit. When I won the championship, that was it for the day. 'Okay, that's done. Next?' So I didn't stay around and went off to San Francisco with Mansour Ojjeh.

SEVENTEEN
Turbo Change

By 1983, several important Williams associations had either been concluded or were drawing to a close. Leyland, having enjoyed a mutually successful liaison, had moved at the end of 1981, Steve Herrick having joined the London-based company CSS Promotions, where he would work closely with Sheridan Thynne as they explored other sources of finance and commercial partnerships for the team. The flow of money from Saudia Arabia had reduced and would end at the close of 1983, as would the association with TAG. Mansour Ojjeh had previously strengthened the TAG connection with Williams, its decals showing prominently on the nose and cockpit sides during 1981 and 1982, but a shift in emphasis on the engine front throughout Formula 1 would see a new direction for Ojjeh.

Following Renault's first win in 1979, turbocharged engines had increased in competitiveness and reliability; the faithful Ford-Cosworth was coming to the end of its useful life. Leading teams accepted the need for a partnership with a major motor manufacturer. McLaren, having used the trusty Cosworth to good effect, committed themselves to an ambitious project with Porsche and came to an agreement with Ojjeh to provide finance.

Williams had not been idle. Frank had entered discussions with Honda in early 1981 and finally signed a contract in February 1983, a few weeks before leaving for the first race of the season in Brazil. Rosberg remained on board as reigning world champion but Daly's contract had not been renewed, which was no surprise to anyone, least of all Daly himself. The parting had been amicable after a difficult year for both sides. Now Frank invited Jacques Laffite to return. Since leaving at the end of 1975, the Frenchman had won six Grands Prix with Ligier. The question was, would Jacques be hungry enough to give Williams the impetus they needed in their final year with the out-of-breath Ford-Cosworth?

Not as hungry as Rosberg, it transpired. Whereas Laffite would finish in the points on just six occasions – his best results being a couple of fourth places at the start of the season – Rosberg was ready to wring the car's neck. He turned the power deficit to his advantage at Monaco by using slick tyres on a track made treacherous by a light shower. While the opposition slithered in all directions as drivers tried to tame unwieldy amounts of turbo power, Rosberg waltzed into the distance and gave Williams their only win of the season. The Honda turbo could not come quickly enough, but when it did come, it was not all plain sailing, as Rosberg discovered when he raced the Williams-Honda for the first time in the final race of the 1983 season in South Africa.

A surprisingly good fifth place at Kyalami would prove a false dawn for 1984, as the team got to grips not only with a totally different engine package but also a new concept in chassis manufacture. The FW10 was the first Williams to use carbon fibre, Patrick's caution meaning that his was the last of the leading teams to switch from aluminium alloy honeycomb. As for the power, the Honda V6 was based on an engine previously used in Formula 2, whereas the McLaren-TAG Turbo, which would go on to win the 1984 title, was designed to the precise requirements laid down by John Barnard, the McLaren designer. Honda engine failures were commonplace, the team often getting through as many as four during a single weekend. It would have been an extremely barren season had Rosberg not shown typical resilience by winning the Dallas Grand Prix, run on a crumbling track in searing heat.

Appropriately in this season of change, the team had left Station Road and the collection of industrial units and Portakabins that had mushroomed during the previous seven years. The purpose-built factory at Basil Hill Road, opened on 16 June 1984 by Michael Heseltine, MP for South Oxfordshire and minister of defence in the Thatcher government, gave Honda a workshop for engine rebuilds on site rather than in Japan. It was a clear sign of how the partners were gearing up for a major effort. A vital element in that effort would be the drivers.

Laffite and Williams parted company on good terms for a second and final time at the end of the 1984 season. Frank had been watching the progress of Ayrton Senna, even going as far as giving the young Brazilian a test drive in the Williams-Ford during 1983, but was not quick enough off the mark for 1985: Senna was snapped up by Lotus after an impressive debut season in Formula 1 with the Toleman team – soon to become Benetton. Senna replaced Nigel Mansell at Lotus, a swap which many at the time saw as a very smart move by the team. Nigel had made an eventful arrival in Formula 1, stunning performances occasionally interrupting a litany of crashes and excuses. It was clear that Mansell did not enjoy the confidence of Lotus, but elsewhere there were dedicated supporters who could see his potential – most notably Peter Windsor, then sports editor of *Autocar*, and Peter Collins, team manager at Williams. Frank was not convinced. His prevarication provoked an ultimatum to make a decision from Patrick at the Dutch Grand Prix in August 1984 and Mansell was signed, more or less on the spot. It was the beginning of a colourful relationship.

Frank and Patrick could have been forgiven for wondering about the decision when Nigel tangled with another car on the opening lap of the 1985 season in Brazil. He then crashed while on his way to the starting grid for the next race in Portugal. The difference between Williams and Lotus was that Mansell was not publicly castigated for his sins. Frank kept his thoughts to himself, sound psychology which Mansell repaid by producing a very impressive drive from the back of the grid to fifth place. This was in pouring rain – difficult conditions at the best of times but lethal when trying to cope with the 700 bhp that the Honda V6 continued to deliver in vicious bursts. The throttle was all or nothing, maximum acceleration or none at all. Frank and Patrick took careful note of Nigel's drive on a day when nine drivers – including Rosberg – spun off, but they also could not help admiring Senna's sheer brilliance as he took the first of his many Grand Prix victories.

Honda addressed the power delivery problem by introducing a new V6 in time for Rosberg to pull off a brilliant win on the streets of Detroit, almost twelve months since the team's last victory in Dallas. The FW10 was coming good, as Rosberg demonstrated by claiming pole at Silverstone with an average speed of just over 160 mph. It was the fastest lap ever recorded by a Formula 1 car at any circuit during a race meeting – and, as the team discovered later, he did it with a slowly deflating front tyre. Plus of course his customary Marlboro cigarette before and after the event. Both drivers were to retire from the British Grand Prix, but that did nothing to lessen the growing feeling that Williams were on the verge of a breakthrough, particularly when Mansell scored his best-ever result by finishing second at Spa-Francorchamps, a driver's circuit if ever there was one.

The same could be said for Brands Hatch, scene of the European Grand Prix on 6 October 1985. Mansell had cut his teeth on the club circuit at the challenging venue in Kent, and it showed when he joined his teammate on the second row of the grid. Senna started from pole and led for several laps with Rosberg pushing him hard. Senna's blocking tactics, outrageous in Rosberg's view, culminated in contact as the Williams driver tried an almost desperate lunge inside the Lotus. Rosberg's frustration knew no bounds when he was forced into the pits with the resulting puncture. It so happened, however, that he rejoined just as Senna, now hotly pursued by Mansell, was completing a lap. Whether by accident or design, Rosberg took his time to move out of Senna's way. In the ensuing confusion Mansell shot into the lead with the outraged Senna giving chase. This was a tough test for Nigel: the pressure from the 120,000 crowd willing him on to his first win; the pressure from a man who had already won two Grands Prix; the internal pressure from knowing that his reputation would be in shreds if he made a mistake now. Mansell did not put a wheel out of place, crossing the line to take the first of many emotional victories.

The second would come in South Africa a fortnight later when Mansell led home a Williams one-two. Rosberg then underlined his potential to win the final round in Australia, his last race for Williams. Frank and Patrick were sad to see him go but Rosberg's replacement, Nelson Piquet, was a double world champion. With the Honda engine getting better by the race and a potentially quick car, the FW11, nearing completion in the new factory at Didcot, there was everything to look forward to in 1986.

DEREK DALY

I really only became aware of Williams when Alan Jones drove the FW06 in 1978. It was a nimble, simple little car that began to run remarkably well. I got the drive in 1982 because my manager at the time, Guy Edwards, initiated it through Charlie Crichton-Stuart. I don't think I spoke to Frank until he called me and said, 'I think I'm going to give you this drive.' They were the actual words he used: 'I *think* I'm going to give you this drive.' It was obviously a situation where he had to fill the seat with somebody. He wasn't really sure what the somebody was like or what they could do, but he was forced to fill the seat because Reutemann had gone.

I went to the factory and met Frank. They took pictures and stuff like that. Frank was the boss and that's the way it was. One of the things that struck me was that he and Patrick would jab at each other all the time: one would slag the other, but all in good humour. For instance, Frank would say, 'I get all the credit and Patrick does all the hard work.' And if something broke on the car, Frank would say, 'Patrick, how come *your* car broke this time?' It was all in good humour and Frank had a great laugh, a great hearty laugh.

I don't remember any sit-down serious discussions as in 'This is our expectation; this is what we'd like you to aim for; this is how we'd like to manage the season; and this is how we're going to work together.' I don't remember any meetings like that. I remember it as 'Let's just go and do it.' Which in a way is how I think most teams operated. The driver was a bit of a self-contained package. The driver did what he did and the team did what they did. If they did it right together, then well and good. But if they didn't, there was no major effort to make sure the two were well connected or in harmony.

I had been with Tyrrell before. Williams was a step up in engineering, but it was a step down in how to integrate the driver with the team. They let me get on with it more, whereas Ken [Tyrrell] would be very involved. Ken was more of a tutor and mentor to a driver. Not a huge difference, but Ken was more that way inclined. Frank was more engineering and get in and do it, and if it works, great, and if it doesn't work, we'll do something else. But the feeling was that I had taken a step up. The expectation was high. Keke had tested at Zolder and was under the lap record and the car was phenomenally fast. Whereas the reality of it was that it was fast, but it wasn't a world-beater at every race.

The mechanics were good, solid, reliable: they got the job done and I really got on with them. I had a difficult season, had a few problems, made a few mistakes. But there was no interaction between me and Frank or Patrick. For instance, if I had a bad race, there was no 'Let's discuss why; let's understand better; let's add more to whatever you need so that we can get the best from you.' Instead, it was simply 'That's what happened; let's move on.' At the end of 1982 Frank did call to tell me that he was going to put Laffite in the car. It wasn't an unexpected phone call because I knew I had not driven well. But in fairness to Frank, he didn't use an assistant, or send a fax or whatever. He picked the phone up and did it himself, so fair play to him. I don't necessarily see my year at Williams as a highlight, but neither do I see it as a low point. It seemed to fit into the Williams vernacular of 'That's it; it's over; it didn't work out; move on.' There was a sort of emotional numbness to it. I never look back and regret anything about it. Not in the slightest.

My downfall in Formula 1 started with the crashes at Tyrrell – so many crashes, not all my fault but being in the wrong places at the wrong time and having mechanical failures. I was almost shaking at the end of the year. By the time I got to Williams I had to rebuild myself, which I never quite did because then I got divorced at the end of the year, so the timing was wrong. But it led me to America and to a completely different life.

NEIL OATLEY

It was a difficult year. By 1983 turbo cars were starting to come on and our car was probably a bit average. Again, Monaco was an inspired tyre decision. We knew the track was damp but there wasn't any standing water. There was a sprinkling but no puddles and the Goodyear tyre engineer said the dry compound was a huge amount softer than the wet compound, so providing you didn't lose it on the first lap or so, you could be there. With twenty cars going round, you were going to get a dry line almost straight away. That's exactly what happened.

We had outgrown the buildings at Station Road. The drawing office had become very cramped but the place continued to have a good atmosphere – everyone could still squeeze into the canteen at tea break! Things were very different at the new factory on Basil Hill Road. It was obviously a much bigger building. The drawing office was at the opposite end to the part of the workshop where the cars were built. Before, you could look out of the drawing-office window and the race cars were down below. With the move, more people joined the team and you didn't always know who they were or what they did. That intimate touch was lost. It became less of a family atmosphere, but that sort of thing was inevitable. The team simply had to expand.

PATRICK HEAD

Keke was quite funny when we raced in the heat of Dallas in 1984. We had sorted out this cooling equipment, which was a skullcap, and Keke was unbelievably self-conscious about it. He didn't want anyone to see it, so he quickly put it on and then quickly put on his helmet. But I think it made a difference. When he removed his helmet after the race, he was able to shake his head and his golden locks weren't matted with sweat. It kept him cool, no doubt about it. But all credit to him. The circuit had broken up and it was like being a rally driver. Keke was good at that kind of stuff.

When the deal was done with Honda to run turbo in 1984, we aimed to get a car out running at the end of 1983 so that we could spend the winter developing. Honda sent an engine to us and it was literally a block with a couple of heads on it and a sump. No inlet manifold, no exhaust manifold, no exhaust system, no data, no thermal balance. The turbos came in a cardboard box.

In those days you communicated by telex, so that was clacking back and forth as we tried to get some information. I sent Mr Kawamoto a telex asking for a complete thermal balance for the engine and various other things such as exhaust specification and so on. He sent back a telex saying, 'Please design what you think.' That was it! We had one guy, Gary Thomas, in the design office, and he liked to get into engines. So we just sat down and worked out the numbers.

BRIAN O'ROURKE

When I started thinking about the first carbon fibre monocoque for the FW10, we were moving to Basil Hill Road and Patrick asked what equipment I needed to do this job. I said I needed to pressure-cook the laminates; I would need an autoclave. After explaining exactly what an autoclave would do, that it was a kind of pressurised oven, I was told to go and get one. I had to be careful about how much we were going to spend. In the end we spent very little in comparison with what we should have done. I spent quite a few months getting it set up so that, when we moved into the new factory, we were ready for all these bits and pieces to come in. I think I ended up drawing a factory extension to do it.

It was a bit of a shock. My original brief over the phone before I joined had been about someone with experience of designing composite-skin sandwich panels. I was a stress engineer. What I didn't bargain for was having to get on the drawing board, do the concept, full detail drafting, work out how to do the tooling, buy the facilities, extend the factory and draw the hole in the wall to fit the autoclave through. It was the whole thing. I wondered what the hell I had got myself into. But looking back, I'm quite proud of that because it started the process that you see today.

I was removed from most of the racing, which was just as well because we were racing the FW09. Patrick used to say it's surprising how good a car looks when it wins. Well, that car won, and I don't remember it getting any better-looking afterwards. I had the feeling that Patrick slightly resented having to go down this carbon fibre route, as in 'Bloody John Barnard has gone and built a carbon fibre chassis for McLaren. Bugger it, now we're all gonna have to do that.'

We hadn't built anything like that before. It was quite a bit of pressure. You need to get a few things wrong to get things right, but we couldn't afford to get anything wrong. You don't look at something and say, 'Blimey, that's going to be hard. Let's just find our way into it gently and gradually build up.' It's like if you don't know how to swim, they say, 'Go up to that ten-metre board and go straight in at the deep end and you've then got to win an Olympic 100-metre sprint. Oh, and you are not allowed to drown in the process.' We had a very small group. I was doing this with six blokes in the composite shop, and that was it. On that of that, this was the first year of crash testing, and that taught us a few things as well.

KEKE ROSBERG

The only time I ever had a cross word with Frank was when he told me Mansell was joining the team. I said I didn't want him and I was leaving. Frank said, 'No, you're not.' I insisted that I didn't want to stay but Frank held me to my contract. Unfortunately, that moment affected my thinking about the team because I decided to leave as soon as I could. I paid my dues until the end and then left, but only because I said I would and without really considering the quality of the team and the promising future if I had decided to stay.

That was the only clash I had with Frank, otherwise I had no problems at all. We got on very well but I don't think that Frank is the sort of man who builds great friendships. He doesn't let you come close. It's not because he's the boss. He's not distancing himself because he's in authority; he's at a distance only because he chooses not to let you come close. Looking back, you ask yourself, 'Did I have many breakfasts with Frank?' Answer: 'No.' 'Did we have many dinners with Frank?' Answer: 'No.' He was always there, but he wasn't, if you know what I mean.

Telephone contact was with Frank whereas face-to-face contact tended to be with Patrick, except at race meetings, when Frank would run the debriefs and so on. But he did have a sense of humour. He was very funny at times and we would always be making jokes at Frank's expense. He was a caring sort of person, but not as much as he liked to think he was. We used to tell a joke about how Frank would go into the workshop and pat one of the lads on the back. 'How's it going, Pete?' he would ask. Pete would say, 'Not so good, Frank. My wife died this morning.' And Frank would say, 'Okay, never mind. D'you think that front suspension will be ready in time for the test at Paul Ricard next week?'

NIGEL MANSELL

It was tricky as Frank had a load of drivers wanting to drive for him but, as luck would have it, he gave me the opportunity and it was wonderful to be teammates with Keke. It was difficult initially because how can one formulate any opinion about someone who slags you off in the press so terribly? I did a bit of soul searching and asked if this guy had anything to complain about or not? I thought *Frank is the team boss, Patrick is one of the directors and if they want me to drive for Williams, then fantastic.* So Keke and I got together to set this straight. I said 'If you think I'm a c***, then tell me. I've read all these things in the press.' He denied this was true. We gelled within a matter of a few weeks, testing and racing. We went from strength to strength.

The great thing for me is I've never had a problem with anybody I've worked for. Patrick will probably be the first one to tell you, I always gave it my all when I was in the car, and if you're a designer or an engineer or actually employed by somebody and they can see their employee working as hard as they know how, you can't do better than that. I always got tremendous support and encouragement. They never questioned if I was trying; if anything, they sometimes said I should slow down a little bit.

Compared to my time at Lotus, the bullshit at Williams was so much less. They were interested in getting on with the job; calling a spade a spade. If people made a mistake, they wanted to know why so that they could improve and it wouldn't happen again. That related across to driving the car for them as well. If I made a mistake then they were interested in why; was it me or was it something that could be done to improve the car? We had to be honest with each other. It was such a good relationship.

Winning my first race at Brands Hatch was sensational but, wonderful as it was, to actually repeat the result two weeks later in South Africa was almost a better moment. Anyone can win a race, but then to win another proves it's not a fluke. Frank said many times on television interviews that I was born and became a winner then. For me, there was no turning back. I was on a new career path with new focus and it was wonderful to have that opportunity.

ALAN HENRY

The occasion was on a Sunday-night flight back from Hockenheim, I think, in early 1983. There had been these rumours about Williams doing a deal with Honda, but as ever Frank would say nothing. I was chatting with Frank over the back of his seat in front of me – about aircraft, as you do, and his meticulous obsession with noting down the registration, plane type and destination of every flight he had been on. Knowing precisely what I was looking for, I asked him to let me look at the entries for the first part of the year. 'Seems to me you took a lot of flights to Tokyo, Frank,' I said. 'You bastard, AH,' he replied.

JOHN CADD

I think it was about 1985, and there was a bit of a mix-up about Frank needing a car taken to his house so that he could go to a meeting. Frank had a Walkinshaw Rover Vitesse and I drove like a lunatic to get to his house. Frank liked to be very punctual. If there was a meeting at ten o'clock, he wanted to be there at ten o'clock, not one minute past. I arrived at the house and Ginny was waiting with a pile of clothes and a towel. Frank was out running and the plan was for him to get changed at the factory. I set off in the direction that Ginny had told me and nearly knocked Frank over as he came running round a bend towards me. Normally Frank drove, but this time he got in the back of the car and started getting undressed. I thought, *Christ, imagine if we have an accident now. He's stark naked in the car, and I'm a mechanic.* He got sorted and we arrived on time.

ALAN CHALLIS

When Frank told me that he'd signed Nigel, I told him he must be mad. 'All he ever does is throw it in the wall.' And Frank just said, 'Well, you'll have to keep mending it, won't you?' But from the day Nigel started, I got on very well with him. Nigel is one of those people who either likes you or hates you. For some reason, he decided – probably because of my position in the team – that he liked me. With Nigel, you always knew that the car wouldn't go any quicker than he could make it go. He was a very quick racing driver. You couldn't ask for more.

DICKIE STANFORD

I was working as a mechanic in Formula 3 and I turned up on the team's doorstep and got an interview with Peter Collins. I was turned down because there were no jobs available in those days. Peter told me to get Formula 2 experience and then come back. Which is what I did. I started with Williams in January 1985.

I had been told that Frank was really a hard person to work for. That was made apparent almost from the start. Frank would come in and check the cleanliness of the car, ask what you were doing; be involved in everything. I found it totally different to the way you work anywhere else. Whereas you do everything when in Formula 3 or Formula 2, at Williams there was a sub-assembly department for the gearbox, the uprights, for everything else on the car. Honda brought the engine fully kitted. That was the biggest thing to get over in the first week. You didn't pull the upright to bits; you didn't pull the diff to bits; somebody else did that. You got it back as a unit. It was like car production. There were three mechanics on each car, and they were pushed to do what needed to be done. I was the number three on Nigel's car, the gearbox/rear-end man.

We won our first race in Detroit with Keke when we did a pit stop. This was planned because we knew, for our car, the tyres wouldn't last. When you look at it now, you would expect the stop to be about five seconds, but in those days ten seconds was considered to be really good. That won us the race.

We went to Canada and Honda came up with some new camshafts for the engine. Suddenly it was like night and day – wins at Brands

Hatch and South Africa. Brands was a big day for me because it was Nigel's first win, and mine. When you are in the lead and, say, there are five laps to go, you are always panicking. You're thinking, *Is everything okay?* I don't care what anyone says. If they say everything is hunky dory, it's not. When you look around the garage and you've done it for about twenty years, you can see what people are thinking. The last five laps are probably the worst because that's when things break. These cars are only designed to do one race.

PETE FOSTEKEW

Frank is a real practical joker. I've fallen foul of him a couple of times. After we had won the Adelaide race in 1985 we'd more or less packed up and two policemen turned up. They were enthusiasts. One of them said to Frank, 'Swap your shirt?' It had been the last race of the season and Frank said okay. Off came our shirts. I put this shirt on and it had two stripes on it which meant I outranked Frank, so jokingly I started bossing him about. I should have realised what might happen when his parting words were: 'I'll have you, you bastard!'

Anyway as the evening progressed, I was at the back of the garage and all of a sudden there was this mighty, booming voice, someone shouting. We looked up to find probably the biggest policeman in Southern Australia. He must have been about eight feet square, complete gold braid – the lot. He looked at me and roared, 'You! Yeah you! Come here!' I'd still got this bloody shirt on. I thought I was going to be court-martialled. 'You want to be a bloody policeman, do you? You can get down there and do point duty. Okay?' I thought Frank had gone. Then I saw his grinning face peeping round the corner.

EIGHTEEN
On the Edge

The Williams mechanics were at the Paul Ricard circuit for the final test session before the 1986 season opened two weeks later in Brazil. It was Saturday 8 March and all should have been well with the world.

The new Williams-Honda FW11 had been competitive from the moment it first ran. Nigel Mansell and Nelson Piquet, arguably the strongest driver pairing on the entry list, were on hand in the south of France to put the car through its final paces. Sponsorship from Canon, Mobil, ICI and Denim was in place. It was a glorious morning and the status of the Williams team was such that Goodyear would pay for every test lap completed. But both cars were on stands with their wheels off, confined to the garage with various mechanical problems, and Frank chose that very moment to turn up. Frank Dernie and the crew could not believe his timing.

Williams had flown to Nice that morning. He had been up bright and early at the start of a weekend that would bring the best of both his worlds. After seeing and hearing his cars on full song – or so he hoped – Frank would return to England and prepare for a half-marathon in Portsmouth the following day. Frank and Ginny had moved yet again, this time to Boxford House, a small mansion – there is no other word for it – near Newbury. Jonathan was at boarding school and Claire now had the company of another brother, three-year-old Jaime. Unlike the threadbare aftermath of previous moves, Frank and Ginny had the funds to renovate Boxford House from top to bottom. Life was hard to beat.

Despite the lack of activity at the racetrack, Frank was in buoyant mood as he called Ginny to say he would be home in time for supper. Peter Windsor, who had abandoned journalism to take up a post as PR coordinator with the team, joined Frank as they walked towards the Ford Sierra hire car for the drive back to the airport. The ninety-minute journey would take them on an interesting mixture of B roads north-east through hilly countryside before reaching the autoroute and heading east towards Cannes and Nice. It was a route familiar to everyone in Formula 1, the first section tempting would-be racers to have a bit of fun before reaching the tedium of the motorway.

About fifteen minutes into the journey, at a point where the road emerged from the hills near the village of Meounes-les-Montrieux, a curve led into a short straight. As the Ford swept through the left-hander, it began to slide. Frank automatically compensated but the steering correction was too fast, too soon. The car swung the other way, then back again before nosediving into a ploughed field several feet below the road on the left-hand side. The car landed upside down, the left-front corner of the roof collapsing and trapping Frank underneath. His life would be very different from that moment on.

PETER WINDSOR

I hadn't actually been a passenger with Frank that often. I had driven with him periodically in his Jaguar XJS, driving quite slowly around the country roads when we went out to have lunch at a pub somewhere; that was the limit of my experience in the passenger seat with him. But I knew from Ginny that he was a nightmare. He was known to switch off the headlights so that he could see if anyone was coming and then he could take the racing line through the country roads at night. And he used to have a stopwatch to time journeys such as Didcot to Heathrow.

But I had never really driven much with him on the roads until that day. It was an Avis Ford Sierra 1600. This was at a time when team owners would have rented a BMW or a Mercedes, but Frank was still not wanting to spend any more than he had to. I had been down at Paul Ricard with some sponsors that day and they had all gone. We needed to get something like a 7 p.m. flight out of Nice. We took the route using twisty roads. In the tight bits Frank was definitely driving fast, but pretty well. The Sierra was a horrendous car. Going downhill on a bumpy road into hairpins, he would brake late and the back end would jump out. He would lock up the front brakes from time to time, but none of this was a big deal; he had it all under control. It was relatively slow-speed stuff.

There is a feeling you get when driving with very good Formula 1 drivers. You go through the Esses at Silverstone and it's okay, but when the back end starts to slide in the middle of Stowe, you think, *Whoa! Now we're in different territory.* We had come out of the mountainous section to where the road flattened out. Frank just lost the back end and I remember a flash thought: *Right, we'll really see what Frank's car control is like, now that we're going quite quickly.*

We must have been doing 70 mph, something like that. He overcorrected and I knew we were going to spin, but as there was not a lot of room on the inside of the road we went over this drop and somersaulted. The car landed upside down, more on Frank's side than mine. Because of the rounded pillars on the Sierra, there was not enough strength to withstand an impact like that. The roof collapsed and Frank took the brunt of the blow, right through the top of his head.

I was obviously a bit shocked, but otherwise okay. There was a smell of fuel and Frank was saying, 'Get me out of the car! Get me out of the car!' We were upside down; the roof had collapsed; our briefcases were open; there was stuff everywhere; and although we had our seat belts on, we were tangled up in the belts. Frank was saying, 'I can't move my legs.' I didn't know if he had pinched a nerve, or what had happened. I did try to pull him out by the armpits while cradling his head, rather than pulling him by the neck or whatever. That's about all I knew what to do as I dragged him out the back of the car. Somebody had seen the accident and kicked in the remnants of the rear window and removed the shards of glass. As he lay on the ground, I remember Frank saying, 'I'm never going to drive fast again. I'm going to drive a Gogomobile.' That was the car that came to his mind – it was a very odd thing to say at that moment.

Someone called an ambulance and I got someone else to go to the circuit and get Nelson because I remembered that his Mercedes had a phone – this was in the early days of cellphones and none of us had mobiles. I knew this would be the best way to get things moving with people like Sid [Professor Watkins] and Bernie [Ecclestone].

JOHN CADD

I was at Paul Ricard. Dickie [Stanford] was working on Nigel's car and I was working on Nelson's. That morning a hose had come off Nigel's brand-new car and there was a fire. The chassis was in the garage and the boys were working on it, trying to repair it. There was quite a lot of damage. Our car had only done five or six laps before the crown wheel and pinion broke. Back in those days we didn't have the luxuries of today where you can get another gearbox and replace the broken one; you used to have to change the damaged parts.

So, there's two cars up on the stands in the garage, everyone working frantically to get them back on the track. Then this silver Sierra arrives – and it's Frank. We're thinking, *Shit! This is a Goodyear tyre test and Frank is getting paid by the lap.* Frank came straight in the garage and you could see the dismay on his face. He came over and asked what the problem was. I said, 'We've blown the gearbox, Frank. We've only done five or six laps and the crown wheel and pinion's gone.' 'How long is it going to take you to fix it?' 'I reckon it's going to be at least an hour and a half, an hour and three-quarters.' 'Well, we'll call it an hour.' 'Okay, Frank.'

You always added a bit on when estimating the time needed. We managed to get ours back together in three-quarters of an hour. Nelson climbed in, went out, shook the car down for one lap, came back in. We checked it all over, then we did a bit of running, got the car on a good balance and that allowed us to start the tyre test. We started whacking tyres on, off, on, off. Nothing was a problem. After a short while, Frank said he was off.

He used to go round and say cheerio to everyone. He shot off and we carried on with the tyre test. Everything was fine. Nelson was doing lots of laps. As he came into the pits at one point, he just missed this kiddie on a motorbike. This kid stopped his bike by us and said, 'Mr Williams! Mr Williams! Big accident!'

Frank [Dernie], Nigel and Nelson shot off in the Mercedes. We put the cars away, closed up for the night and went back to the hotel. I saw Peter Windsor later on that evening. He'd come back, his shirt covered in blood. He filled us in on a few details and then we decided to stop the test and go back to England. We were going through Marseilles airport just as Ginny and Patrick were arriving. From that point we were waiting for news back at the factory.

VIRGINIA WILLIAMS

Frank phoned me up – I can't remember the exact time, but I think it was about four o'clock – and said he was just leaving the circuit. He would be back through the door at about eight o'clock and could he have pasta for dinner that night because he was doing a half-marathon the next day? He asked if I wanted to come down to Portsmouth with the kids to watch. I said that would be lovely.

Then I got a call from Peter Windsor about an hour later saying, 'Ginny, Frank won't be home tonight because we've been in a bit of a ding down here, so he just wants you to know that he won't be home tonight and we'll catch up with you later.' To start with I didn't want my imagination to exaggerate. But after an hour I started to get a bit panicky because I thought, *Why didn't Frank phone me? Why wouldn't he have phoned me to say that he had to go and get his leg put in plaster?*

Then the doorbell rang and it was Patrick. As soon as I opened the door and saw him, I could feel my heart thumping out of my chest. I can just remember Patrick saying, 'Ginny, he's not dead.' We went into the kitchen and at almost the same time Bernie phoned and asked if Patrick was with me. When I was watching Patrick, he turned full circle away from me so that I wouldn't see his face. I remember thinking, *We're in trouble.* Patrick said they were going to operate on Frank because he had a couple of problems. He and I were going to go down in Bernie's plane first thing the next day.

In the morning Bernie phoned again and Patrick was quite clearly upset because Bernie had told him about the difficulties they were having. I don't think they expected Frank to survive. In the end, Patrick and I went straight to Heathrow and got on some dreadful plane on a scheduled flight as it was easier that way. We were reading *Private Eye* and keeping ourselves amused, much as you see people talking and laughing at funerals. That way we were able to get through the flight to Marseilles.

I'd learned that Frank had been driving and I wasn't surprised that he'd had the accident. He was a pretty hairy driver. I had said to him that I thought he would kill himself in a car. I didn't like driving with him at all. I remember going to a party at Jackie Oliver's, and I was white and nearly sick by the time we got there. I think it worried me far more later on because when you've got three children under ten you don't really want to be driving like that. I *loathed* it. He always says that I drove very fast, and I did drive very fast, but I always felt I was much safer than Frank.

PETER WINDSOR

It was a weird time, one of those occasions when you are in the hands of the doctors. First of all they took Frank to Toulon, and then after about an hour and a half they put him into traction and said they couldn't do much there and he would have to go to Marseilles. I think they realised it was an incurable spinal injury even at that point.

Nelson and I and Frank Dernie followed this Citroën ambulance. Nigel was sitting with Frank. At Marseilles we just hung around outside the operating theatre for hours and hours. Eventually Sid, who had obviously flown in, came out and said, 'It's okay. I've seen Frank; he's sitting up; he's pretty cheery. The operation went well. I watched the operation. There's not much I can do now. I would suggest you go back to bed or if you have work to do, go back to England.' So that was very encouraging obviously. Everyone flew back to England. Ginny asked me to stay. It was just the two of us for about five days.

PROFESSOR SIDNEY WATKINS
(F1's chief medical officer, from his book *Life at the Limit*, Macmillan, 1996)

Bernie had placed his Citation jet on standby at Biggin Hill and I flew down that night. The hospital was pretty quiet when we arrived and Nigel, Peter and Nelson and myself had a brief chat about the accident. Frank was already in the operating theatre, so I changed my clothes and went in. I introduced myself to the operating neurosurgeon, Dr Vincentelli, who was expecting me and was very welcoming. I had a look at the X-rays and saw what I had feared most – there was complete dislocation at C6–C7 (the sixth cervical vertebra on the seventh) with gross reduction of the diameter of the spinal canal. It seemed highly likely that the spinal cord had been irretrievably damaged and one could only hope for the best.

PETER WINDSOR

We had to do the nitty-gritty, find a hotel, get to the hospital every day and so on. The first time Ginny went in to see Frank – I think it was a couple of days later – she came out of the IC unit completely shocked.

He had an oxygen mask on; he looked as white as a sheet. It was horrendous. This went on for another day.

We had a private meeting with the head of the IC unit and he said, 'Well, we think it's time for your husband to be flown back to the UK.' I asked if that meant he had improved enough to be flown back, to which he replied, 'Well, Monsieur, put it like this: we do not want there to be a big problem here in France.' To which I said, 'So, basically, you're saying you do not want him to die in France.' And he more or less said yes.

I got on the phone to Sid and said this did not sound right. 'The picture painted two days before is different to the one we're getting now. Ginny is very worried and I think we should be doing a lot more.' He said, 'I'm sure you're exaggerating, but to put your mind at rest I'll fly out one of the best anaesthetists.' I arranged to have him flown out in an air ambulance, met Dr Yates at Marseilles airport at 3 a.m. and drove to the hospital, where it took a while to get into the IC unit because they wouldn't let him in. He came up with the bogus story of hearing how wonderful they were and wanted to see for himself.

Dr Yates came out about forty-five minutes later and said, 'Right, if we don't move Frank in twenty-four hours, he is going to die. I was in the intensive care unit. It was empty and they have all gone off on a coffee break. They haven't even got the technology to do a tracheotomy, and if we don't get the fluid out of his lungs, he's not going to live. We need to get him back to England in twenty-four hours.'

There had been a point when Ginny rang me and said she had been asked if she would give permission to switch off the life-support machine. I said if Frank has a brain and can talk, he can still run a Formula 1 team. He is fit and he is a fighter. Ginny said she agreed 100 per cent. She didn't give permission. There was quite a lot of surprise at the time, not only within the hospital but within the motor racing world as well.

I made contact with an air ambulance service in Switzerland. Sheridan Thynne got on to Mark Thatcher, who organised a police escort from Biggin Hill. I didn't have a lot more to do with it for a couple of days. Ginny took over. She was very organised, a fantastic lady. She was always there with Frank. She kept the whole thing running.

VIRGINIA WILLIAMS

I had to push *very* hard. The first thing Frank had asked me was, 'Have they told you that I'm paralysed?' He even said, 'from the neck down'. And I said, 'Yes.' He knew about the state he was in. That's why I called my book *A Different Kind of Life* because Frank had said to me, 'As I see it, I've had forty fantastic years of one kind of life. Now I shall have another forty years of a different kind of life.'

I think he was in such poor condition that most people – and I'm not blaming anybody at the hospital at the time – probably thought, *With this guy there's no point.* But it was because of Frank that I thought I can't go their way when he's told me that he wants to live. I can't be the one that makes that decision; I've got to tell them that they've got to fight. I'm not having him fighting and them not fighting. So we did have quite a hairy few days. Peter did play a very active role. We did have a bit of trouble getting some help from England, but only on the medical side. Bernie said we could get a plane and Prof ended up sending Dr Paul Yates to assess the situation because I was giving Prof such a hard time and he was utterly fed up with me.

Frank was freezing cold in the corner; there was no nursing. They tried to keep us out and Peter was always trying to get me in. When Dr Yates arrived, I wasn't allowed to go in with him. When he came out, he said Frank should be taken back to England straight away, but it was difficult because he wasn't sure if Frank would survive the flight. I went back to the hotel. The next morning Peter knocked on my door and said, 'We're flying Frank back this morning.' I can remember being hysterical. I said to the anaesthetist, 'You said last night that we couldn't fly him because he couldn't survive the journey, so why are you telling me this?' And he said, 'Because he's going to die there or he's going to die on the aeroplane, so we've got to make this choice. We've got to go for it.' It was terrible. Absolutely terrible.

My girlfriend and her husband came down and they joined me and Peter on the flight back in the private plane Bernie had sent down. Frank was not far ahead of us in the air ambulance. I had no idea whether or not Frank would be alive when we reached England. The flight seemed to take for ever.

BERNIE ECCLESTONE

I got a plane to bring them back. I spoke to Professor Watkins at the time and I asked him what was going to happen to Frank. He said, 'I'm sorry. Frank is going to be like this for ever.' I remember thinking, *Christ, that's not nice.* I went to see him every night once he got back. I knew Frank was one of life's survivors but I really didn't know if he was going to pull through this.

NIGEL MANSELL

We went to the scene of the accident. It was touch and go. Everything had been going so well with the team. It was a beautiful day, but it was one of those situations where for a very small error in judgement, you pay an incredibly high price. Normally on any other road, any other corner, it wouldn't have been a drama at all; you'd have just gone 'Oops!' and pulled back a bit. But there was nowhere to go. I think he was very, very unlucky, especially when you have someone else in the car walk away.

ALAIN PROST

I remember this very well. I was at Paul Ricard at the time and we heard about the accident. The reaction was we were terrified. We did not think about the team itself, more about Frank. He was a passionate guy doing a lot of sport, jogging all the time, and when you have this kind of life and that sort of thing happens it is … I was terrified.

NEIL OATLEY

I had left the team and I was at Ricard that day for a test with the Beatrice team. Williams were there and unusually Frank was there. I'm not sure why he was there. Our car was actually quite good and I think Frank was a little worried that we were actually so close to the Williams lap times. Frank was sniffing around in the pit lane. Probably he was bored in Didcot and just wanted to go and get a fix of seeing his racing cars run. Then we packed up and went off home. Communications in 1986 were nothing like they are now and I remember flicking on the radio when I woke up on Sunday morning. That's when I heard the news. There was a very real chance that he wasn't going to survive. I spoke to Patrick a couple of days later, and even at that stage I think Patrick thought it was the end.

FRANK DERNIE

Frank was thrilled to bits as we were going really well and he left Paul Ricard full of the joys of spring. We'd had a problem with the car but because we were blindingly quick compared to anybody else and feeling fairly optimistic, I thought there was no point in risking anything; better to call it a day.

While we were packing up, a French youth on a moped appeared with a message that Frank had had an accident and he was asking for me. I thought to myself, *Silly bugger. He's slid off the road because he drove very fast and he just needs a bit of a shove out of a ditch or something.* We got there just before the ambulance. Frank was lying there with his head on his briefcase, saying, 'My arms are fucked. Have a look at my arms,' and I was thinking, *He's got a little mark on his head and he looks fine. What's all this about?* He'd obviously taken a whack on the head.

The ambulance arrived and they started putting him in this pump-up thing. I thought that was a bit strange but I had no real idea of how bad the accident had been until the ambulance set off at 5 kph down the hill. I thought, *Jesus, they're obviously a bit worried*. Then they stopped in a layby and a car with a police escort arrived. A doctor jumped out, got in the ambulance and started working on him. That's when we realised it was pretty serious.

Nelson, who probably had one of the first car phones in Christendom, started trying to ring Bernie, but with surrounding hills the phone kept cutting off. As soon as we could, I rang Patrick to tell him Frank had had a shunt and that he looked quite bad. When we reached Toulon hospital there was a young doctor in charge. The main man wasn't there but showed up later, and clearly he'd had a few drinks as he'd been having lunch with his mates. He didn't know I spoke French and he stormed in saying, 'What are these clowns doing in my hospital?' He looked at the X-rays and said, 'Well, he's going to die. I'm going back to my guests.' And fucked off, leaving it with the young bloke.

I had a chat with the young doctor, who was shitting himself. It was obviously very serious. It was a very famous person he'd got there and he didn't know what to do. He said he'd never had an injury like this. He showed me the X-ray, and you could see the broken vertebra had moved. He said that it had moved by probably more than the diameter of the spinal cord so it was almost certainly severed.

Frank was moved to Marseilles. When we eventually got in to see him, Frank looked at Nigel and me and said, 'Who the fuck's testing then?' And I thought, *He'll be all right*.

HOWDEN GANLEY

When I heard about the accident, I didn't know at that stage that he would be paralysed. So I remember thinking that he was pretty wild on the road and this was not such a surprise. When I was racing with him and we went to a couple of places, eventually I banned him from driving.

KEKE ROSBERG

I remember being really shocked. But, to be perfectly honest, once the news began to sink in, I don't think anyone was really surprised. Frank was a hooligan on the roads. Many of us were hooligans in those days and Frank actually did us a great favour. His accident really shook us with a reminder that we were not immortal. We thought we were. We thought, *We will be here for ever, we're so wonderful.*

Everyone knew the corner; we knew the exact place where he had gone off. We had been up and down that road so many times, it was like having an accident happen in your own backyard. There was a big message in that accident for all of us. We were just very happy that Frank was still alive even though the news of his condition didn't sound good.

SHERIDAN THYNNE

I got a telephone call at about six o'clock that evening. Part of my family lives in Spain and we meet every so often. When Ginny rang I was standing in the hallway and about to leave for London. Ginny didn't really know what had happened at that stage. Had it been another occasion I would have said that I'd come over. But I asked her to call me later because I had no means of knowing and I don't think Ginny had any means of knowing how serious it was at that time. I wasn't going out to dinner; I was going to a family meeting of people who live a thousand miles apart and don't meet very often, to discuss some very important matters, so I was guilty of not doing what prob-ably ninety-nine times out of a hundred I'd have said. But because I didn't envisage – and I don't think she envisaged at that stage – what it was, I was therefore inaccessible for the next five hours. I can't remember if I heard that night or first thing the following morning. I think it was that following morning that Patrick addressed the entire factory to explain things to everyone. But I really don't think anyone fully appreciated exactly what it meant at that stage.

LADY SARAH ASPINALL

I was with friends in Monaco when I heard. Until Frank's accident I didn't realise the full implications of disability; I didn't realise what it meant. My son Jason was paralysed in a road accident in 1995, and by then I was better prepared for the full implications of disability. I thought about Frank and what it might mean to him. Someone who was a live wire, never still. He really loved his classical music and I think that gave him great peace. He was thirsting for knowledge, life and everything else. And he still is, I'm sure. But I found it hard to comprehend the effect of an accident on a man like that. I just wanted to turn the clock back, so quickly and so badly. I just don't know how Frank and Jason cope. I couldn't deal with it, I'm sure. Neither of them sit and moan. Frank went to see Jason after his accident; he was incredibly helpful and kind.

NINETEEN

Back from the Dead

F rank managed to survive the flight and was swiftly transferred under
police escort to the London Hospital on Whitechapel Road. A week
later he was moved from intensive care to a side unit on the neurolog-
ical ward. News of this small step forward was welcomed by friends,
family, supporters, colleagues and employees around the globe – not
least in Rio de Janeiro, where the teams were gathering for the first race
of the 1986 season. A win for Nelson Piquet in Brazil would be a boost
for Frank, but he suddenly had more serious matters to contend with.
Not long after his move from IC, he was rushed back in with the
doctors' worst fear: pneumonia.

The medical staff fought for the best part of a week to stop his lungs
filling with fluid, and it was made clear to Virginia that this was but a
small battle in an ongoing war. Later on, six weeks after the accident,
when Frank was breathing on his own, there was still a possibility that
he might not live. However, Frank's determination and fitness were
clearly assisting his recovery as it edged towards the two-month mark.
He was emphatic that he did not wish to undergo rehabilitation at the
spinal unit at Stoke Mandeville, and Ginny supported the view that he
would be better off at home, so the dining room on the ground floor
at Boxford House was converted to deal with Frank's needs.

On 28 May, twelve weeks after his cheery departure for Heathrow
and the flight to Nice, Frank returned home. A couple of days after that

he visited the factory. It took Ginny and two nurses to get him out of the front seat of the Jaguar. He looked pale and desperately frail, and there was no getting away from the fact that he would be unable to use his legs and lower arms for the rest of his life. Since all voluntary functions had ceased beneath the level of his upper chest, he was unable to breathe by expanding his ribs, but he would overcome that, his extraordinary willpower charged by the adrenalin that continued to pump as strongly as ever as he paid a visit to his beloved team.

VIRGINIA WILLIAMS

Frank was very fit and his heart rate was very slow, which was good. I stayed in the hospital for about three months. Because nurses changed a lot in intensive care and work on rotation, they never ever leave the patient. There's always one nurse right there, but they never recognised when Frank stopped breathing. So I was put in place, by Frank largely, to sit there watching him. If he stopped breathing, I would say to the nurse, 'He's not breathing! He's not breathing!' They'd come and revive him again.

He never faltered, and I don't know whether the fact that I was the person he was relying on to keep an eye on him played a part. If you're determined to live, I think it does. But even at six weeks we were still quite fearful of losing him. I can remember one night when I was quite low and the anaesthetist said to come and have a cup of tea with him. I was low because we'd tried to give Frank a sip of something and we couldn't because it always went into his lungs. You then had to use suction and the tea had to be coloured so that you could see if it was mis-routing. There was this anxiety on my part because I wanted him to be able to achieve putting something into his mouth rather than being fed through the nasal gastric feed. The anaesthetist said to me that we could still lose him.

I was quite surprised because I thought we'd got through six weeks and we'd always been able to revive him every time. I wasn't expecting to hear that. He also said that he might never be able to feed by mouth, and at that point I can remember getting very, *very* low and thinking, *Well, what's the point? Why would you want to live if you can't even swallow a cup of tea?* It shows how greedy I am because that would probably be my priority. Frank liked his tea and I just thought, *What kind of quality of life is this going to be?* But at the back of my mind I didn't quite believe it. I'm not sure that I also didn't believe that he would remain paralysed. I think that whatever they told me I thought, *Oh well, they can tell me that and I can be depressed today, but I'm sure that Frank will find a way of beating it.*

One of the reasons that I wrote my book was because I was so ignorant of spinal injury and I felt that most people were. I didn't understand that if you severed your spinal cord, it didn't matter who you were; you were never ever going to be able to have movement below the point of injury. I still, at that point in the London Hospital, believed that Frank would overcome it. I think that Frank believed that he'd overcome it too.

Williams got me a room at the Tower Hotel, and I used to go back for two or three hours in the night. I can remember going to the hotel at about five o'clock in the morning to have a shower and I got a phone call to say that I had to go back because they were losing him. It was raining and there was a taxi queue of lots of businessmen staying at the Tower Hotel. I can remember running up and saying, 'Can you let me go in the first taxi because my husband is dying and I've got to get back to the hospital.' I think they looked at me thinking that was a good excuse to get to the top of the queue. I got back and he survived. He survived quite a few. I think there were at least a dozen occasions when he was dead and revived again.

FRANK WILLIAMS

One night I found I couldn't breathe. The nurse raised the alarm and they came and shoved the suction tube into my lungs. It was a very unpleasant thing to have shoved down your lungs. They could not stop the stuff coming. I remember thinking my spit tasted of yeast and they couldn't understand it. What had happened was, I was on a nasal gastric feed and the tube had come out of my stomach and gone into my lungs. That's where all the food was going. The consultant arrived and he realised straight away. I could have died then or on any number of occasions. But I had no idea that it had been such a close-run thing. I really was not aware.

IAN ANDERSON

People didn't really appreciate the seriousness of it at first. They knew Frank was badly injured but didn't really think there was a touch-and-go situation. When the realisation dawned, we were pretty shocked. Patrick said, 'We are a team and the infrastructure is there, and everybody is supposed to know what they're doing, so we'll carry on.' But it put an enormous strain on Patrick – and everyone close to Frank, really. It was amazing that Frank actually came back, as was the time scale of him coming back.

DEREK DALY

I thought that would be the end of the team. What I did not factor in was Frank's mental resolve. One of my weaknesses was that I didn't have the mental skills to absorb Formula 1 and handle it. Frank does. So when he had his accident I quantified his continuation with the team from *my* mental platform and just didn't realise how different Frank's was. I don't think I could have absorbed it and handled it and processed what happened the way he has.

PETE FOSTEKEW

Obviously it came as quite a shock when we first heard about it because of course we didn't know the extent of his injuries other than the fact that he'd had a very serious accident. So I think everyone wondered what was going to happen. There were all sorts of theories floating about, such as Patrick taking over completely. But then you thought,

Well with the greatest of respect to Patrick, he isn't the businessman; that's Frank's job. So, I couldn't see that working and I thought it was all going to fold. But as time progressed, we learnt that his injuries were serious but he was still capable.

The day he came back – there were about sixty of us then – the whole place stood and applauded when Ginny brought him in. I was quite touched by that and I don't think it would happen in many other industries.

BERNIE GOBLE

I was off work for some reason on the day of the accident. I came in the day after, and as I drove through the gate there were press and loads of flowers. Patrick called a meeting in the race bay and told us what he knew. I guess he probably felt he had to say it, but he said that although Frank was not going to die as far anyone could tell, he had problems. But the company would function for the foreseeable future. Although your first concern is for Frank, the next thing you think about is your job, and is it safe? Most people are committed, bought houses, got mortgages and some have kids. But after that reassurance they kept us informed about how Frank was doing pretty much on a daily basis. We just focused on the racing and did it for Frank.

ALAN CHALLIS

I was back at the factory. We had a phone call more or less straight away. It must have been a few days before I realised exactly what had happened to Frank. I went down to see him in hospital, obviously a little while after he was brought back to London. You'd walk into the room and think, *Bloody hell!* Naturally, people back at the factory were worried about their livelihood; it was a natural reaction. It was almost a case of no Frank, no Williams. That's how it seemed initially. But I was told in no uncertain terms in the hospital, 'Things have got to go on, carry on as normal. Get on and get it done.' Which we did.

PATRICK HEAD

If such a terrible thing was ever going to happen, then it came at a time that kept the upset to a minimum. The car was quick, and in a Grand Prix team that papers over all sorts of schisms and problems. We had Sheridan Thynne as our marketing manager and we had some brilliant mechanics taking care of things – people like Dickie Stanford and Alan Challis. We had some very, very good people in the team – Frank Dernie for instance. So, in terms of actually running the team, there wasn't really a problem.

With the sponsors there probably would have been a problem if we hadn't been fast. But if you're finishing first and second, or your only problem is one driver complaining about the other because he's taken a win from him, then your sponsors can deal with that. So that made us able to get through the year.

JONATHAN WILLIAMS

I had turned eleven a few weeks before the accident. The last memory I have before the accident was around my birthday. I was at a boarding school near Andover and my mother and father had come down on a Saturday. They brought the latest Grand Prix Scalextric set, which had a full track and two cars, one of which was an FW07 and the other a Brabham BT49, two iconic cars of the time. I was not allowed to take the cars out of the box at that stage as I was likely to break them. I had to choose which track layout I wanted, and then someone back at the factory would create the diorama on a piece of plywood by making grass and trees and then delivering the finished article to our house near Goring. That was my last memory of Dad walking.

I got called in to see the headmaster, a gentleman called Francis Floyd. I remember he said, 'Look, nothing to worry about. Dad's been in a bit of a smash. He's in hospital.' It was a Catholic school, and if a boy or a member of his family were ill they would be asked if the combined school could pray [for them] during morning prayers. I remember being asked if I wanted this and it took me about three days to agree.

There were daily newspapers in the library, but because they wanted to mask the severity of what had occurred the papers were removed each morning, because of course the accident had created quite a bit of news, particularly as Nigel Mansell was driving for the team. Eventually I became aware of the full story and it was arranged that I should visit Dad at the London Hospital. I think I was more apprehensive than anything else; I don't remember being particularly shocked. But I do recall that the family routine had gone because my mother was obviously at the hospital. All the parental duties were being handled by my uncle and his then wife. And I do remember feeling a bit edgy when what was the ground-floor dining room of our family home was converted into a medically orientated bedroom with a mechanical contraption that was a bed.

One of the day boys at the school had told me in a very caring way that he had read that my father was paralysed. Having access to the outside world, as it were, he had read this in one of the papers. When my mother called me from the hospital in France, I actually asked her the question. There was a moment or two of silence, and then she confirmed it. I guess she couldn't say anything else. Then she said something along the lines of 'We'll have to explain to you at an appropriate time what that means.'

Me being at school was a help to my mother. There was a geographical separation from it all. We didn't have mobile phones and in those days computers at school were just the rather rudimentary BBC one. There was no Internet and limited access to TV.

To be honest, I probably learned more about it when I read my mother's book in 1991. I did find that very emotional. These days I have assumed quite a bit of the man-about-the-house duties because my father can't do certain things any more because of his disability. Even though they are not big things, they are the sort of things my father would have done when the racing schedule allowed before his accident. I don't live at home but I have a modern barn conversion which is nearby, about 150 yards away. There is independence but a lot of close proximity.

TWENTY

Business as Usual

It was a sure sign that Williams was reasonably unaffected as a race team when their drivers spent much of the 1986 season falling out with each other. According to Nelson Piquet, he had been promised number-one status in recognition of his two world championships. Nigel Mansell, on the other hand, believed his seniority in the team should mean equal top spot. Nigel had replied to Nelson's victory in Brazil with a win in Belgium followed two weeks later by another in Canada – results that put him within striking distance of championship leader Alain Prost in his McLaren. When Nigel then won in France, it not only moved the Englishman to the top of the table, it also put him fifteen points clear of his increasingly frustrated teammate. Just to bring things nicely to the boil as the teams headed for the next round at Brands Hatch, Mansell was not slow to put his case to British media eager to massage the story into something tasty.

'That's what I like about Williams,' said Nigel. 'I'm equal number one. There's no bullshit in the contracts. They don't have a driver as absolute outright number one, and they don't say you are number two.' Piquet felt differently, but unfortunately for him the man with whom he had negotiated his contract was recovering from a life-threatening accident.

Frank was able to experience the mounting tension at first hand when he made his first public appearance at Brands Hatch, although all

190

seemed sweetness and light as his two drivers hunkered down for photographs with their boss in his wheelchair. Mansell and Piquet, along with everyone else, rejoiced at Frank's return, but that was the only point on which they agreed.

Bernie Ecclestone had arranged for Frank, Ginny and a nurse to be collected from Boxford House and flown to the circuit. This was on the first day of practice, and Frank received a standing ovation as he was wheeled into the media centre. When they finally reached the inside of the circuit, Frank and Ginny were greeted by a large banner opposite the pits: WELCOME BACK FRANK – FROM BRANDS HATCH. Frank would return on the second day for a few hours, but to the obvious relief of his medical team decided to spend race day at home in front of the television. The British Grand Prix would make compelling viewing.

Mansell's race appeared to come to a very premature end when a driveshaft broke as he snatched second gear away from the line. Then all hell broke loose when a multi-car collision going into the first corner caused the race to be stopped. Mansell was able to restart in the spare car, but the good news for Nigel was accompanied by very bad news for Jacques Laffite. A hapless victim of the melee, the popular Frenchman had been forced off the track and head on into a crash barrier. The resulting leg injuries would end his Formula 1 career.

The spare Williams had been set up for Piquet as it was his turn to have use of the back-up car, so Mansell took a few laps to settle in before moving into second place behind his teammate, who had started from pole position. For the next twenty laps they ran nose to tail, until Piquet, perhaps unnerved by Mansell's menacing presence and the obvious bias of the 120,000 crowd, missed a gear. Mansell grabbed his chance and took the lead.

Piquet's only hope was a scheduled pit stop for tyres. He stopped first, which gave the Brazilian the advantage of nicely warmed tyres two laps later when Mansell emerged from the pits, still ahead. However, Piquet's one chance to take the lead was foiled by a backmarker dutifully trying to stay out of the way. That was it. Victory was Mansell's, and with it an eleven-point lead over Piquet in the championship. It was an emotional and dehydrated Mansell who made his way to the podium, the spare Williams lacking on-board drinking water. But the most poignant moment came when Ginny, who had made the trip to Brands Hatch, raised the gold cup and held it aloft. This win was for the team but above all everyone knew it was for Frank.

Piquet was not best pleased with Mansell's tactics – Frank got to hear about it from Nelson, allegedly in tearful detail, when he made his first trip to Hungary for an entire race weekend. He then had Mansell moaning in his ear at the end of it. Piquet had found that the FW11 was better suited to the tight corners of the Hungaroring with a special differential. He had kept this to himself even though the differential was common knowledge around the debriefing table in the team's motorhome. Mansell had felt the full effect of Piquet's ploy when the Brazilian actually lapped the championship leader while on his way to an easy win. Nigel, who had finished third, was furious.

It continued neck and neck between the Williams drivers as they won a race apiece in Italy and Portugal. At the penultimate round in Mexico Nigel might have wrapped up the championship had he not had difficulty finding first gear at the start. He recovered from the unfortunate fumble to finish fifth while Piquet was fourth. But by finishing second Prost moved into second place on the championship table, six points behind Mansell and one ahead of Piquet. It would be all to play for at the final round in Australia. Williams had already won the constructors' championship with a record 141 points, and Mansell was clear favourite to take the drivers' title, particularly when he claimed pole position on the streets of Adelaide. Prost was fourth-fastest and seen as the championship outsider.

At the one-third mark Mansell looked in good shape. Third place would be good enough, regardless of where Prost and Piquet finished. Mansell's chances improved even more when Prost suffered a puncture and had to stop for fresh tyres. Prost's discarded tyres were checked by Goodyear as a matter of course. Wear seemed minimal, and this was reported to Williams, the advice being that pit stops for fresh rubber were unnecessary. That may have been the case on Prost's car but the Williams pair were working their tyres harder thanks to more power from the Honda V6 and the fact that they were running more wing angle, thus forcing even more heat into the rubber.

Prost, having rejoined, worked his way past Mansell, Piquet having done the same some time before. The order was now Piquet, Prost, Mansell. Nigel was still on course for the championship. Then it all went wrong. Powering down the back straight at around 180 mph, Mansell's left-rear tyre exploded. The Williams made a terrifying sight as, with its stiffly sprung right-front wheel pawing the air, it bucked and lurched between the concrete walls flanking the track. With sparks pouring from beneath the car as its rear scraped the track, Mansell somehow wrestled the Williams to a halt in the escape road, the wrecked rear wheel giving a jolt like a death throe as the engine finally stalled.

Piquet looked set to win the title but Patrick Head, alarmed by what he had seen on the television monitors, knew there was no option but to bring Nelson into the pits for fresh tyres. The subsequent stop made Prost favourite for the championship, but it was not over yet. As Piquet gave chase, setting fastest lap in the process, Prost watched his fuel read-out as anxiously as the pit board informing him of the Brazilian's advance. Prost's on-board computer showed empty as the McLaren started its last lap, his nothing-to-lose charge through the field having taken its toll of his fuel. All Prost could do was push on and hope the computer was inaccurate. It was. The Frenchman crossed the line four seconds ahead of Piquet. Watching from the BBC Television studios in London's Shepherd's Bush, Frank had got up in the small hours to witness the championship slipping through his team's fingers.

VIRGINIA WILLIAMS

That was a very emotional time at Brands Hatch. I wasn't prepared for what happened. Frank wasn't fit enough to come on the Sunday and I went. I don't know why exactly. I think Patrick had said that I ought to, or Frank had said, 'Why don't you go?' Patrick said, 'Will you come on the podium?' and I said no. He said that they'd like me to. I said I would, but only if he came with me. Jonathan thinks that I'm the only Formula 1 wife who's ever been on the podium. I was terrified and I thought I mustn't cry. That was all I was focusing on – not standing there and sobbing. I felt after that I couldn't even look at Nigel and Nelson. I couldn't acknowledge or look at anything. It was very emotional.

NIGEL MANSELL

Nelson's done it with every team he's been in, and he had Frank Dernie in his pocket. They kept a different diff in Hungary and there wasn't the transparency between the engineers at that time. Full marks to him. He had something that worked beautifully in the race. Not a problem. It would have been nice to have had the same but I liken it to the fact that when my car broke down at Brands Hatch in '86 I had to jump in his spare car and I beat him in his own car. I was very grateful for the way he had set it up.

The tyre failure in Adelaide is a haunting experience, even today. To come so close and be robbed of a world championship. Had I never won the world championship, it would probably haunt me even more. We radioed we're coming in for tyres, and everybody thought it was best to stay out on those tyres, and Goodyear said the tread depth was okay on Prost's car. There was not a problem – the lap times were good – so they said stay out. I was perfectly positioned to come in, have a slow stop, go out again, but it's just one of those things. There's probably half a dozen or more things that cost the championship that year but that was the most visual one at the last race. I felt quite sorry for Goodyear because it was such a horrific thing to watch on television. They got blamed for me not winning the world championship, but it wasn't just down to them.

NELSON PIQUET

In 1974 they inaugurated a Formula 1 circuit in Brasilia and Frank had a team there. That's when I first met him. At this time I was building up a small Supervee team and I needed to buy a lot of small things – batteries and stuff like that. Frank sold me all these things. It suited him because these items were old and it gave him money. It also meant he didn't have to carry a lot of these things back to England and yet he would be able to buy new when he got back.

When I came into Formula 1 with him, I didn't get to do much with Frank because, as soon as I signed the contract, two months later he had the accident. At the end of every race I kept going to the hospital to see him. But it became a big mess for me with the accident because I had a very easy contract with Frank but he was gone for one year. It was complete shit in the team from my side. When I went there, I was already twice champion. In my contract I was number-one driver. I had the spare car, everything. When I came to the first race, it was not like this.

I love Frank. I'm very, very impressed with all his power and the way he is able to do things. I admire him very much. I try to work with him because he is fantastic. I know my time there was not very good because Frank was in hospital and Patrick Head did not like me very much. In the end, when I was out of Williams, I became friends with Patrick, but when I was in the team, the situation was not very good.

JOHN CADD

We went to Japan after the last race in Australia. I was working on the cars and we went there to do some running demonstrations around some of the factories. I stood there and Murray Walker, being the way he is, bless him, said to Nigel, 'Do you realise, Nigel, if you'd had the shunt earlier and hit the wall and stayed in the middle of the circuit the race would have been stopped and you'd have been world champion.' He said, 'Christ, I don't want to hear that, Murray.'

ALAN CHALLIS

I was in the debrief in Hungary. I don't think Nigel realised that Nelson was going to have that diff in his car. The diff itself was a bit iffy – there was no guarantee that it would last the race – but it was an open book. You could walk in and look at the engineers' sheets. All the information was there. There was certainly some screaming going on in the motorhome afterwards. I'm not sure how much difference it made, to be quite honest with you, but it suited Nelson's psychological bit to know that he'd put one over on Nigel. It got to the stage where the two drivers would have their little groups of people in the team. That was a bit difficult sometimes, where you had to say, 'You don't work for Nigel; you don't work for Nelson; you work for Williams. Get on.'

DICKIE STANFORD

We didn't know in Hungary what Nigel and Nelson had agreed or disagreed on; we just knew there was a bit of a ruckus after race morning warm-up, and by then it was too late to do anything. Nigel came in and said to us, 'He's not playing fair.' There was always rivalry between the two, to the point where you wondered if we were actually in the same team. Even his mechanics were a bit surprised. There were two different sides to the story: according to Nelson all the information was there about what he had done over the weekend, and Nigel claimed it wasn't.

FRANK DERNIE

After Frank's accident it was felt that a team principal needed to be at the Grand Prix, which hitherto had always been Frank, so it hadn't really mattered what Patrick and I were up to. I think Patrick felt that if he was going to be at the races as team principal, while he could deal with the car he needed somebody else that he felt comfortable with to run the technical side if he got dragged off for a couple of hours for a meeting or something. So it was decided we'd both go. I ran Nelson and Patrick ran Nigel.

The differential story has grown out of all proportion, if my recollection is correct. Nelson and Nigel by then didn't want to talk to each other very much. Some teams keep the drivers' briefings separate so that one driver can keep things secret from the other, but Williams never did. Patrick and I used to go through everything once the drivers had gone, so the story about not knowing about the diff is bollocks. Nelson didn't make a big thing about how brilliant the diff was, but it was known that he had it in and it was known he was keeping it in. He had run it and said, 'There's not that much in it.' But he would say that, wouldn't he?

In Adelaide clearly we had a tyre failure. We decided to stop Nelson for new tyres because there could be a fatal accident. It's preyed on my mind quite a bit as Nelson should have been world champion. You see the '86 season as not being fair because Nigel crashed at the last race and he was robbed. That goes to show from a psychological perspective that the last race seems to be much more important: everyone remembers Brazil 2008. If you imagine the season had been turned round and in the first race Nigel had had a tyre failure and crashed, nobody would have noticed he hadn't scored any points. It just goes to show that it was very emotive at the time, but the fact is you can lose the championship at any stage of the season, and that was a particularly public way of doing it, but it wasn't the only way.

DICKIE STANFORD

We didn't see the tyre go. We were in the pit lane and in those days the mechanics didn't have radios. If you were a really rich team, everyone had a radio and you would hear all the information. The first we knew was when we heard the commentator say Nigel had had a big crash on the main straight. We didn't know until a little later that he had travelled all the way down the main straight. We thought we were looking good. You have to say we were cruising around.

When Nigel had the shunt, the engineers knew straight away that the suspension was damaged and there was no chance of getting the car back to the pits. So everything switched to Nelson. Goodyear told Patrick they were concerned about the tyres. Nelson was brought in; it was better to be safe than sorry.

It was a big blow for everyone, even the guys on Nelson's car. We felt cheated. It was a case of pack up and get the hell out of there. It was not a case of having another race in which to try and pull it back. That was it. Being Australia, we couldn't leave that night. We saw the whole thing for the first time on TV news that night. That didn't help.

VIRGINIA WILLIAMS

I went to the BBC studio in the middle of the night with Frank to watch Adelaide. It was quite extraordinary because they had a big banner and it had NIGEL, NELSON AND ALAIN because it looked to be Nigel's championship, with Nelson being the second favourite and Alain the least likely. They were ready at the end of the race to move the banners behind Steve Rider. Steve is very professional. When we arrived at the studio, he ran through a few of the questions he'd ask Frank when we won the championship. That was the assumption. We drove home in absolute silence. We couldn't believe we'd lost that championship.

STEVE COATES

I joined at the end of 1985 as a mechanic looking after the trucks. In 1986 the Honda had unburnt fuel collecting in the exhausts. It kept flashing but not exploding. In Estoril it got worse, unbeknown to us. The car had been sitting between practice and qualifying. Les Jones started it up and there was an explosion, like a flame-thrower. It spewed out flames and knocked Frank out of his wheelchair. He banged his head on the floor. Les came off worse, because he was bent down. Frank was directly behind him. As a first-aider, I started on Les straight away.

As soon as the medics arrived, I went to check on Frank. And there he was, back in his wheelchair, wheeling around the garage, singed hair and a bit red in the face, like he'd got rouge on. But he was having none of it. It was like nothing had happened.

DAMON HILL

The Mansell–Williams effect was very important for me because I can remember I had already set in course my ambitions to get into Formula 1 and to win. Seeing Mansell in a Williams just planted that seed, that grain of thought that this is not so impossible; he's done it. He showed that there was potential to achieve things and actually win Grands Prix. When he started beating Piquet, that inspired me in a way that can't be overestimated.

When Nigel won his first Grand Prix at Brands Hatch in 1985 I stood and watched him go into Paddock Hill Bend. I watched every lap; I didn't move from the spot the whole way through. This was the big breakthrough. I really wanted him to win because I knew that would mean I could win as well. It was very key in my thinking, the fact that it was a British team. Frank and Patrick probably represented the closest I could get to my dad, if you like. They seemed to have all the same character traits and attitudes that I think my dad carried. Williams were very powerful for my imagination, particularly that race in 1985. From that point the floodgates opened for Nigel. It just got stronger and stronger. It was fantastic.

So you can imagine what it was like when he was in with a chance of the championship in 1986 in Adelaide. I watched it in my flat in Wandsworth. We stayed up all night. We had a party, and just for a laugh I watched it wearing my driving overalls. When he went out, it was devastating, just devastating. Nobody could believe it. We had got ourselves revved up, all excited. I know that emotion. I wasn't young, twenty-five at that point, and I still had this ambition. So when it happened to me eight years later – at the same circuit – I knew precisely what it was like for others sitting at home.

TWENTY-ONE
Sayonara Bonjour

Frank attended every race in 1987. In the course of reaching this personal target he discovered the severe difficulties faced by quadriplegics on commercial flights. There was nothing else for it but to purchase a Learjet. The aircraft, bought early in the summer, took Frank through the remainder of a season that seemed perfect as Williams-Honda won both championships for the first time since 1981. But beneath the surface there was dissension.

Nelson Piquet became world champion standing in the Williams garage at Suzuka watching Mansell crash out of the penultimate round. Nigel, Nelson's only rival at this stage, attempting to match Piquet's pole-position time, spun backwards into the barrier and severely hurt his back. Nigel was airlifted home and was not sorry to go. In truth, he was glad to see the back of the season. There had been one or two highlights, including a truly remarkable comeback drive to victory after a pit stop at Silverstone, a win made all the sweeter because Mansell had taken the lead from Piquet with the bravest of brave moves going into Stowe at 180 mph. It was classic Mansell. But Nigel was convinced that Honda were supplying better engines to Nelson. True or not, this was a minor issue for Frank and Patrick in the light of developments that had been brewing for the best part of a year.

Adelaide 1986 had been bad luck for Williams for more than the obvious reason. Soichiro Honda, the company's founder, had paid a rare visit to a Grand Prix confident he was about to witness a Honda-powered driver win the world championship for the first time. Mr Honda was put out when Piquet and Mansell lost out at the eleventh hour, a failure he attributed to the Williams drivers being allowed to fight among themselves throughout the season to the detriment of the team as a whole. It also seems at least possible that Japanese business culture had difficulty with Frank's quadriplegia. It mattered little that Williams functioned as well as it would have had Frank not had his accident. Although never openly stated, the Honda view might possibly have been that a man in a wheelchair did not project the proper image for a company figurehead.

Meanwhile, Honda had become increasingly enamoured of Ayrton Senna, particularly after agreeing to supply his team, Lotus, with engines for 1987. Williams probably did not help matters by thrashing the Lotus-Honda 9–2 in wins. Despite having another year to run with Williams, Honda informed Frank in July 1987 that they would be terminating their contract that December. Not long after, Piquet told Frank he would be moving to Lotus-Honda, further feeding Mansell's suspicions of preferential treatment. Frank would agree a financial settlement with Honda, but in no way would that compensate for the dismal season that would unfold in 1988, the only high point for Frank being his CBE, awarded in the New Year for the team's efforts in 1987.

One of Piquet's three wins that year had been at Monza, a result that would mislead the Williams technical team. The FW11B had been fitted with a complex active-ride suspension system, and the win prompted the belief that this avenue was worth exploring on the 1988 car. The FW12 would be smaller than its predecessor, which made the mounting of the active-ride components more difficult, in particular keeping the electronic components away from the hotter parts of the car. That heat would be generated by the Judd V8, built by John Judd, a talented engineer who ran a comparatively small engine business in Rugby.

Given the limited choice at such short notice and the fact that turbocharged engines were about to be phased out, Williams had opted for a normally aspirated engine. But whatever its merits or limitations, no one would hold a candle to the new combination of McLaren and Honda as Ayrton Senna and Alain Prost won all but one of the sixteen 1988 Grands Prix. It was no consolation for Williams to know that it would have been a clean sweep for McLaren had Senna not tripped over one of their cars while lapping the FW12 at Monza. The Williams was driven by Jean-Louis Schlesser, a stand-in for Mansell, who was indisposed. Two weeks earlier in Belgium Mansell's place had been taken by Martin Brundle.

Neither substitute would improve a dismal season for Williams, the highlights of which were two podium finishes for Mansell among a sad catalogue of retirements with technical trouble, many of them caused by the active suspension. It was a measure of the team's refusal to be beaten that a last-minute decision at Silverstone would see the FW12 converted overnight to normal suspension. Mansell rewarded the super-human efforts of mechanics and engineers with a second place in wet conditions that diluted the power advantage of the Hondas.

Given half a chance Nigel would give it everything, but most of the time in 1988 he had what he considered to be no chance at all, so much so that he brought his golf clubs with him to the racetrack in Mexico, a blunt hint that his time would be better spent on the golf course than inside the active-ride FW12. It was no surprise when he seized the opportunity to sign for Ferrari in 1989. Piquet had been replaced by Riccardo Patrese for 1988. Despite having just two wins to his name with Brabham, the likeable Italian was to settle in easily for a five-year stint at Williams, during which time Riccardo and Nigel would work together once more. In the meantime, for 1989 and 1990 Patrese was joined by Thierry Boutsen, another easy-going individual with a great deal of natural flair. And the good news for them both was a very important development on the engine front.

There was no doubt in the minds of Frank and Patrick that they needed a relationship with a major engine manufacturer. As soon as Honda had begun to prevaricate, Frank, assuming the worst, had opened negotiations with Renault. The French firm had not been directly involved with Formula 1 since the move by Lotus to Honda engines in 1987, but its engineers at Viry-Chatillion in Paris had been working on a normally aspirated V10 to conform to the forthcoming regulations. Frank made sure he was heading the queue. A deal was done for 1989, initiating a remarkable decade of achievement for both sides.

PATRICK HEAD

I went up to Japan after the 1986 championship had ended so badly in Australia. Yes, we had won the constructors' championship but we had lost the drivers' championship, and Honda weren't impressed. They said we had lost because we were fair to both drivers. If we hadn't been fair to both drivers, we would have won the 1986 championship, but what's the point of justifying what you do? That's what we did; that's what happened. Frank was out of it for most of the year. He turned up in Budapest, but he was a shell. He was almost just proving that he was still alive. He was not making any contribution.

It was a bloody difficult year. I went to Japan fifteen times in 1986 as well as going to every single race and quite a lot of the tests. By the end of that year I was a dead man.

Honda were lovely people to work with but they were – and I think with very good reason – hugely enamoured with Ayrton Senna. It was because of Senna that they took on Lotus. And they pretty much told us Lotus were going to piss on Williams in 1987 with Ayrton Senna. So there was a certain amount of pleasure to be had when it didn't work out that way and we wiped the floor with Lotus.

It was very annoying because I had been working with Katsumi Ichida, who was their chief designer, and telling him that their engine was ridiculously high because it had all kinds of stuff underneath the crankshaft that had no reason to be there. At the meeting after Australia in 1986 he took me into the development area and very positively showed me the new sump that would allow them to lower the engine by forty millimetres or something enormous. It was exactly what I'd been going on at them about for a long time. We were working on a car that was much smaller and lower and more compact, so when I saw the new engine I thought, *Fantastic! This will be really good.*

I was called into a meeting with Gerard Ducarouge, who is a really nice man. He was telling them that they [Lotus] didn't need the new engine; the old engine would do. The engine was so good that in the Lotus chassis it would beat everything. He said they didn't need the new lower sump and they told me it was 'not happening'. It went into the McLaren for 1988 – the low sump, everything I had been pushing for. But such is life.

Honda were quite sure that Lotus and Ayrton were going to blow us away in 1987, and they were a bit nonplussed that we won the constructors' championship. We were so upset by what we thought Honda had done to us but we wanted to throw everything at the car in 1988 and blow Honda away. First race of the year we almost did it. I think they must have been pretty horrified because what they regarded as a pretty basic Judd engine brought us closer to them than they expected. But the active ride really wasn't well enough developed both in its software, its control but also in its hydraulic system. The car was an ogre. The longer it ran, the more it became like being suspended on rubber bands.

So we had to withdraw the active ride at Silverstone in 1988. We did a big overnight job. There was no pre-planning to it; we literally made the decision at three o'clock on Saturday afternoon to convert to standard by race-morning warm-up. The back end was reasonably easy to do. The front end literally meant designing and making our own dampers overnight. The most phenomenal amount of work was done. It was a case of 'This is a complete and utter cock-up; we've got to do something different.' It was one of those many achievements in Formula 1 that just go quietly under the radar. We made new dampers, by which I mean dampers that had not been in existence. This was a damper that was on the end of the push rod that had a very big piston diameter and a very short stroke. We converted the active-ride strut into a damper overnight. It was a major piece of work.

I have to say to be fair to John Judd that his engine really wasn't bad. Had we done a better job of the car, we could have had a much better season. We had all sorts of problems with the active-ride system. We didn't cool the oil very well and that caused the engine to have problems. We finished second at Jerez, second at Silverstone, but we really could have won races with the Judd engine. When Renault came along it was what we needed to get back with a manufacturer, somebody with resources, with gravitas. Judd was fantastic to work with, but a little company up in Rugby wasn't the same thing as being with a manufacturer.

FRANK WILLIAMS

I think Honda left us because I broke my neck. The boss of Honda turned up in hospital and I'm sure it was to see if I was going to make it or not. I think at that point they lost confidence. And at the same time Ron [Dennis] was saying to them, 'I've got Senna. I've got this; I've got that. I've got Prost. It's a dream team.' We had won both championships in 1987 but I think they felt they were getting a better deal.

NIGEL MANSELL

No doubt 1988 was a challenge. What chance did a normally aspirated runner have of winning a race? None, none at all. The active ride didn't work. It did all sorts of nasty things to you but it was part of the development. It was a very difficult year. We just tried to wring the car's neck, whatever it was. Get the best out of it.

MARTIN BRUNDLE

I think I first met Frank pre- his accident at a charity shoot at Gleneagles. I'm sure I would have talked to him to try to get a test in his car or something because those were my Formula 3 years.

I went to see Frank in his office. I was looking for a drive because it was *the* team to go to. I had meetings and it was all very polite but, as with all team bosses, they will see almost any reasonable candidate because they learn something about what the other teams are doing and also it holds the marketplace up. You always have to temper an apparently enthusiastic meeting with the knowledge that they've probably got twenty-five other guys on the phone every day.

In 1988 I was their test driver. I think it was when they were testing these twin disc brakes on the active car and it spat Nigel off the road too many times. He was more or less saying, 'Put a monkey in it; I'm not driving it any more.' So, I was the monkey. But it was a really good experience because I wasn't in Formula 1 at the time; I'd gone off to do the World Sportscar Championship.

Nigel got chickenpox and at the very last minute, on the Thursday of the Belgian Grand Prix weekend, I was told to go over to Spa. I met Frank in the Dorint Hotel and we cut a deal that included all expenses and the whole year's testing that I'd done for them risking my life in that bloody thing. I'd be testing at Monza, and twice a day it would just flop on to the ground when the active gave in. That's why Nigel wouldn't drive it. But it was good experience for me. I asked Frank for an amount of money that is not much more than I get paid for an after-dinner speech now, and I swear, if he could have, I thought he was going to get up out of his wheelchair and hit me! He had such a good way of putting shock on his face. And the audacity of me asking for such a number! And the numbers were stupid – as in very low – now I think about it. It was crazy really. I jumped into Nigel's seat, which was a very comfortable rubbery thing. I tried to drive it out the garage and I couldn't turn the wheel because it had Nigel's little doughnut of a steering wheel on it. I was quickest in the wet and finished up seventh in the end because two cars were disqualified for some reason.

I'd never driven a car that went round corners like that. It turned out that I wasn't really fit enough to be fully on it for a Grand Prix distance around Spa. New tyres used to have stickers on the tread in those days and they would – or ought to – disappear quite quickly. I went out. These white things are flicking away – no sign of them being worn away. You have to remember all I'd done so far was drive a Tyrrell and a Zakspeed. I went through Eau Rouge and I thought, *Oh, that didn't move*. I think it was fully three laps before I got the wheels to spin. I had no concept of the amount of grip that car had. Then I was away. I thought it was absolutely brilliant. I just remember Patrick and the engineers being at a whole new level of engineering excellence and car performance – even with the Judd. He didn't want to be at power circuits like Spa and Monza with the Judd. I was glad of the opportunity. It was very straightforward – no BS, not too many wasted words. It was slightly different, I'd imagine, because I was parachuted in at the last minute. I'm sure they weren't expecting too much from me. If it was a cham-pionship campaign, then it would have been slightly more aggressive.

JOHN SUTTON

I was a budding engineer frustrated with the rate at which you could progress as an enthusiastic youngster in a big company. I looked at racing teams as somewhere to be pushed harder more quickly. I wanted real engineering. I wrote to most of the Formula 1 teams. Williams said there was no job available but my letter had been filed. I moved house and thought this was a good opportunity to notify the change of address and ask if anything was going. Patrick wrote back saying my qualifications and persistence certainly warranted a chat. That chat lasted for about an hour. After forty minutes he was still telling me about himself and the history of the team. I thought, *I'll go away and he won't have any idea whether to hire me as he won't know anything about me* but he was checking I didn't have two heads. I butted in to tell him what I'd been doing. He sent me away to think about whether I really wanted to be a design engineer in Formula 1. He didn't say, 'Yes, I'd like to offer you a job,' or, 'I'll think about it.' It was a different approach. He warned me off thinking it was living the high life. Instead it was fifty-, sixty- and seventy-hour weeks, seven days a week. If I was any good, I'd be paid quite well.

This was August 1988. I saw Patrick on a Thursday or a Friday and left it until Tuesday, believing that was reasonable time to mull over, although I decided immediately. Around that time they announced the engine deal with Renault and I thought it was a smart move going to a team with a great heritage which was having a lean patch. I knew Renault had been phenomenal in the turbo era. It was really nice to go to Williams as a junior engineer at a point when they weren't on the crest of a wave. You felt in step with the progress of the team.

JOHN CADD

Nigel was a fantastic driver. When he got in that car he was like a brick shithouse. I wonder if today's drivers have the same mentality to set the car up the way those guys did as they worked really closely with the engineer. As mechanics we were always changing things. A lot of that doesn't go on at the circuit because they haven't got the time now.

I used to wire Nelson's road car up so that when he touched the brakes it would squirt water out the steering wheel at him. He came to Estoril with his own BMW with a fully modified engine. His girlfriend at the time, Sylvie, told me he'd asked her to hold his car keys and not to let me have them. I persuaded her to give me the keys. The car had headlight washers and they were twice as powerful as the windscreen washer. So I set to, and in a couple of minutes I had it all wired up – job done. Testing finished and Nelson said cheerio. Trouble was, a lot of people found out that I'd done it. Nelson and Sylvie walked to the car and got in. Nelson looked down and, where the race truck was, he saw all these feet beneath it. He knew something had been done to his car.

He drove from the circuit to the hotel without touching the brakes. In the hotel car park he locked the car so Sylvie couldn't get out. Nelson felt around and found the hose, pulled it down, stood on the brakes and soaked her, bless her. She came in the next day and said that's the last time I ever do anything for you. She had been soaked from head to foot.

RICCARDO PATRESE

The first time I met Frank was in 1977. I was driving with Alan Jones at Shadow and Frank was building his new team. The following year he wanted to have a new driver, so he came to me and asked if I was interested. He told me that the plan was to have only one car and that he had a new sponsor. Frank was not really on top at that moment. A new team, Arrows, was coming and it looked like it was going to be a better opportunity. Alan was also waiting because he thought the same thing.

In the end the situation was that Frank wanted either me or Alan. They chose me but I said, 'No, Frank. Sorry, but I prefer to stay with Arrows in 1978.' So he signed Alan Jones.

I was driving for Bernie Ecclestone in 1987 and he started to think that Brabham was not a team that could go on for long. So he proposed to Frank and Patrick to test me. That was very unusual for a team owner to give a driver to another team. Bernie wanted to help me and thought it would be a good opportunity. I went to Imola and tested for two days for Williams. I went very quick. They knew they had to get a driver for the following year and they liked what I did at the test, so I had a contract for 1988.

Unfortunately, immediately after the test Honda decided not to continue with Williams. But I knew this was one of the best teams and they said something good was coming. So I went there with a lot of enthusiasm. The 1988 car was not quick but for me this was nothing new. I worked very hard that year. Then in September 1988 I did the first laps with the Renault V10 at Paul Ricard. I knew straight away that this was going to be a successful period.

TWENTY-TWO

Making Way for the Warrior's Return

In the summer of 1988 Boxford House was sold. Since that fateful day two years before, it had become a nursing home, a place without the intimacy and privacy associated with a marriage and children. Staff, friends and helpers were constantly toing and froing as Frank and Virginia tried to come to terms with the massive changes to their respective lives. It had been an extremely difficult time, particularly for Ginny. She was leaving a beautiful house that represented both her happiest and saddest moments. She would use an apartment in London as a place to rebuild her independence for a couple of days each week before going back to the former rectory they had purchased near Newbury to join Frank when the children returned from school at the weekends.

For Frank this was the next stage in his 'different kind of life'. It had become clear over the previous twelve months or so that his limited dexterity had improved as far as it could. Nelson Piquet had bought him a hands-free telephone, a boon for someone who liked to spend much of his time communicating and catching up with gossip. After endless practice, Frank was able to at least scrawl his initials with a pen held in a special hand splint. He could manage for the time being and shunned devices designed for the disabled. He rebuffed Ginny's attempts to get him an electric wheelchair, preferring to be pushed by his nurses and personal helpers at the time, Robin Kinnell and Iain Cunningham, and refused to display a disabled parking badge on his car, wanting to be treated as normally as possible.

Frank was more interested in getting on with his work and fostering the relationship with Renault. It was a difficult season in 1989 since the FW13 was not one of the greatest cars to emerge from the Williams drawing office, although Boutsen applied his delicate touch in wet conditions to win in Canada and Australia. Second place in the constructors' championship may have sounded satisfactory but a quick look at the table showed McLaren-Honda once again the dominant force, with twice as many points. It would be worse in 1990, even though Renault took a step forward with a new V10 mounted lower in the latest chassis, the FW13B. Patrese won at Imola and Boutsen held his nerve to win the Hungarian Grand Prix despite enormous pressure from Senna's McLaren for most of the seventy-seven laps. But McLaren were champions yet again and Williams had been overhauled not only by Ferrari but also Benetton. Something needed to be done. Frank and Patrick were about to make two key appointments.

Nigel Mansell had enjoyed mixed results at Ferrari. His first year, 1989, had got off to the best possible start. The Ferrari employed a semi-automatic gearbox operated by paddle shifts on the steering wheel. This novelty, which was more or less untested and had caused problems in practice, was not expected to last a lap, never mind the entire Brazilian Grand Prix. Nevertheless Mansell won in Rio to end a lean period for Ferrari. In the absence of a quick teammate, Mansell attained the status of instant hero in Italy. Nigel was relaxed and happy, and this was reflected in his driving.

It would be a different story in 1990 when Ferrari signed Prost. There were no team orders at Ferrari, the only rule being that whoever was in front should be allowed to stay there. Mansell led the British Grand Prix with Prost gradually moving forward before dutifully sitting in second place. All was well until intermittent gearbox trouble saw Mansell falter and Prost take the lead on Nigel's home patch. After his gearbox packed up completely, back in the paddock Mansell wondered out loud why his car was always the one to break. Not long after the race finished, Mansell called the media to the Ferrari motorhome and announced he would retire at the end of the season, a statement he would reiterate at Monza about six weeks later in order to stem the flow of rumours about an approach from Williams.

A few weeks after that, a press release from Mansell's home on the Isle of Man revealed he would, after all, be returning to Williams in 1991. Mansell cited huge support from fans asking him not to quit. While Nigel had undoubtedly captured the imagination of the British public like no driver since James Hunt fifteen years before, more cynical members of the media felt the offer of £4.6 million for a one-year contract probably had a lot to do with his about-turn. It made Mansell Britain's most highly paid sportsman at the time and, just for good measure, he said he would be the number-one driver ahead of Patrese.

While Frank was dealing with Nigel, Patrick had been in discussions with Adrian Newey, a promising designer and aerodynamicist who had cut his teeth in IndyCar racing and with Leyton House, a small Formula 1 team. Newey's signing in 1990 would play a huge part in the successful period that was about to unfold for Williams Grand Prix Engineering.

PATRICK HEAD

I think we should have made a better car in 1989, the first year with Renault, but in truth we carried forward the FW12 that we'd done for the Judd. Integrating a completely new engine is quite a lot of work. We won twice in 1989 but the car for 1990, the FW13, was really an abject failure. We had moved our wind tunnel from the original factory and the commissioning of the wind tunnel in the new factory had been done extremely badly. In the keenness to get it up and operating, the proper check to see it was functioning had not been done. We had done a test in the wind tunnel that showed that a high nose and front wing had given us 150 pounds of downforce and we thought that was the way to go – we'll do a chassis with a high front on it. I asked for the test to be done again and the 150 pounds of downforce had disappeared. We thought there was no point in doing that for nothing, so we didn't.

Halfway through 1990 it had been obvious to me that the Leyton House was pretty special. I didn't really know Adrian – I didn't know his history, his IndyCar work. But he knew his onions on aerodynamics whereas our guys quite clearly didn't. By then Frank Dernie had moved on to Lotus and was working with Nelson. We needed someone with a lot more knowledge and experience. Leyton House seemed to be in a bit of a mess, particularly as it was being run by an accountant who sacked Adrian because they hadn't qualified in Mexico, only to have that car very nearly win in France.

I gave Adrian a ring after Mexico and asked him if he'd like to come and work for us. He'd been with us a week and I thought, *This guy's pretty astute; he knows much more about racing cars that just aerodynamics*. Meanwhile, it was quite clear in many areas that he didn't know much about hydraulic systems, gearboxes and so on. I said to Adrian, 'Look, aerodynamics these days are dictating the car layout, so why don't you become chief designer, operating on aerodynamics? I'll look after the gearbox, the active-ride system, the brakes, the uprights, the systems and whatever.'

I had a company I was running with 320 people, so it wasn't as if I could stand at my drawing board the whole time and design the car. Adrian agreed and said, 'Yes, that sounds fine. By the way, that gearbox you're doing is no good: it goes right through my diffuser.' So I closed my door and spent six weeks designing what would become our first semi-automatic paddle-shift gearbox. Literally, every drawing has *PH* on it because I knew there was no way we'd achieve a completely new gearbox system design going through the normal system of democracy.

Integrating Adrian into the company was very interesting. I think everyone realised that he was very clever, but Williams, being quite conservative, had a bit of trouble integrating with a guy who says, 'Well, you may think you can throw a stone that far but I'm telling you, you're going to throw it that far.' Adrian just expects all that to happen. He's a very clever lad, but he only deals with half of the story. You have to set up your company to be able to use his talent but still keep a disciplined system operating. I liked working with Adrian: he was challenging, adventurous, full of good ideas, amusing – a good guy.

THIERRY BOUTSEN

Williams had experience and a great reputation for engineering. It was my first really top team in Formula 1. The FW12 was difficult to set up – no, not difficult to set up, there was only one set-up that worked. It needed to be as hard as possible.

I had a big accident during testing. The suspension broke in turn one in Brazil, and that threw me into the wall at 250 kph, or something like that. It was the kind of an accident where it hurts in your whole body. Afterwards, some days you feel good and some days you feel really bad and you don't know why. When I made a check some time later, I discovered that the corners of five vertebrae were broken and my whole body stamina was changing from day to day. It didn't seem bad when I had the accident, because it was only hurting and I could live with that, but in fact the consequences were much harder than they first appeared. This handicapped me for some races. I was really not in good physical form and it took me over a year to recover.

For Frank and Patrick, this was simply a business. They wanted to win races – that's why they employed me and I could achieve that – but there was very little emotion in them, certainly in the beginning. At the end of the second year I had a little bit more personal contact with Patrick but, with Frank, it was purely business, which I understand and I approve. It's his way of doing things and he's won many championships this way.

I felt very, very good after my first win in Canada. It was a big relief for me because I should have won Mexico two years before that with Benetton. So I knew that I was capable of winning but never had the material to do so. Adelaide was different because when we started with that car, the FW13, I could hardly qualify it. It was handling so badly, and yet a few races later I won in Adelaide, so that was a big achievement, a really big achievement.

In Hungary in 1990, let's say I took a big risk. I analysed the performance of the car. It was very good on one lap in Hungary. Lasting the distance was another thing, and I knew that if I could start on pole and be first at the end of the first lap, nobody would overtake me. That would be the only way for me to win and it meant I had to run non-stop. If I had to come into the pits to change tyres, I would have lost the race. So I took the risk to go to the end with the same set of tyres. I ended the race with no rubber whatsoever on the left-rear tyre. Also, the brakes were totally worn out at the front. I couldn't have done two more laps, so it was very marginal. But I made it and I kept Ayrton behind me. I was very proud of it, because I went against all the advice from Patrick, who didn't think that was possible.

Once I had finished on the podium and done all the television and media interviews, I went back to the Williams motorhome. It was empty. Everyone had gone. Maybe I was the wrong one to win that day because they had just told me that I would not be part of the team for 1991. I have no idea why everyone had gone. At the time I was totally pissed off. But now I realise that business is business and you have to live with these kind of things. I've survived. There are more important things than that.

I have absolutely no regrets. It was a fantastic two years because I was in a great team. Working with Renault was amazing because they had incredible potential. Canada was only the sixth race with Williams and Renault working together, and winning their first Grand Prix with a normally aspirated engine after such a short time was really amazing.

ALAN CHALLIS

Patrick was abrasive: he didn't mind having a shout at you, whether he was right or wrong. Fairly early in the piece he used to shout during the day and it always seemed to be my fault. Come the evening he'd come and pat me on the shoulder and say sorry. I'd say, 'What was that all about?' and he would say, 'I know I can shout at you and you ignore me and just get on with the job. If you didn't agree, you'd say you didn't think it should be done that way.' It was a good working relationship. I must admit, when Adrian first arrived, I thought, *Hmm, I'm not sure if this is going to work*. But it obviously did.

DICKIE STANFORD

The relationship with Renault was good from day one. In general, the problems were solvable. Like any new engine, there were big blow-ups to start with, but they just got better and better. They were good to work with. A lot of the Renault people were from their own Formula 1 team, so they knew how it worked – you were not trying to teach them anything. I had been asked to go back to the test team in 1989, which I did, and then at the end of the year I was asked if I would like to be chief mechanic on the race team.

JOHN SUTTON

In terms of recollections of Frank and the spirit of the place, I look back really fondly on the occasions when you'd bomb down to the workshops quite late on in the evening to look after something you're working on, and you'd bump into Frank, who was wheeling himself around. He'd stop and say, 'Right. What's the great gizmo? What's the thing that's going to cost me a bomb, that's going to put the wind up Duncan [the accountant] for the next race or the next test?' He was always really enthusiastic. He'd say, 'Come on, what have we got? Bamboozle me with something I won't understand.'

IAIN CUNNINGHAM

We thought that because Frank had been so fit and so determined in his able-bodied life, he would put more effort into regaining more movement and having more independence, but he didn't. He just got on with his life. He very rarely complained. Occasionally, in the car in the mornings, he would say his arms were giving him gyp. He would say he was out of sorts; he was not feeling that good, that there was a bit of pain. There would be a slight explanation, but he would never court sympathy.

Interestingly, when I got to know him a bit better, I made the point that he could use his disability a little bit more when it came to getting the sympathy vote when dealing with his sponsors or whomever. He said he was aware of that, but he was reluctant to use it because it would show weakness.

He said that he never missed his exercises or his running. But he did miss being able to wander off down the paddock and see people. He refused point blank to have something like an electric wheelchair. 'No way,' he would say. 'I'm not going to look like an effing Dalek!'

He wanted to look as normal as possible. He was fastidious about his appearance. I remember on one occasion we went to Renault for the launch of an engine and I hadn't straightened his trousers. As they were taking the photos, I suddenly realised. Even now, when I see that photo, I get so angry about it. Something like that was important to Frank. It was important to me as well. It was the little details that mattered.

MICHAEL CANE

I was team manager from 1989 until the end of 1990. I found my time there, particularly getting to know Frank, very enjoyable. He was in his wheelchair all the time of course, but there was never an ounce of self-pity. He was a charming man. He had the ability to talk to anyone, no matter where they stood in the organisation. He's obviously very intelligent and he had this drive just to keep going to get back to the top. We never had a cross word. The only disagreement we had was over someone who had worked for the team for many years. It suddenly didn't suit the structure of the team for that person to be there and Frank told me to get rid of him. But since this person had been there for so long I felt that should be Frank's job, and said so. To the best of my knowledge, that person was still there several years later.

Frank has a great sense of humour. But that will not be evident unless you know him. The pictures you see of Frank on television are of someone concentrating totally on something at that particular moment. He's massively focused, but if you look at people in a similar position in the pit lane they are exactly the same. When it's all over, he would relax.

Frank is very good at taking any misfortune that comes along. He doesn't seem to look backwards; he's always looking towards the next objective. There was a clear division between the technical and the commercial side, and it worked very well. Patrick didn't want to get involved with the commercial aspect and he was free to do whatever was necessary to make the cars competitive. Frank worked with Sheridan on the commercial side and it seemed to be a very good arrangement.

Frank had his own private plane by that stage and I would travel with him to a lot of the races. We didn't say a great deal either then or at any other time. I am not a great conversationalist myself and we would maybe chat about the tyres we were going to run or something like that. But otherwise not a lot was said, and that seemed to suit us both.

A lot of the criticism that came his way at the time was because of the way he appeared to fire his drivers for no good reason. I wasn't surprised at all to see him let some of the drivers go because he was very pragmatic about these things. The team wins and they see the drivers taking most of the glory. The team owner knows what it's like to run a business, with a great number of people working very hard, and suddenly the media are interested only in the driver. I'm sure that can be irritating at times. Certainly, Frank tends to see most of his drivers as no more than another employee. But, above all, he likes a driver with fire in his belly, one who has it there every time he gets in the car.

STEVE COATES

Frank doesn't like motorbikes, he never has. Whereas I'm a big biker. When I first came for the job at Williams, I was a truck mechanic and I used to service Williams's trucks at the local garage. I got an opportunity for an interview with the team and was accepted for the job of repairing the trucks if they broke down, which was a dream job for me. I arrived at the factory on a Friday to drop off my toolbox ready to start on Monday. I turned up in black, dirty overalls – they were really minging because I had been under trucks all day. Not knowing where to go, I walked into the posh reception area. The receptionist was looking at me as if to say, 'Tradesman's entrance is round the back.' I panicked slightly when Frank arrived and asked who I was. When I told him, he just said, 'Oh, right. Nice to meet you. See you Monday.' There I was, a biker, covered in tattoos and wearing an earring. He never bothered how I looked; there's never any judging a book by its cover.

One day Frank had a meeting with one of the executives from Camel or ICI in his office on the top floor. It was warm and all the windows were open. I was down in the truck bay when Ian Anderson came to see me, asking for a favour. He said the FIA were implementing speed traps in the pit lane. We had bought one and needed to calibrate it and make sure it was working properly. Would I go out on my bike and do speed checks while he used the hand-held radar gun? We used the road outside the factory to do these tests. For the first two runs Ian missed me. On the third he got me doing 86 mph. The trouble was, each time I was going faster and faster, trying to beat my own speed, bearing in mind this bike was in race spec – it was bloody quick and noisy, not a lot different to the race car going up and down the road.

Frank could hear the noise and was getting more and more agitated. The guy he was with suddenly got up and shut all the windows, but they could still hear me thundering down the road. We finished the tests, and about an hour later Frank's nurse turned up to tell me Frank was absolutely fuming and wanted to see me. I started to do the usual thing of keeping out of his way, which I managed for a few weeks. But when we got to the next race, I had nowhere to hide. Frank had not long arrived before I was summoned. He said, 'Coates, you're sacked. You don't know how serious this is.' I tried to tell him what I'd been doing, but he wouldn't have any of it. I got myself into a right old state and had to go and find Ian [Harrison, team manager] and ask him to explain. It all backfired on me because of course Frank was winding me up. He succeeded.

JOHN RUSSELL

I arrived in June 1989 having trained in the nuclear industry at Harwell. I was desperate to get into motor racing, and when an advert came up for a design draughtsman I successfully applied. I was very much in awe for the first three to six months. I felt out of kilter. This was my first professional motor-racing experience and these guys were legends. There was a strict code of discipline and engineering correctness, but outside that framework I found I was working with a bunch of talented individuals with a great spirit of teamwork and humility in what they did.

I met Patrick for a second interview for a design engineer's job. I was bricking it when faced with this hero. I had heard all about Patrick and expected a grilling, but we just had a chat instead. I was flabbergasted. I met Frank as he was pushed around the area downstairs where we were located. I was amazed at Frank's attitude to his disability: he makes no recognition of it and treats every employee on an equal footing. No airs and graces. You can go and tell him what you think, and he'll give you a response, always well measured. He must be a frightful poker player. But a truly remarkable individual.

TWENTY-THREE

No Wheels, No Gears

I f there were doubts within the team about the wisdom of inviting
Mansell to return, Nigel blew those away with just one lap of Estoril. It was during a winter test, and Mansell took the FW13B round the
Portuguese track faster than it had ever gone before, confirming his
continuing aggression and speed as well as the thought that perhaps
the 1990 car was not so bad after all. In fact, rather than model the
next Williams on the FW13B, Adrian Newey was basing his concept on
fresh ideas. Patrick, meanwhile, was working on a semi-automatic gearbox. The FW14 would represent a major step forward.

The team was installing a new wind tunnel facility so large that it
would not fit inside the existing building at Basil Hill Road. Capable of
accommodating a 50-per-cent-scale model, the structure would require
concrete pylons twenty feet deep to support it. The tunnel was visible
from the 10,000-square-foot Williams Conference Centre, built in
1989 as an additional revenue stream, with two meeting rooms, the
Piers Courage Suite and the Alan Jones Room, and a display centre for
the seventeen Williams Formula 1 cars gathered over the years.

The conference centre was used to host the now traditional pre-
season media lunch, Frank bracing himself for the banter likely to come
his way for re-hiring a driver he had allegedly been glad to see the back
of in 1988. Frank parried the obvious question by saying that Nigel

had matured in the two years he had been away, but had not lost any of his burning desire to drive the wheels off the car and win. His return had done much to motivate the entire factory. Frank also went to great lengths to praise Patrese, saying he was 'a good man, as well as a very good racing driver'.

Riccardo was to prove that by qualifying faster than Nigel in the first seven races of the 1991 season. Patrese secured three pole positions and was never off the front two rows during that time, Mansell slipping back to the third row just once. But race results did not reflect the promise of practice and qualifying. Ironing out problems with the electronically controlled and hydraulically activated gearbox occupied the first few races, but by the time they reached round five in Canada a win seemed finally on the cards, particularly when Mansell led from the start and never looked like being troubled.

In fact, the drive had been so easy that the novelty of winning a race for only the second time in almost as many years prompted Nigel to savour the moment. He began waving to the crowd while completing his last lap, forty-seven seconds ahead of his nearest rival, Nelson Piquet. The far end of the Circuit Gilles Villeneuve is a hairpin flanked by grandstands. As Nigel arrived in the midst of this horseshoe of admirers, the crowd rose as one. Nigel continued waving while changing down to first gear for the hairpin, but allowed the engine revs to fall too far. The transmission baulked between the gears and there was insufficient electrical charge left in the system to enable the hydraulics to select a gear. Mansell desperately flicked the selector paddle on the steering wheel, but there was no one at home. The engine stalled and the Williams rolled to a silent halt. Almost a minute later the incredulous Piquet passed in his Benetton to win the race.

Mansell's embarrassment was forgotten in Mexico two weeks later when the Williams pair started from the front row and finished that way, Patrese leading home the team's first one-two since 1989. Nigel began a roll with a win in France, followed by two more in Britain and Germany, results that moved him into contention for the title. Ayrton Senna, the championship leader, fought back with wins in Hungary and Belgium, Mansell responding with a fine victory in Italy. With four races to go, the pair were separated by eighteen points as the scene shifted to Portugal.

Patrese took pole position with Mansell fourth. Splitting the Williams drivers were the McLarens of Prost and Senna. Mansell made a storming start, passed the McLaren drivers and settled in behind his teammate. When Patrese duly let Mansell into the lead, everything appeared to be going well. Then came a scheduled stop for tyres. The pit crew had Mansell away again in 7.75 seconds, but after less than fifty metres the right-rear wheel parted company with the car. The error was compounded as, against regulations, the car was then worked on in the so-called fast lane of the pit road. Mansell rejoined in seventeenth place, but the officials eventually got their act together and showed him the black flag. Disqualified, Mansell was understandably enraged. On this occasion he had done nothing wrong. Patrese won the race, with Senna second, but that did little to lessen his anger at the fumble in the pit lane.

Never one to give up, Nigel clawed back some of the lost ground by winning in Spain after running wheel-to-wheel at 190 mph on the main straight with Senna in one of the most dramatic and iconic sights in the history of Formula 1. When Senna finished fifth that day, it gave Mansell a chance. But only if he won at the penultimate round in Japan. The championship slipped beyond reach when Nigel, lying third behind Senna, slid into the gravel trap. It summed up a season when Williams were almost, but not quite, in contention. To win consistently, they would need a faster car than the McLaren.

ADRIAN NEWEY

Patrick gave me more liberty, a lot of freedom. I set about designing the FW14 for the '91 season, which, bearing in mind I'd started mid-July, was a fair time pressure. At that time Williams had its original very basic quarter-scale wind tunnel and the use of the wind tunnel in Southampton in which we could put the 40-per-cent scale model. So I elected to do all the top surface aerodynamics, which are considered to be slightly less critical, in the quarter-scale tunnel at Williams, and the rest in Southampton.

The car that I based the FW14 on wasn't actually the 1990 Williams but the cars I'd been designing for Leyton House for 1991. I used that knowledge but blended it with the huge expertise and resource that Williams had. It was also the same time that John Barnard's semi-automatic gearbox concept was clearly the way to go, and Patrick, in addition to providing the overall technical direction of the team, got his pencil out and set about drawing and designing the gearbox himself, which was in the days of a fair mixture of drawing boards and CAD systems. Patrick and I never converted to CAD. My title was chief designer, which traditionally would mean the nuts and bolts and mechanical design of the car. But I also assumed the position of head of aerodynamics, which suited me absolutely fine. I tried to blend the mechanical design of the car with the aerodynamics because to me the two are intricately linked. You can't separate them out. You have to come up with a package which is cohesive. We evolved the car in a very short space of time.

We didn't get a lot of pre-season testing, but gradually we started to demonstrate some pace. At Montreal I was on for what would have been my first win in Formula 1. Then Nigel went through the famous waving to the crowds on the last lap. I remember standing at the back of the garage and feeling so depressed, having been so close to a win. I just couldn't believe it. But we picked ourselves up and went off to Mexico, where we looked very competitive in practice. Riccardo picked up a stomach bug and Saturday morning he came in looking really green and weak. I think he did one timed lap in the morning and that was it. He got in the car for qualifying and did one timed lap which was good enough to stick it on pole – quite a remarkable performance by Riccardo that day. So we had the front row, with Nigel second.

In the race Nigel did one of his funny falling-asleep periods. Then he suddenly woke up and reeled in Riccardo, much to Renault's consternation as the two of them were at it hammer and tongs. Renault were trying to say, 'Hold on! Let's have a formation finish.' But that was one of the strengths of Frank and Patrick: they always believed in allowing drivers to race. Riccardo went on to win and I finally got my first victory. After some gearbox problems we finally went to Suzuka, where frankly we were on the back foot. Not winning the championship wasn't a big let-down because we didn't expect it. It was disappointing, though, as we had the quickest car that year, but were unable to convert that into the championship win.

RICCARDO PATRESE

Patrick used to be shouting a lot even if he is a bit more relaxed these days, but I remember he felt that he had to rev me up a little bit during qualifying. So, before I would go out for a qualifying lap, he would be trying to make me a little bit angry. One of these occasions was at Estoril in 1991. Nigel was still fighting for the championship and we knew it was important for me to be on the front row with Nigel. That way we had the two cars against Ayrton for the championship. My engine blew up after my first run. I spent ten minutes walking back to the pits feeling a little bit cross because I wouldn't be able to use the second set of tyres.

Patrick was waiting and he said I had to go out in the T-car [spare car], which was set up for Nigel. I said, 'Patrick, why do I have to go in a car that I have never made a single lap in, and which is prepared for Nigel? There are five minutes to go and I only have one lap; it's not possible!' He shouts, 'You have to go in the car!' I say, 'It's not possible!' 'You have to go in the car!' 'No, I can't go in the car!'

There was a discussion like this for two minutes and then he got me, really quite physically, and he threw me into the car, which in the meantime my mechanics had adjusted a little. As I put my helmet on, Patrick is shouting, 'You go out and you try. You go balls out, you have to do everything you can!'

On the out lap from the pits, the car felt very good. So I thought, *Hmm, maybe this is not so bad.* I pushed for maximum speed and, bang, pole position! Of course, when I came back in, everyone was smiling and Patrick said, 'See, I was right. You didn't trust me, did you?' So I admitted that he was right. It was a happy story in the end. I led for a while and then I let Nigel through so that he could go for the win. Then his pit stop became a mess, so I won.

PETER WINDSOR

I offered my resignation after the pit-stop drama in Portugal and Frank said, 'No, no, definitely not. We need to find the cause of it. But I want you to carry on, absolutely.' He was very supportive. Patrick didn't really talk to me very much and was pretty cold after that. One of our mechanics was pretty negative about my role in that incident. But everyone else seemed to be of the opinion – which is my opinion – that it wasn't my fault at all.

When I joined as team manager, one of the things Patrick raised early on was how tardy the Williams pit stops were relative to Ferrari and McLaren. I set up a pretty arduous practice routine over the winter. We had heated uprights mounted on the race shop floor with the wheel assembly at exactly the right height for the guys to have wheels on and off. Having a car available for wheel-change practice all the time is actually a very difficult thing. Cars never exist as a complete item other than at racetracks. And when testing, the race team mechanics are not always there, so you can usually only practise your pit-stop routine during a race weekend.

I changed the whole thing. I started to get the guys on a fitness regime; practised the whole thing hour after hour and eventually we were pretty good. But in doing all that, it was pretty clear that the boys felt that McLaren and Ferrari were quicker, particularly at the rear of the car. It was more difficult to locate the wheel and get it on and off the Williams.

Dickie Stanford and I worked out a system where I was the lollipop guy – a job, I think, I did pretty well. I'm not very good at some things but I am quite good at distances, gaps and speeds. So I was very comfortable in that role. But instead of me cueing off the four guys putting their guns in the air when the wheels had been done, we would save time by cueing off the jacks. The rear jack would cue off the rear guys putting their guns in the air; it would be the same for the front jack. It was just taking one of the steps out, but we felt we could do it because we were under pressure to take between one and two seconds off our time. It worked perfectly: we did find time, and all our pit stops were very good.

But in that race, on the right rear the mechanic got the wheel off, put the new wheel on and the nut became cross-threaded. How that happened is immaterial. So he took the gun out to put his hand in and do it manually. But when rear jack man saw the gun come out, he thought, *He's done.* When the left-rear gun came out, the jack was lowered. I was looking at the traffic coming down the pit lane. I saw the rear jack go down; I saw the front jack lowered, so I raised the lollipop and Nigel was away.

I think the only mistake we made was not to practise a procedure in the event of a wheel nut jamming and what the jack man should do, under pressure, when he sees the gun coming out. But there's loads of things which in hindsight you feel should have been done.

The ludicrous thing about it was that there was no pit lane speed limit, and although the regulations had the pit lane divided into lanes, the pit lane in Estoril was so narrow there were effectively only two lanes.

When the wheel came off, I and a few others ran to the car but not a single marshal showed a yellow flag because the car was in the outside lane. We were near the entry and cars were blasting past us at 100 mph. They disqualified us for working on the car in the pit lane. What were we supposed to do? It was ridiculous. Nigel could have been in the points in that race.

Peter Warr was in charge of the stewards. I went up to see him and asked why Nigel had been black-flagged and he said it was because we had been working on the car in the pit lane. He said he was bringing Nigel in. As soon as you bring a guy in, you're stuffed. Frank didn't want to protest afterwards. I felt he should have.

JOHN RUSSELL

I came in as a completely green engineer who just about knew which way the tyres went on. I was engineering Riccardo's car. I'd never run a car in my life apart from three tests. The car was a rocket ship but we had a few technical issues with the gearbox which hurt us at the beginning of that season. Riccardo loved the car. You had a naïve race engineer with a very experienced driver. Adrian hung around to stop me making too many stupid mistakes, but he did it in a very non-patronising way. It set me up and taught me a lot about race engineering.

SHERIDAN THYNNE

Frank combines a massive capacity to infuriate with an enormous persuasive charm. I had to make it clear very early on that he could set goals that I'd try very hard to achieve, but I didn't need or wish to be told how to get there. He was very good at that and I suppose he knew that telling Patrick how to get there wouldn't have worked very well either. He had the skill to recognise lots of us who were confident at what we were doing and in whom he needed to have trust. Thus we had to have the freedom to get on with the job and if we failed, he could take steps.

Sponsors had enormous respect for him and what he's achieved. There was a guy called Wally McDonald at Mobil who was a board member, not just of Mobil Oil Corporation, but of Mobil Corporation, the parent company. He was extremely supportive and had a huge respect for Frank. He arranged for us to go and have lunch with the president of Mobil Corporation in New York. The reason was that they were having trouble getting other divisions of Mobil to make financial contributions and Wally said that he was sure if they could send out a picture of the president of Mobil shaking hands in head office, then the people who weren't supportive before would suddenly discover that they were supportive. We did that and it worked.

Frank initially took the view that sponsors were a necessary evil, somebody you gave the minimum amount of support to. I got through to him fairly quickly that looking after sponsors was quite hard work but finding new ones was much harder work, and therefore the ones that you had would be worth trying to keep. Periodically I'd say, 'Frank I want you to do this ...' and I would only say that on the occasions when I *really* wanted him to do it.

Patrick didn't need to talk to the sponsors at any great length. They wanted to talk to Frank, as the boss, and most of them saw Patrick as a superboffin. Patrick would shake hands with them, but he didn't need any dialogue with them. Which I didn't encourage in case he said things that I wouldn't want him to say.

I used to have very good relationships with the chief mechanic. If I wanted to do something that interfaced with the team, then I'd talk to the chief mechanic first about the feasibility. In the days when we had Barclay as a sponsor, Patrick came to me and said he was going to run at Hockenheim with a rear-wing endplate about a quarter of the usual size. Since this carried the Barclay logo, I might want to warn them. So I thought about that and went and spoke to Alan Challis and asked him to predict what would happen. Alan said, 'Riccardo will do one standing lap, one flying lap, come in, and say, "Patrick! No fucking way!" and then we won't run them again.' Sure enough, that's exactly what happened. One flying lap from Riccardo, a pungent comment to Patrick about the ineffectiveness of the wing endplate and I had no further worries about explaining to Barclay why their exposure on the car had been dramatically reduced.

TWENTY-FOUR

14B for Bully

If ever a car was made for Nigel Mansell, it was the Williams FW14B. Appreciating the benefits of active suspension despite the torrid experience of the team's first venture in 1988, Patrick Head joined Adrian Newey to explore this avenue further with FW14B in order to gain a performance advantage over McLaren. A simple concept, active suspension offered control of the car's ride height, which in turn allowed the engineers to optimise the aerodynamics – in other words, produce more downforce and make it go faster, more consistently. The FW14B was actually a stop-gap while the team researched active suspension during the heat of battle, but such was the car's immediate dominance it remained in service throughout the season.

Mansell's physical strength allowed him to bully the car, and he put down an impressive marker by winning the first five races of the 1992 season. He would have won the sixth at Monaco had a wheel not worked loose, forcing a pit stop. He then hounded Senna in his McLaren but was unable to overtake. Needle between the Englishman and the Brazilian continued in Canada, where Mansell made an ill-advised lunge down the inside of the McLaren and ended up with bits of blue Williams flying in all directions as he had no alternative but to straight-line the chicane. There was, however, consolation when Senna and Patrese both retired, leaving Mansell's championship lead intact.

Under the terms of his contract Nigel should have been able to rely on Patrese giving way to him, but Riccardo felt otherwise inclined after learning from Frank that his services would not be required in 1993. Mansell and Patrese were first and second fastest during qualifying for the next race in France, but Riccardo took the lead and showed no sign of giving up his advantage. Fortunately for Nigel a light shower caused the race to be stopped and allowed Patrick to have a few words with Riccardo. What was said became obvious when at the restart Patrese led for a few laps before pulling to one side on the pit straight and waving Mansell through. Such a dramatic gesture was unnecessary, but it was clear that Patrese had been told to put the interests of the team above his own. Nigel required no assistance at Silverstone, where he delighted the partisan crowd with a powerful drive to his seventh win of the season.

That same weekend rumours began to surface that Frank was in conversation with Alain Prost concerning 1993. Naturally, Mansell was not entirely happy about this, but concentrated on the here and now by winning in Germany and then clinching the world championship by finishing second in Hungary despite there being five more races to run. It was well deserved. Williams may have provided the equipment, but Mansell had delivered and felt that was enough to warrant his continuing as number one for another year. The dilemma for Frank was that half of his working budget – reputed to be in the region of £25 million – was supplied by Renault and their fuel and oil supplier Elf in the form of engines and technical support. It had not escaped the notice of the French firms that Prost, a triple world champion, was sitting around doing nothing in 1992. It was intimated to Frank that Prost's presence in a Williams-Renault would be good for the team and good for business in France. A story emerged from the Williams celebrations in Hungary that Nigel had agreed to share number-one status with Prost in return for an additional US$1.5 million. Honour seemed be satisfied all round.

Enter Ayrton Senna, still at the top of Frank's wish list. There had been discussions on and off over the years, but now Senna said he would drive for Williams for nothing in 1993. This was Senna's way of expressing his annoyance that Prost was in front of him in the queue to drive for Williams. This may have been a wind-up but did nothing for Mansell's peace of mind. Nigel's worst fears were realised a few days later when he allegedly received an offer worth much less than the figure agreed in Hungary. Williams had been told a cut was necessary since it seemed likely that Elf would be bringing less money to the table in 1993 following a drop in profits for the first six months of 1992.

Discussions with Mansell continued through the next race in Belgium. Two weeks after that, Nigel gave a press conference on the weekend of the Italian Grand Prix which degenerated into farce when last-minute furtive messages from Williams failed to dissuade the emotional Nigel from announcing his retirement at the end of the season 'due to circumstances beyond my control'. The British media led with the story, provoking outrage over such shabby treatment for Britain's new world champion, the first since James Hunt in 1976. Williams battened down the hatches, determined to ride out a storm that had blown up out of nowhere.

In any case, there was business to be done on the racetrack. Mansell won in Portugal, a race in which Patrese was fortunate to escape unhurt from a spectacular accident. A misunderstanding led to Riccardo running into the back of a car slowing for the pits, the 160-mph impact sending the Williams skywards. Just as it looked like flipping over backwards, the car crashed back on to the track, narrowly missing the underside of a bridge. The wreckage travelled some distance before rattling against the pit wall, where, remarkably, Patrese was able to climb from an intact cockpit. Patrese would round off his time with Williams on a happy note when he won in Japan, Mansell having gifted the race to help him in his ultimately successful battle with Senna and Michael Schumacher for second place in the championship. Even though both cars were to retire from the final race in Australia, the constructors' championship had long since been done and dusted.

Mansell then left for pastures new, Sheridan Thynne ending his long association with Frank to travel with him to the United States. But Nigel's turbulent association with Williams was not yet over.

PATRICK HEAD

Nigel was outstanding in 1992, quite brilliant. The active-ride FW14B was a massive step forward for us, but it was difficult. It was changing all the time according to the software so it didn't necessarily give the feedback in real time. It told the driver, 'Don't worry. I've got the grip – you're okay.' So you had to know that, later in the corner, it would sort itself out and the grip would be there. Riccardo didn't like that whereas Nigel would just say, 'I know the grip will be there.' Bang. Total self-confidence.

I wouldn't say we developed the car much during the year; it was mostly about keeping it reliable because it was quite a complex car. It was something I anguished over. I knew we had a very good car, and I thought it quite possible that even with the FW14 developed, we could win the championship without active ride. We were always able to go back to a conventional car if we had to, but while the active ride was proving itself reliable and quicker, that's what we stuck with.

ADRIAN NEWEY

The active suspension was a three-legged system that AP [Automotive Products] had developed for road cars. It was a very simple system which offered good ride height control and therefore allowed us to optimise the aerodynamics. As a spring and damper suspension, however, the vehicle dynamics of the suspension were actually very poor, and that was its weakness. But we were able to develop aero-dynamics which, combined with the ride height control we had, gave us huge amounts of downforce.

We realised in the wind tunnel that if we lowered the rear and raised the front, you could stall the diffuser and that reduced the drag of the car significantly. So we put a button on the steering wheel which the drivers could push once they were on the straight. The button lowered the rear, raised the front. I can't remember the figure but that would give them something like an extra 10 kph. It was a great system, an aerodynamicist's dream in terms of what we could then develop.

At the last test of the winter there was a failure in the system. It wasn't serious, but Nigel was very worried and wanted to run the passive car at the first race in South Africa. We said we believed we could get it reliable, and we also believed we needed the performance it offered, otherwise we were going to be beaten. We started with the active system, and it was good as gold. It was very robust and gave us no problems as well as offering the performance advantage. Plus there was the fact that McLaren had got themselves completely and utterly lost trying to run V10 cars and V12 cars. In truth, they went backwards over the winter, and we went forwards.

The 1992 season was the easiest I've ever had in motor racing, without a doubt. It was very interesting between the drivers. In 1991, while Nigel was generally the quicker of the two, on his day Riccardo could beat Nigel. In 1992 the active car was perfect for Nigel because, first of all, it was before we had power steering and, because of the amount of downforce it had, the steering loads were very high. Nigel had this tremendous upper-body strength, so he could cope with the steering loads. And because the suspension system was quite crude, the car used to move around and give all sorts of slightly funny signals to the driver. Going into the corner, if the rear started to move in a slightly Citroën 2CV-like way, Riccardo's understandable reaction was to lift off the throttle, whereas Nigel had this total belief in himself and his ability to control the car, so he would keep his foot on it. By carrying his speed, he'd keep up the downforce and through the corner the car would go.

But Nigel was very clever as well. He realised that his principal rival for the championship was going to be Riccardo and that he'd better set about destroying him from the outset. He did that very effectively in one simple move. Riccardo had been training very hard through the winter in order to get his weight down and get himself really fit. I think that was the first year we had the driver weigh-ins. Nigel, who never appeared to take gym work very seriously and wasn't too careful about his diet, set about dehydrating himself for a couple of days. Then he stripped everything out of his overalls, took all the lining out and removed the lining from his helmet. At the weigh-in, he managed to come in about half a kilo under Riccardo, who was mentally destroyed by this.

At Monza in 1991 Nigel had been very quick and very good at jumping the chicanes, so Patrick asked him what his secret was because Riccardo seemed to be struggling. The 1991 car had a cockpit chassis structure that came over the top of the steering wheel. Nigel said, 'Well, what I do is, I jam my knuckles against the inside of the cockpit. Then, when I jump the chicane, the steering wheel can't move.' So Patrick duly went back to Riccardo and told him what he had do. Riccardo went out and came back after one lap with blood all leaking through his gloves! Nigel was very good at winding people up.

Nigel had a very close relationship with David Brown, his race engineer. We didn't have a huge amount in the way of data recording in those days. But we did have three knobs in the cockpit which were for low-speed front ride-height, high-speed front ride-height and rear ride-height. The drivers could use these to adjust the handling of the car during the race. Nigel would go out, adjust it to what he wanted and then, on his in lap, change all the settings. Those settings would go down on the set-up sheet. Riccardo would duly try and copy Nigel's settings, which of course were hopelessly off. David was in on the act but kept his mouth shut. So there were all these little wind-ups going on, which to be fair to Nigel was clever of him. He had sussed that his main rival was Riccardo and he needed to go about outsmarting him.

When it became evident that Frank had signed Prost and in the process had allowed a contract that put Nigel out of a drive, I felt it was wrong. What that did mean was, when we started talking about extending my contract, I asked that I should be involved in major policy decisions including driver choice, recognising that of course Frank and

Patrick could outvote me ultimately. But I wanted to be in a position to put my tuppence in. So I re-signed in 1993 for one year. But in the middle of 1993 Ferrari basically couldn't get their active car to work at all, so miraculously the FIA decided to ban active suspension.

RICCARDO PATRESE

I was an Italian driver but I had worked with English teams before. Frank had worked a lot with foreign drivers and he could understand my Latin attitude. I think one of the reasons I stayed so long in Williams – five years – was because the relationship with the mechanics and the engineers and everyone was fantastic. One of my characteristics is that I'm a driver who always wants to look after the enthusiasm and wants the best morale of the team. It is important that if you want the results you always have to have a nice atmosphere and everyone motivated. The driver needs to be motivated because, in the end, he is the man who is going to get the result through a lot of hard work. I loved the team and the team loved me. I finished second in the drivers' championship. Okay, every driver likes to be champion, but you can't have everything you want in life.

Nigel and I are very good friends, but to work with him can be hard because, as you know, he likes to have all the attention for himself. He was a fantastic driver and he deserved to win the championship in 1992. He was a little bit quicker than I was. Working with Nigel went very well but I have to say that for me the most important thing was the best interest of the team. Nigel wanted to have everything for himself.

IAN ANDERSON

From a technical point of view, that car was unbelievably impressive. It had active ride, which I know a lot of people had on their cars later on, but I don't think anyone made it work as well. It had a power-shift gearbox , hydraulically operated throttles and ABS. To make it reliable was very impressive. Of course, Nigel will tell you it's all down to the driver. We did have the theory that we ought to put straps under the car. When Nigel asked what we did that for, we would say, 'Well, if it breaks, you can carry it across the line.'

NIGEL MANSELL

I had two very good years in 1991 and 1992. There were a few problems with the semi-automatic gearbox, otherwise we could have really challenged for the championship in 1991. It was tricky in 1992 because Frank was trying to replace me, but fortunately I had a good strong contract, otherwise I'd never have won the championship. I wasn't afforded the same opportunity to do it again in 1993 because they wanted a French driver and a French-engined car to win the championship.

PETER WINDSOR

The bottom line was that Nigel was annoyed that Frank had signed Prost. The only way he was going to stay was if he got twice the amount of money Prost was getting. I don't think Nigel was in the mood to spend three months negotiating. He was world champion; he was king of the castle and wanted an instant response from Frank. He wasn't going to get it because Frank never gave in that quickly. He wasn't being mean. He was trying to do the best job for himself and his company. There were a lot of people around who were fanning the flames. To me, it was simple: Nigel wanted the money and Frank was either going to pay it or he wasn't. He did offer it in the end, and to this day I don't understand why Nigel didn't accept that very late offer and stay. Okay, you could argue that Frank was asking for trouble by bringing Prost into the team, but I think he genuinely felt that Mansell and Prost were the best driver combination for 1993, and from Renault's point of view it was the right thing to do. If Frank had made the final offer a couple of months before, the deal would have been done.

FRANK WILLIAMS

Put simply, I think it was a matter of two hard-headed idiots who couldn't make a deal, couldn't communicate at the right time. It's still my firm opinion that if Nigel hadn't had that press conference at Monza, announcing what I thought was a grossly premature decision to retire, by Monday evening or so – away from the track – both of us would have calmed down. He'd have been away from all his syco-phantic followers, who were advising him badly in my opinion, and we'd probably have made a deal.

DAMON HILL

I had an enormous responsibility in the 1992 British Grand Prix: it was my first F1 race and I had to let Nigel pass four or five times or I'd have had 150,000 people on my back. I've never looked in my mirrors so much! When Nigel crossed the line, I was right there and this bloke ran out in front of me. I was doing 100 mph-plus coming across the line. I had already backed off, but this guy didn't even think there was another car coming. Then we got stuck down at Copse. We all came to a grinding halt because of spectators pouring on to the track to greet Nigel. We were stranded there, our cars lost in the crowd. I remember thinking, *If they take my Brabham apart for souvenirs, it's no loss to anyone!*

TWENTY-FIVE

French Toast

Everyone said 1993 would be Alain Prost's year but circumstances seemed to be against him before a wheel had so much as turned. An administrative mix-up in the office at Didcot meant the Williams entry form arrived after the FIA deadline. A late entry required the approval of the other eleven teams. This should have been a formality, but Williams had been dominant and looked likely to continue on top. Rivals saw this as an opportunity, some calling for a ban on the technical advantages exploited so brilliantly at Didcot.

There was a problem too with Prost. Or, more to the point, his relationship with Max Mosley. The FIA president, barely in office for a year, had taken offence at alleged criticism of the governing body by Prost when working as a media pundit during his sabbatical in 1992. Both matters were eventually resolved, but that would not be the last time the Frenchman crossed swords with authority in 1993. Prost's state of mind was not helped by the assumption that he was a shoo-in for the championship simply because he had what was likely to be the best car – a point of view put forward by Senna at every opportunity, particularly as McLaren had lost their Honda engines and the Brazilian had been saddled with a less competitive Ford.

The FW15 would make its appearance about six months later than planned. With the FW14B having blown the opposition away in 1992, there was time to incorporate the lessons learned into the new car. After all the shenanigans Prost was joined by Damon Hill. Promoted from the role of test driver, Hill would be a useful asset when it came to explaining to Prost the intricacies of active suspension.

There was a moment just after the start of the first race in South Africa when observers thought they were about to see the Williams team wipe themselves out. Prost had a poor getaway from pole but Hill went in the opposite direction and shot from fourth to second. The excitement was too much as Damon thought about challenging Senna for the lead. The Williams spun, and almost took the other one with it. Both recovered, only for Hill to tangle with a Lotus. Prost made amends by taking the win everyone had predicted.

Senna then scored two superb wins in Brazil and in the European Grand Prix at Donington Park, Prost responding with maximum points at Imola and Barcelona. It was Senna's turn again at Monaco, his sixth victory in the principality beating the record set by the father of the man standing next to him on the podium. Senna was touched by the graceful tribute paid by Damon that paved the way for an amicable but all too brief working relationship in the future. Prost, however, was outraged by a ten-second penalty imposed because of a jumped start, his fourth place at Monaco helping Senna open a five-point lead in the championship. Wins for Prost in Canada and France turned the tables, Alain's championship lead stretching with victory at Silverstone, but only after Hill was denied victory by a blown engine with eighteen laps to go.

Hill began to wonder if he was jinxed when two weeks later in Germany that maiden win was snatched from his grasp yet again, this time by a puncture. Prost was the beneficiary once more, although he was far from happy about another ten-second penalty, imposed on this occasion for taking to the escape road on the first lap. Prost had not gained any advantage and pointed out to no avail that he had been forced to do so in order to avoid a spinning car.

Prost's mood was not helped in Hungary when he stalled on pole position, was obliged to start from the back and then had a lengthy pit stop for repairs while on his way to twelfth place. This time, however, the gods smiled on Hill, who led from the first lap and finally took that overdue win. Having broken his duck, Hill rattled off two more wins, the second coming at the expense of Prost just as he was poised to settle the championship at Monza – an engine failure less than twenty miles from home delaying the coronation of the 1993 world champion until the Portuguese Grand Prix two weeks later.

Prost chose that weekend to announce his retirement at the end of the season even though there was another year to run on his contract. The spectre of Senna had struck once more, Frank finally getting the Brazilian's signature on a contract even though he knew it would enrage Prost. Pragmatic as ever, Frank had gone for who he considered to be the best driver for his team in much the same way as he had announced a two-year deal with Rothmans the previous July. This had not only prompted the departure of RJ Reynolds and their Camel brand, but also outraged Canon, previously a main sponsor, and caused the Japanese sponsor to quit after nine seasons with Williams. Frank remained tight-lipped in the face of criticism from Tokyo. What was done, was done. As ever, he was thinking of the next race. He had Ayrton Senna on board; what more could anyone ask?

FRANK WILLIAMS

The partnership with Renault was outstanding. Then when Adrian arrived he and Patrick made a fantastic combination. Those were the days. The 1992 and 1993 cars were brilliant. In fact, I think it's fair to say the FW14B is one of the all-time great racing cars. It suited Nigel perfectly.

PATRICK HEAD

Alain Prost was a very measured driver, very clever, massively talented. A couple of races didn't go his way but he pulled it together and just went bang, bang, bang, bang, and won the championship.

Alain was one of those not only exceptionally talented drivers, but one who was massively in control. He knew when to be quick, when to take it easy; he didn't need to prove himself in every race. So, when he'd won his championship – I'm not saying he was tugging – but there was no way he was going to extend himself in the last couple of races. Ayrton won those, although in truth – and nothing against Ayrton – the McLaren active-ride system had by that time surpassed ours. If active ride had continued into 1994, we would have run on something I suspect even better than McLaren. We were just running what we had because it was so dominant that year; we didn't have to develop it. The FW15 was an outstanding car. The active-ride system was clever, but it wasn't the ultimate.

DAMON HILL

I had obviously heard of Frank because of course I had come from a racing family. Frank once told me a story about how he got a lift back from a race in my dad's plane. He hadn't eaten all day – you know, the usual Frank story. He hadn't got any money and was bumming a lift back to England and my dad took pity on him. They were four hours or so into the flight – it used to take hours across Europe in those small planes – and Frank found a sweet in his pocket. So he popped this sweet in his mouth and sort of savoured it. It got him through the flight. When they got out at the other end and were heading off my dad went back to the plane to check if he'd left anything. He found the sweet wrapper and shouted across to Frank, 'Oi! You! Is this yours?' Frank got a ticking off, which I can see happening. That story completely rings true.

So I knew a bit about racing, even though I was into bikes and racing them up until about 1983. Then I started looking at cars and going racing on four wheels. In terms of watching the unfolding of form in Formula 1, it was quite apparent that Williams were definitely coming into their next phase with the arrival of Adrian Newey and the Renault engine; they really were going to be hard to beat. So it was a godsend that I had the opportunity to test, develop and work on the car that Nigel drove to win the championship. I was thinking to myself, *I can drive that car, and he can drive that car and win races with it. I know where I stand.* That really gave me a strong feeling that, given the right opportunity, I could give it a go.

I became so familiar with the team that it was almost like an extended test session when we went to a race meeting. You knew the terrain, you knew the people and you knew the form. I was aware very much with Williams that if you didn't come up to their impression of where you rightfully should be, then you hadn't got a place there. I was very mindful of that. Average wasn't good enough for Williams; that's how it is.

I won my first race in Hungary. It was a nightmare getting from the Hungaroring to the airport and somehow they had managed to wangle themselves a helicopter. I'd won my first race and I thought, *Well, I'm definitely entitled to this now.* So I went with Adrian, Patrick, Frank and somebody else from the team in what I can only describe as a Mr Magoo helicopter. You could see they had painted it with a paint-brush – it was agricultural in the extreme. As we land, Patrick turns to Frank and says, 'You know, Frank, perhaps it's not wise for all of us to travel in the same helicopter.' This was after we'd got in the thing, flown across to the airport and questioned it for most of the way. Obviously, given my family experience with flying and so forth, there was poignancy to that. It was typical Patrick. And Frank loves it: he just gets a run of adrenalin out of the whole thing.

ALAIN PROST

I started to talk to Frank the day I left Ferrari at the end of 1991. I was already in Australia, talking to Ferrari about not just being a driver but also having some responsibilities for the team. And then suddenly we had to stop. I hope that one day they will tell you exactly what happened!

So I was in Queensland and I had a call from the Elf people. We started to talk about the 1992 season. They were telling me that maybe they could have the opportunity to replace Nigel. To be honest, I didn't know what to say. On one side you are happy because people are interested in you. But on the other side it was not good to be in the middle of a polemic. That was only the Elf people – they were quite important at the time from a business point of view with Renault. So I said, 'Okay, we wait until next week when we come back to Europe and we see what happens.' It took a good week or two before they told me it was not going to be easy. I said, 'Okay, it's not a problem.' I had some contact with other teams, but I was not interested. So I said maybe we could enter into a discussion for 1993 and I would take a sabbatical year; that could be quite a good thing to do. Then we went into a discussion with Renault and Elf and Frank. I don't remember exactly when we signed the contract but it was around the time the 1992 season started.

Then I had all the problems before we even started racing in 1993. I always had the support of Frank and Patrick, but I didn't understand very well what happened at the time. It looked like maybe some people were not very happy for me to come back. Even now I cannot say. We had a problem with the FIA and then we had a problem during the Monaco race, which was very, very bad for me. I had a very difficult time after the second race in Brazil and then Donington, two races when it was wet. I felt a lack of support with the French press, and not a great deal of support from Renault at the time.

But it was a very strange year for me because, in a way, I got on very well with the team, with the engineers, with the mechanics – everybody. Yet there was a strange feeling with the Renault people. I felt very well inside the team but outside the team it was a very strange ambience with the press. When I was winning, the press in France saw this as absolutely normal because I had the best car and I was with the best team – more horsepower than Ayrton's car and things like this. It's very difficult to motivate yourself when it is like this.

Above: Thierry Boutsen won his first Grand Prix in Montreal, leading home Riccardo Patrese to a Williams one-two. The Williams welcome would be less than effusive when the Belgian driver won his third race in Hungary a year later in 1990.

Right: Riccardo Patrese: five happy years at Williams, even if Patrick Head wound up the Italian from time to time.

Above: A victorious Nigel Mansell gives a lift to Ayrton Senna, whose McLaren had run out of fuel at the end of the 1991 British Grand Prix at Silverstone.

Left: A drop of the hard stuff. An exhausted Nigel Mansell recovers with the champagne at Monaco in 1992 after failing to wrest the lead from Ayrton Senna during the dramatic closing stages.

Below: Easy does it. A relaxed Sheridan Thynne (first left) and Peter Windsor confer as Nigel Mansell lounges against his Williams-Renault FW14B before the start of the 1992 Hungarian Grand Prix, the race which would give Mansell his championship title.

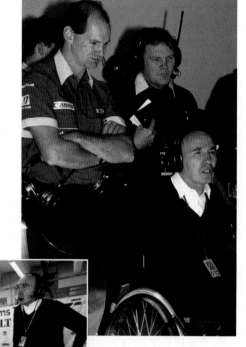

Right: Winning combination. Adrian Newey (left) and Patrick Head study lap times with Frank Williams in 1992.

Below: Not much to say. Alain Prost in discussion with Frank Williams – probably on the pained subject of Ayrton Senna – before practice for the 1993 German Grand Prix at Hockenheim.

Below: Second place in Portugal with the Williams FW15C was enough for Alain Prost to clinch his fourth world title.

Above: Jason Plato's Williams Renault Laguna battles for the lead at Thruxton during the 1997 British Touring Car Championship.

Left: Doesn't look right, somehow. Heinz-Harald Frentzen (left) and Jacques Villeneuve at the launch of red Williams FW20 in 1998.

Below: Ralf Schumacher (left) and Jenson Button: team-mates in 2000. Despite an impressive debut season, Button would be on his bike when Williams took up their option on Juan Pablo Montoya in 2001.

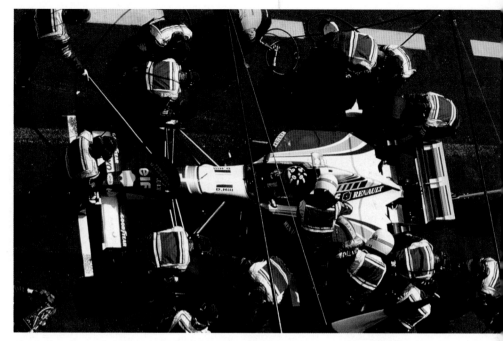

Above: Another well-drilled pit stop as Damon Hill receives fuel and fresh tyres on his way to second place in the 1995 French Grand Prix at Magny-Cours.

Above: Highs and Lows. Damon Hill (above left) celebrates finishing second at Monaco in 1993 and (above right) walks back to the pits after hitting the tyre barrier while leading the 1996 Italian Grand Prix.

Left: The Big One. Damon Hill, winner of the 1996 Japanese Grand Prix and the World Championship.

Below: Highland fling. David Coulthard is hoisted aloft after his first Grand Prix win at Estoril in Portugal, 1995.

Above: Michael Schumacher helps his brother Ralf celebrate a Williams one-two with Juan Pablo Montoya in the 2003 French Grand Prix at Magny Cours.

Right: Tough act to follow. Sam Michael (left) stepped into Patrick Head's shoes as Technical Director.

Below: Nearing the end of a tough season for Williams. Mark Webber (left) and Nico Rosberg before the start of the 2006 Chinese Grand Prix.

Above: Dramatic pit stop in 2008 during the floodlit Singapore Grand Prix, where Nico Rosberg finished second.

Below: A rare moment of solitude for Sir Frank Williams.

It was day and night all the time. When you lose a race like Donington, people did not want to realise there were many reasons for this. Ayrton's car was technically a different car when it was wet. For sure Ayrton was very fast, but in these conditions the McLaren was much better. Winning is one thing but you need to win in a good ambience. At Imola I had to drive with a sticking throttle and I won. I don't know if it was one of the best wins for me, but it was a good one. And that is when I realised there was no objectivity. Why should I be attacked when it was wet at Donington? And yet nobody said Imola was a good race because they saw it as being a perfectly normal race. It's never that simple, never black or white.

Then we had this story in the middle of the year when Renault asked me about my position with Ayrton. This went back to the discussion we had in the winter of 1991. I never asked to be a number one or a number two; I never asked anything like this in any team I was with. The only thing I asked when writing the contract was that they would not have Ayrton in the same team. Then in the middle of 1993 Frank called me. I knew already from a few weeks before that he was having some pressure from Renault. I was in the south-west of France. Frank asked if he could see me and I said, 'Yes, of course, but you know I am on holidays.' He said, 'Yes, I know, but don't move. You have worked a lot, tested a lot; I will come to see you.' He came from London. I always remember this day. He said he had pressure over having Ayrton and he wanted to know what I thought.

I said, 'Okay. If you want to take Ayrton, you choose. I want to compete against Ayrton, but not in the same team. I want to fight him on the track. I want to be with your team and together have the best chance possible to beat him on the track. But I have been with him in the same team before, and I know what that is like.' So Frank had to make a decision. A few weeks after that I said to Renault, 'Okay, you are pushing for Ayrton and you gave me aggravation this year. I have a two-year contract. You pay me the second year of my contract and I leave.' And that's what happened.

It was a different ambience at Williams compared with McLaren or Ferrari. The Williams ambience suited me very well – the English part was very good. I didn't need to say hello all the time, every day. I am much closer to this mentality. I knew what was needed to do the job and I had a good relationship with Adrian and with Frank and Patrick – with everyone there. You don't need more than that. It was more the external parts that were the problem. Frank's team is sometimes not prepared for the external part. The inside is very good. But just in the middle between the inside and the outside, you find the grey part.

JOHN RUSSELL

Damon was very eloquent at describing how the car responded and was an admirable test driver to back up the plan. It was a great car to work with and even if you screwed up massively, you were third on the grid. I look back on 1993 as one of my happiest seasons. Damon came from nowhere. No disrespect, but he almost had to be pointed which end of the car to get in. He did an absolutely fantastic job: he won three races, ran Alain close on pole quite a few times.

MARTIN BRUNDLE

At the end of 1992, when Nigel decided he was going to America, I was just getting the hang of beating Schumacher in a Benetton. At Monza I beat Michael and I finished second to Senna. I'd already had some meetings with Frank and I really thought I'd got the drive. I think I made the mistake of trusting too many people. On the Tuesday night I had the drive and by the Thursday night I hadn't got it. I think it was a lot of pressure. With the Mansell name going, Hill was a bigger name to have. So that was thoroughly disappointing. Frank asked me to go and see him and he'd explain it all, but I've never done it. Whatever the answer, I don't want to know it. Not even seventeen years later.

DAVID COULTHARD

I first came across Frank when I was in British Formula 3 driving with Paul Stewart Racing. Because I knew Iain Cunningham, and because of his relationship with Frank and Frank's condition, he would spend a bit of time talking to Frank, so I had access to Frank in a way that you wouldn't have general access to other team principals. He arranged for me to go and have a walk round the Williams factory, where I had an introduction to Frank. He was a very important person to me as a young driver, because he was operating one of the most successful Grand Prix teams of the time. That eventually led to me having the opportunity to test for Williams.

The first test was at Silverstone in 1992. I can remember having my first run and thinking, *Wow, this is fantastic!* It led to a slightly bizarre informal testing agreement. It was informal in that there was no contract and no payment, and it was always explained to me that because of Elf having an association with the team, and them having a number of French drivers at that time, the French were always pushing for French drivers. But because I had always done well and had done well in Formula 3 and Monaco and that sort of thing, Williams were keen for me to carry on doing the testing.

I didn't actually have a formal test contract until part way through 1993, at which point I was paid the vast sum of £20,000 for risking life and limb to test all the new-fangled test-spec items they'd conceived. In those days Formula 1 was still quite creative in what you could actually test. So you really were a crash-test dummy for a lot of the items. Nowadays Formula 1 is so restricted of course that you're lucky to test a different covering on the steering wheel.

It was a good old British mug-of-tea, proper British racing team. Down under the towers at Didcot was a very enjoyable place to serve your apprenticeship. Frank would have his push-rounds in the morning – that would be his exercise. He'd go around the race bays and the machine shop. He'd be exercising by taking himself around so he had a really good feel of what was happening on the shop floor. It was very interesting when I eventually went to McLaren in 1996 because very rarely did Ron ever walk round the factory, and that was because he was always busy doing other things and his schedule allowed him to use his time in a different way. Whereas part of Frank's day is the exercise necessary to keep what muscles he has in his shoulders going, and so he has a more intimate relationship with his team.

DEREK DALY

Ten years after I left Williams I suggested that I would love to have a run in the car Prost used to win the world championship. This was just before the active cars were about to be banned and I wanted to see what they were like. That's when they had the Ricard test for me, John Watson, Jochen Mass and four or five others – and that was down to me asking Frank. He asked Patrick and came back and said that it was okay. So I obviously maintained a certain amount of professional relationship and credibility with them in that he was confident to let me run in the car all those years after I'd left. I found that at the test the team were totally professional. The FW15 was the finest racing car I have ever driven, absolutely without any doubt. It just did everything right.

TWENTY-SIX
Imola

The joke in later years was that FIA stood for Ferrari International Assistance. The jibe was probably coined in 1994 when Formula 1's governing body ruled out many of the technologies which Williams had mastered, but which Ferrari, among others, had failed with. Whatever the reasons for the rule alterations, Adrian Newey had to make wholesale design changes. The result, the FW16, would prove that such things cannot be done with the sweep of a pencil, no matter how talented the designer.

When Damon Hill drove the 1994 Williams-Renault for the first time, he knew life was going to be difficult, at least in the short term. Hill's vast experience as a Williams test driver – more than 25,000 miles – had been mainly in cars with active suspension. Now he was back in a so-called passive car, and it didn't feel good. Was this how it was supposed to be? Had he been spoiled by the driver aids associated with active suspension and the other gizmos that had now been banned? Then there was the fact that his new teammate was one of the most famous names, not just in motor racing but in world sport, but Hill doubted even Senna could succeed in the FW16. Senna respected Hill's experience with Williams cars and was looking for answers, but Damon had none to satisfy himself, never mind the driver who was expected to bring Williams a third successive championship almost as a matter of course.

Williams knew they were in trouble when Senna spun during the opening race of the season, a rare mistake made more galling by the fact that it happened in his home Grand Prix. Senna's skill had wrestled the FW16 on to pole position, but seventy-one seconds was one thing, seventy-one laps quite another. Second place for Hill in Brazil was recognised for the display of tenacity and perseverance it clearly was.

There was no time for a decent fix as the cars were shipped directly to Japan and the next round at Aida, an obscure track in the hills above Okayama. Once again, pole position for Senna had more to do with the driver than his car. The thought of eighty-three laps around this tight circuit was daunting, the only respite being brief pit stops, as refuelling was now permitted again after more than ten years. But Senna would not get as far as his first stop. In fact, he would not get beyond the first corner, a touch from behind sending the Williams sideways to be struck by the Ferrari of Nicola Larini, the pair ending their race in the gravel trap on the outside of the corner. A minute later Hill was also in trouble, the result of an adventurous attempt to overtake the second-place McLaren of Mika Hakkinen. Hill was at least able to restart in ninth place, but another impressive drive into second came to an end when the transmission broke with more than thirty laps to go.

Senna, meanwhile, had spent his time watching Michael Schumacher head towards his second win in succession for Benetton-Ford. The Brazilian was sure the Benetton was using traction control, a device banned for 1994. Despite later investigation by the FIA, this was never proven. Of more immediate concern was the fact that in his previous ten seasons Senna had never failed to score in the first two races, let alone win, something he had achieved eight times. In his mind he simply had to win the next race, the San Marino Grand Prix at Imola on 1 May. There was no pressure from within the team; the stress was coming from outside Williams. The next issue of *Autosport*, dated 21 April 1994, carried the headline MICHAEL 20, AYRTON 0, the British magazine following that up a week later with, under a picture of Ayrton wearing a troubled look, 'SENNA. CAN HE TAKE THE HEAT?'

Williams had been busy with modifications, which included making the driver more comfortable in the extremely tight cockpit. In many ways Imola, the first race in Europe, represented a fresh start for the team, but it would be one of the most catastrophic Grands Prix of recent times.

Practice had just begun on Friday when Rubens Barrichello crashed his Jordan while coming through a chicane on the approach to the pit straight. The car, flipped into the air by a kerb at 140 mph, appeared to be heading for a fence in front of a packed grandstand but mercifully ran along the top of the crash barrier before landing upside down on the track, Barrichello escaping with a cut lip and a broken nose. The incident was spectacular but seen as just one of those things. Saturday would produce an accident which could not be dismissed so lightly.

Roland Ratzenberger, attempting to qualify his Simtek-Ford, slammed into a concrete wall at high speed. The thirty-one-year-old Austrian, in his first season in Formula 1, died from multiple injuries in hospital later that afternoon. It was twelve years since a driver had lost his life in a Grand Prix meeting and eight years since a death during testing. Many of those in F1 had never before experienced anything like this, Senna among them. He visited the scene of the accident and went to the medical centre, where Professor Watkins told him gently that Ratzenberger was beyond help. Seeing how upset Ayrton was, Watkins urged him not to race the following day. Senna, after a moment or two's thought, said there were certain things over which he had no control. He could not quit. He would carry on.

The tension on race day soared when two cars collided on the grid. When JJ Lehto stalled, most of the field managed to take evasive action, but Pedro Lamy, starting from the back, was unsighted and slammed into the back of the Benetton. Both drivers escaped serious injury but bodywork and wheels flew in all directions, some of it clearing fencing and injuring several spectators. The safety car, a relative novelty in Formula 1, was dispatched; it never became clear why the race was not stopped and restarted, as permitted by the regulations. Senna had led from pole position with his new nemesis, Schumacher, glued to his tail.

Reaching the end of the first lap, they found the start/finish line strewn with debris. Catching the safety car – an Opel saloon hopelessly inadequate for the job – the field completed four laps at a crawl. The safety car pulled into the pits and the race was on again.

Schumacher continued to hound Senna as they completed another lap and set off for the seventh time towards Tamburello, a long fast left-hander. At 193 mph Senna's Williams failed to follow the line of the bend, veered right and less than two seconds later ran into the concrete wall lining the outside of the corner. The right-front wheel was torn off, a jagged piece of the suspension penetrating Senna's crash helmet. Professor Watkins, ready for action as always in the emergency response vehicle, was quickly on the scene. There was not a broken bone in Senna's body but one look at the head injury told 'The Prof' that his friend would not survive.

ADRIAN NEWEY

Having active suspension banned was a big setback to our 1994 programme. I have to admit that in designing the 1994 car I underestimated how important it was going to be to get a very broad ride-height map again. I think, having been away from passive cars for longer than anyone else, I disadvantaged us slightly. So when the FW16 first came out it was too ride-height sensitive, which made it very tricky to drive, even for someone of Ayrton's huge talent. It was very difficult to handle over a race distance.

We were hugely privileged to have Ayrton driving the car. He was a fantastic guy. But we were to have a disastrous start to the 1994 season. We took the car to Nogaro in France for a test with Damon. Nogaro is quite bumpy and this was the first time I had been able to go out and watch the car. It just looked horrific. It was clear that we needed some fairly major surgery. I came to the conclusion that the side pods were too long. If you're tempted to run the front low, which you always want to do with a racing car, it would stall the whole underside of the car and become inconsistent. So we started working on much shorter side pods.

In the meantime, of course, we went to Imola, which was a horrible weekend. On the Friday Rubens had a big accident, and this happened just as I was walking into the circuit. I was on the outside and saw this car going along the catch fencing on its side. And then Roland had a front wing come off his car during practice and, in my opinion from what I was able to ascertain, that could have been a cause of Roland's accident the following day.

That accident hugely affected Ayrton; he knew Roland quite well. At the same time Ayrton had got tangled up in the first corner in Japan and he had then spent the rest of the race watching from the marshals' post. He was absolutely positive that Schumacher's car was running traction control. So, you had this situation where Ayrton was hugely upset by Roland's accident, he knew our car was very difficult to drive and he was convinced that Schumacher's team were cheating. He was late getting changed for the race and I had that conversation with him in the back of the truck, just before the parade lap for the start of the race.

He was hugely determined to win that one. I don't think we'll ever know what happened. The popular belief was that the car understeered off the road. It didn't; it oversteered off the road. That is clear from the data accumulated afterwards and from the onboard camera from Schumacher's car. You can see the rear of Ayrton's car step out, and then it goes off to the right. If you look through what we could find from what was left of the data recorder, Ayrton went to half throttle at the same time as the steering torque reduced, but did not go to zero. That would be consistent with the rear stepping out: in other words, lift off the throttle and reduce your steering torque. After that he comes off the throttle and gets hard on the brake. The steering torque falls further. I think at that point Ayrton realised he wasn't going to hold it and he went into minimising the accident. So it doesn't appear to be consistent with a steering-column failure. There's no doubt the steering column broke, and there's no doubt it had fatigue marks in it. It was badly designed. But I don't believe it caused that accident.

My personal belief is that he probably had a right-rear slow puncture from the debris on the start line. That would be consistent with everything. You can also see that on the second lap [on which the accident occurred after the restart] he bottomed far harder than the previous lap. Considering his lines were the same both times and the tyre pressures should have been higher on the second lap, he should have bottomed less. But he didn't. That would be consistent with a slow puncture on the right rear, but the tyre was destroyed, so we couldn't tell.

It was without doubt the darkest moment of my motor-racing career. And I think both Patrick and I separately asked ourselves if this is what we wanted to be doing. It was a horrible time.

PROFESSOR SIDNEY WATKINS

When Roland had his accident, Ayrton was beside himself. He had not been close to death at a circuit before. The last tragedy we'd had at a race meeting in Formula 1 had been in Montreal in 1982 when Ricardo Paletti was killed at the start of the race, before Senna's career had reached Grand Prix level. Although he was totally aware of and accepted the dangers, we'd had a long run without a fatality. So many accidents in the past twelve years, so many serious injuries, but nobody irrevocably lost. I had got to know Ayrton very well over the years. He broke down and cried on my shoulder after Roland's accident.

PATRICK HEAD

Ayrton moved to us at a time when we had been very successful: we'd won the constructors' championship in 1991, the drivers' and constructors' in 1992 and 1993. We started 1994 with a car that was quite peaky, quite difficult to drive. Ayrton was a very powerful personality and quite broody. He projected his unhappiness with the way things were going to the whole team. Before Imola we'd done a test at Jerez, where we'd made a significant improvement. We went to Imola thinking we were going to get on top of it. Ayrton was quite determined to win that race.

Barrichello was a young Brazilian – not an acolyte but he certainly saw Ayrton as his mentor. Whether Ayrton saw it that way, I don't know, but that accident certainly affected Ayrton. Then Ratzenberger's death on Saturday hit him very badly.

There were problems with cracking on the side walls of the tyres. It put Goodyear in a very difficult position. They hadn't had a tyre fail, but quite clearly there was movement going on in the tyre. Ayrton would have been well aware of what had happened in 1987 [when Piquet crashed at Tamburello due to a tyre problem]. Ayrton wasn't a stupid guy, quite the opposite. He would have realised the possible consequences of a tyre failure in Tamburello. He was very worried about that and had a lot of meetings with Goodyear. It was a very tense race meeting, I mean, massively tense.

The biggest pressure was winning the Grand Prix and getting his points tally off the ground against this young upstart. He also had some personal problems, which were causing him a lot of anguish.

Looking back at what happened on race day, it was a weird sequence of events. Somebody ran into the back of JJ Lehto on the grid; there was carbon fibre and stuff all over the place. There were several laps under the safety car coming through all this debris on the start/finish line. I think we said to Ayrton on the radio, 'Stick to the right; all the carbon fibre is on the left.' But we never talked to him; we never asked, 'Is everything okay?' He never said a word to us over the radio. Not a word. Total silence.

So you think now, *Why didn't we have a chat?* It was not an unfriendly relationship but it was always tense with Ayrton. We could quite clearly see how stunning he was, but we never developed a human relationship with him as a driver. There was never any intention not to be friendly with him, but it was always a very tense atmosphere, particularly with his first two races not having produced any points.

Then there was the accident. It all happened so quickly. I don't think we necessarily saw those dreadful pictures of the car. You never saw it hitting the wall. It went in off to the side and then came back in. We never saw the severity of the impact.

I don't want to name names but an official came into our garage and told us that Ayrton was okay: he'd cut his arm and might be out for a race, but he would certainly be back after that. I'm not sure that we believed it but that's what we were being told by the FIA. Then Charlie Whiting [race director] came to see us and said the car had been brought back to one of the lock-up garages. He asked if I wanted to go and have a look at it. I said that I did. I could see the steering wheel was missing and that the steering column had broken. The right side of the chassis had caved in, so the front wheel had come up and pushed the chassis down into the area where the steering wheel was. It didn't surprise me the steering wheel was broken off the column. I think we thought the power steering might have had a failure, so we told Damon to drive the rest of the race without power steering.

We never thought – and to this day it's not really proven either way – there had been a mechanical failure in the steering column itself. But looking back I have to ask, How did we ever start Damon in that car half an hour, or whatever it was, after that accident? At the time of course we were being told that Ayrton was okay.

After the event you anguish over it. We are involved in an activity which is thoroughly dangerous. If you don't realise that people can get killed in racing cars, then you're a fool. People say racing cars are safe now. That's nonsense. They can never be completely safe. They have open cockpits. The Tom Pryce type of accident can happen at any time.[2] Open-cockpit cars are dangerous. Motor racing is dangerous. I considered retirement afterwards. I considered stopping. Then I thought to myself, *Well, Patrick, if you'd been involved in contributing to this failure in any way then, if you carry on, at least that knowledge might help make it sure it doesn't happen to another driver*, sort of amortised that in my mind, but it was a horrible event. It was obviously dreadful for Ayrton's family and it was very tough for the team.

---

2. During the 1977 South Africa Grand Prix the Welshman Tom Pryce struck a marshal running across the track. The accident happened just beyond a blind brow taken at 170 mph. Pryce was killed instantly when a fire extinguisher the marshal was carrying struck him on the head.

FRANK WILLIAMS

The thing that really hurt – apart from the obvious – was that we had so little time with Ayrton. We would probably have won the championship four years running. In 1994 it was pretty obvious there was some cheating going on and it took us a while to get our car sorted because it was very difficult at the start. But then it got sorted and dear old Damon did a great job with it.

But Ayrton in that car would have beaten Michael. By the second of the two races that he drove for us, he had worked out that the Benetton was cheating. He said, 'There is no question those cars are cheating.' Ayrton had a very strong opinion on this but no charges were ever brought against Benetton despite an investigation. I'm convinced that before he left the line at Imola Ayrton said to himself, *There is no way, before my maker, that he will beat me today.*

Patrick in particular had a lot to put up with after that: he was always being attacked in the press by statements that were not only very unfair but also very untrue. We were fighting for the championship and you don't think whether it's fair or not or that it shouldn't be happening to us. You don't think like that at the time. You want to get to understand what happened. The lawyers want to make a name for themselves. It's an international court. With the racing and the championship going on, after a certain point we didn't spend too much time wringing our hands. But certainly for me and for Patrick it was quite an emotional shock. I've always said that once every ten years or so a genius turns up. There was Michael; before that it was Ayrton; right now it's Lewis, and so on. The trick is to think who the next one might be. But it was a very difficult time.

DICKIE STANFORD

At the time the top drivers were Prost, Senna and Mansell. You wanted one of them in your team. I had met Ayrton a couple of times before and it's fair to say there were big expectations when he came to

Williams. Prost had retired, Nigel was racing in the United States and the feeling was that we'd finally got Ayrton Senna. We were going to wipe the board and repeat what we had done with Prost the year before.

There were new aero tweaks on that car but I'm not sure that we understood them straight away. We knew that it was a quick car, but we also knew we weren't getting the best out of it when we started the year.

I was in the pits at Imola. After the restart I was standing in the garage when someone said Ayrton had gone off. You didn't realise how big a shunt it was until the race was stopped; then you knew it had to be pretty bad. We had a radio message saying, 'Just concentrate on what you're doing. Don't listen to anybody else. No one knows what's going on; just concentrate on the job in hand.'

I remember being on the grid with Damon and his engineers, and it was a matter of simply focusing on that. The only thing we knew was that there had been a big shunt and we thought Ayrton was being taken to the medical centre. Straight after the race we learned that the car had been taken down to one of the garages near the entrance to the paddock. I was told to go down there with the police and make sure no one touched the car. The police were looking in the car; it wasn't covered over. At one stage I was handed Ayrton's crash helmet. I remember looking at the helmet and thinking, *This is bigger than they're telling us.* A minute later the helmet was taken off me and put back in the seat. But I had seen enough to know things were not looking good.

Frank stayed on and we kept back about four mechanics so that the rest of the team could go off to the airport and just get out of there. Once the police were satisfied, the garage was sealed. I went back to the motorhome. Frank told me that Ayrton was dead. He said Ayrton had died after the accident, but no one had been told. This was probably about two hours after the race.

We finished what we were doing. We got the trucks away and five or six of us went back to Frank's hotel, stayed the night and flew back with Frank in the morning in his plane. Not a lot was said. It was a difficult thing to take in. It was a really bad time for everyone here. It was the first fatality I had been associated with. I've been around a long time and seen accidents; I know this sort of thing can happen. But this was still a big shock.

VIRGINIA WILLIAMS

Frank and Ayrton had an extraordinary relationship. It was like a father and son. Ron [Dennis] probably wouldn't like to hear this, but Ayrton always used to come and have dinner with us – I think even before he was at McLaren, when he was still at Lotus. That's when the relationship with Frank started. He and Frank would have *very* long conversations after races, even during the McLaren time. I always knew when Frank was talking to Ayrton because Frank would be silent. I'd go in, and he'd just shake his head so I knew he was talking, and I'd realise it was Ayrton. There would be these very long silences with both of them.

Ayrton came to Battle House. We were going out for dinner and Ayrton was driving. I can remember thinking, *Oh, this'll be interesting.* I think he had a Mercedes. We got in the car and we drove to a restaurant which was about twenty minutes away. I don't think I've ever been with anyone on the road who drove as slowly as that. I thought we were never going to get there. Having been used to Frank, I was understandably quite nervous about being driven to dinner by Ayrton Senna, but it was like being driven by a ninety-year-old woman. I even said to Frank, 'Were you expecting to be driven so slowly?' He said no.

When Ayrton signed, Frank was thrilled. We were all really thrilled and *very* excited. We were riding for a fall because I think we thought, and everyone else thought, that Ayrton and Williams and Renault would be the golden combination and no one would get near him.

I was at Boxford House and I had been watching the race on television. I turned the television off. I don't know why I turned the television off, but I think they were panning in a bit, but I didn't think he was dead at that point; I just didn't want to be watching it.

Iain Cunningham, who was helping look after Frank, phoned me from the track and said that Frank wanted me to know that it was very bad. I asked how bad, and he said *very* bad. I was sitting there by myself and I could see two people walking down the drive. I remember thinking, *Who on earth is coming because this is the last thing we need?* I went to the door just to pretend that everything was normal, and one of the men said to me, 'Can you tell us your husband's reaction to the death of Ayrton?' This was within an hour or two hours of the accident. I don't think I responded.

It was a horrible time for Williams. People laid masses of flowers at the factory. Frank flew the flag at half mast and I remember going up there and thinking that I'd never wanted to see the flag flying at half mast. But everyone had been lulled into a false sense of security with Formula 1.

It was as bad for everyone. Patrick had always said that he never wanted anyone to die in one of his racing cars. I think for Frank losing Piers was very difficult because he was a very good friend. But at that time there was a one in ten chance that would happen, and we lived with it. They were like fighter pilots: some weren't going to come back. It was different in 1994, which in some ways made the impact of Ayrton's death even worse. Frank never got his time with Ayrton, which is sad.

IAIN CUNNINGHAM

I actually learned that Ayrton had died when I was at the airport. I was very conscious as I watched the McLaren people arrive at the airport that it was much worse for them than it was for us. Ayrton had driven for McLaren for six years and won championships and races. We had done nothing with him. It might have been easier for us if Ayrton had done a season with us, but we had achieved absolutely nothing and lost all. That made it worse for Frank, much worse. Having finally got Ayrton on board, he hadn't been able to give him anything. And as we believed at the time and now know for certain, Frank could have given Ayrton so much. They could have achieved a great deal together.

Everyone at Didcot was devastated. Ayrton had come round a couple of times. He'd said, 'Look, we're having a really tough time but we are going to get better because there is plenty of potential.' He was so upbeat and it gave everyone a tremendous lift. I took him round the factory the first time and he had photographs taken with everyone. And I mean everyone. There was an old boy called George who swept the floors. As Ayrton went by, he spotted George sweeping up behind a milling machine. 'What about him?' he asked. George got his photo. All of that made it so much harder for everyone to take, particularly when the photos arrived about a week after the accident.

There was no emotion from Frank at the time but I remember speaking to Robin [Kinnell] about a week later and asking how Frank had been. Robin said Frank did cry on the flight back from Imola. That was the only time I heard of any real emotion. I knew how much Ayrton meant to Frank. I remember at the time of the contract Frank had no real interest in the terms and conditions; just sign it and get it sorted. Frank even took an interest in Ayrton's overalls and sent different Nacional [Senna's sponsor] badges for him to look at. I'd never known Frank take such an interest in a driver's welfare before. It was a very genuine friendship and there is no doubt that Ayrton looked up to Frank.

It was so difficult to know what to say to Frank afterwards. I went up to him and said, 'I'm so sorry.' He said he had been through this before in his life. But this was probably the worst. There were pictures taken of Frank as he sat along with Ayrton's coffin in São Paulo. You could see that he was extremely distraught. I thought, *If he manages to survive this, I will be amazed*. But he did.

IAN ANDERSON

I had been on the test just before Imola with Senna, doing a lot to the car. I had obviously been aware of Ayrton, but this was when I met him for the first time. It wasn't long after that when the accident happened. We'd had accidents before, but never something like that where a driver got killed. Everyone was shell-shocked. 'Good Lord, how could that possibly happen?' 'Why did it happen?' In the background Roland Ratzenberger had been killed and Rubens Barrichello had had a serious accident, but this hardly got mentioned because Ayrton Senna was a superstar and in the public eye all the time.

PETER WINDSOR

I was thinking about coming back to Europe to do a Formula 1 team with Tetsu Ikuzawa. I was watching the race on the Eurosport feed at my gym. Unlike BBC TV, they stayed on Ayrton's car for about five minutes. I rang Ginny not long after the accident and asked if everything was okay, because the pictures did not look good. I know that Frank has never allowed emotion to come into any of his racing decisions – ever. He had recovered surprisingly quickly from Piers Courage's accident in a way that I or you would never recover from an accident like that. And he would recover in the same way from the Ayrton accident.

PETE FOSTEKEW

When we saw the accident on television, our first reaction was that something had broken. So your next reaction is to question whether you've done something wrong. We drew into ourselves rather than think about Frank or Patrick or anyone else. And when the talk about the steering column came up, I knew that definitely wasn't true. That's not the standard we work at.

BERNIE GOBLE

I watched the Imola race on television as usual. They said he'd been hurt and flown to hospital. That was all we knew. When we heard later that night that he had died, it was a shock, a big shock. You had seen other drivers crash and thought they would have been killed, and yet they just walked away. So the first instinct with Ayrton was that he had been concussed, nothing more than that.

ALAN CHALLIS

I was fortunate to be at the test Ayrton did at Donington in 1983. Frank was coming to run that test and he was late getting there. So I rang Patrick and said, 'What do we do?' and typically Patrick said, 'Just get on with it.' So I got Ayrton out and ten laps later I rang Patrick again and said, 'This bloke's a bit quick.' When he asked what I meant, I told him the lap times, which were quicker than Keke had gone, and Ayrton had done these times very early in the test.

I wasn't racing in 1994. I was watching it on television – as I still do with every race now, even though I have retired. I knew it was a big one. Obviously I knew the corner and I knew that to go in there at that sort of speed was not good, particularly when he didn't jump out afterwards. The fact that he didn't move was worrying.

It was very hard to take, particularly when you read all these stories about the car failing. Patrick went into his shell around that time. But you could see the car had bottomed quite badly and had stepped out of line. I think Ayrton had been quite affected by what had happened the day before. When I was a lot younger, it was a regular occurrence for drivers to be killed, but for young drivers in 1994 it must have been very very difficult to take on board.

STEVE FOWLER

I was watching the race on television and I just had a horrible feeling. I still have the video, as I videoed them all until that point. I didn't video them after that. I keep saying I should destroy Imola 1994, but I've kept it. I've never looked at it since. There was something not right about the picture of him sitting in the car. I felt that things weren't going to be good.

BRIAN O'ROURKE

There had been a test a couple of years before at Imola. Patrese had gone off big time. I had a video provided by the circuit and I used it during lectures on impact tests to show the reality of a big accident. Riccardo went off at Tamburello. He spun through 360 degrees, but having said that, he hit that wall. The thing that really stuck in my mind about that accident was that he actually split his helmet. At first we couldn't work out how that had happened but it turned out that there had been enough elasticity in the belts that, when the car hit the wall, his head went over and actually slapped the concrete, just enough to damage his helmet. He finished up a long way down the track. He was a little concussed. This was a week before the race and yet he went back and stuck it on pole, which confirmed my suspicions about racing drivers!

Ayrton was clearly unconscious and I thought, *Oh my God, he's hit that wall.* When talking to groups of students or engineering societies about crash testing, I was always keen to say, 'Look, we've done all this work, and cars are very much better than they were before 1985, but you can't argue with the laws of physics and statistics. These are open-wheel open-cockpit cars, and at some point or other things might happen that won't give you the result you have become used to, such as seeing a driver climb out and run back to the pits.' I was always aware of that but, if the survival cell was intact, then the driver had a chance.

JOHN RUSSELL

For every man in the team, and most people in Formula 1, 1994 was a hard year. Working alongside Ayrton was an enormous privilege which I'm glad I had. I was running Damon's car, and to be so close to the events at Imola was shocking and very difficult. But in a way it's made me a richer person. We didn't know what had gone wrong, so we turned off the power steering on Damon's car as we were unsure whether that may have contributed to Senna's accident. Damon drove a race not knowing the outcome of Ayrton's injuries even though it obviously looked very serious.

DAMON HILL

In the team – and I understood this – I was always the understudy, and I didn't have a problem with that, given the fact that I was thirty-three when I got the opportunity. I was really grateful to be there. Ayrton was very different to Alain Prost. He needed to win and he was fighting with a car that was difficult to drive in the sense that racing cars can sometimes be difficult to drive. It wasn't a beautiful experience to drive that car. It got better as the year went on.

The 1994 car was classic Adrian Newey – no knuckles left. You had scabs on the knuckles from being scrunched up in there. It wasn't quite set up right, having gone back to passive suspension, so it was tricky to drive. I now know what we should have been doing, which is the annoying, teasing thing in that you only learn later. Ayrton was new to the team, so he was asking me, 'Is this normal?' and I'm saying, 'Well, I'm relatively new here as well. I was hoping you'd be able to tell us!'

After Imola everyone's life in Formula 1 changed. There's no question that it was a defining moment for the team and led to the beginning of a new phase in the sport – the Schumacher phase. It was also a marker between teams like Williams and what they believe the sport should be about, and what other teams believe it should be about. I don't think Williams are a win-at-all-costs team. How the team conducted itself through that phase, and went on to carry on the fight, was typical of Williams and their character.

TWENTY-SEVEN
Moving On

The Grand Prix had been restarted at Imola, but as the terrible truth about Ayrton Senna emerged most people in F1 wanted to be done with the weekend. Damon Hill had completed the outstanding fifty-eight laps and finished sixth. It may as well have been sixty-sixth for all anyone cared at that moment. The next race would be held as surely as night follows day. Frank and Damon had been to Ayrton's funeral in São Paulo and witnessed what had effectively been a day of Brazilian national mourning; that sadness pervaded Monte Carlo two weeks later. Hill would be the sole Williams representative of a team in need of an uplifting result but tangled with Hakkinen's McLaren at the first corner, the Williams coming to a halt a few seconds later with broken suspension in Casino Square. The walk back down the hill to the pits seemed one of the longest and loneliest of Hill's life.

In eighteen months Hill had gone from test driver to carrying the success of the entire team on his shoulders. Plans were in hand to find a replacement for Senna, an impossible task at the best of times and all but hopeless with the season under way. The FIA inadvertently helped Frank and Patrick come to a decision by introducing an immediate series of technical changes to reduce performance. Paradoxically, the slashing of downforce would make the cars – and the Williams in particular – even more nervous than before, so it seemed logical to have someone who knew the team and was familiar with the FW16. David Coulthard, Hill's replacement as test driver, was the obvious choice.

Meanwhile, Renault, unconvinced that Hill could lead the team, were making noises about persuading Mansell to return from the US, where, having brilliantly won the 1993 Champ Car title, Nigel had seemingly fallen out of love with just about everyone and everything connected with this American series. Hill produced a timely riposte by scoring a brilliant win in Spain, where Coulthard's promising debut was ended prematurely by electrical trouble. David then scored his first points in Canada but had to give way to Mansell for the French Grand Prix. It was a brief return, Nigel showing great form by joining Hill on the front row but then doing precious little else before retiring. Damon finished second to Schumacher. It was the Benetton driver's seventh victory, making the championship almost a formality.

Damon wanted to win the British Grand Prix at Silverstone above all others and produced another stunning qualifying lap to take his second pole in succession. With Schumacher joining the Williams on the front row, all seemed set for a tense afternoon.

Schumacher was so keen to get going that he shot ahead of Hill at the start of the parade lap. Overtaking at this stage was forbidden, and when Schumacher, having dropped back, did it again, Williams were sure a penalty would be imposed. Unfortunately, the officials were not well versed in their own rules and failed to send the Benetton to the back of the grid. Once realisation dawned, they had no option but to issue a five-second penalty. This should have been carried out in the pits, and when the Benetton failed to appear in the pit lane, officials showed Schumacher the black flag, which he promptly ignored, a crime more heinous than his original sin. Confusion reigned, and by the time Schumacher took his penalty in the pits the race belonged to Hill. It was an emotional moment for Damon as he stood on the podium and collected a trophy which had eluded his father seventeen times.

A special meeting of the FIA World Council fined Schumacher $500,000, disqualified him from second place at Silverstone and suspended the German for two races. Before the ban took effect, he won in Hungary but was excluded on a technicality from another victory in Belgium, handing that win to Hill. By the time Schumacher returned from his enforced absence, Hill had won both races and the Benetton driver's lead had shrunk from twenty-one points to just one with three races to go. Schumacher then beat Hill at Jerez, extending his lead to five points as the scene shifted to Japan.

It was wet at Suzuka on Sunday 6 November but that did not stop Schumacher and Hill storming away into a race of their own. The rest of the field caught up when the safety car was deployed after eight laps due to the appalling conditions, and then not long after the restart the race was stopped when a car spun off and broke the leg of a marshal attending to another stricken car. When the race finally got going again, it had been decreed that the result would be decided on aggregate times from the two parts. Hill made one more stop whereas Schumacher, gambling wrongly that the race would be stopped after three-quarters distance, was locked into stopping twice more but had the benefit of fresh tyres for his final sprint. Schumacher had 6.8 seconds in hand, his lead when the race had been stopped, meaning he would not have to overtake Hill in order to win, whereas Hill had to push himself to the limit in truly atrocious conditions against an unseen rival. The Williams did not handle as well as the Benetton and had the added handicap of having to race the full distance on the same wet-weather tyre, Hill's mechanics having been unable to remove the right-rear wheel during his pit stop.

Schumacher's aggregate lead as they went into the last lap was 2.4 seconds. If Hill failed to win this race, his championship was as good as over. If he left the road, his reputation would never recover. Damon drove the lap of his life, teetering on the edge of adhesion for the entire 3.6 miles. He completed it, still first on the road, but the result would not be known until Schumacher crossed the line. Everyone held their breath as the computer did its work. Finally the result came – Hill was 3.3 seconds faster on the final lap and had won. He was still in the championship with a shout at the final round in Adelaide.

The first thirty-four laps of the Australian Grand Prix were the best of the season. Once again Schumacher and Hill were in a league of their own, the Williams glued to the gearbox of the Benetton. By coincidence, both made their pit stops on the same lap, rejoining to continue their incredibly tense battle. As the race approached half-distance, Hill was briefly detained by a slower car, Schumacher taking the opportunity to open up a lead. Schumacher then ran wide at the exit of a corner and brushed the wall. Hill did not witness the impact. Rounding the corner, Damon saw the Benetton rejoining the track and assumed Michael was recovering from no more than a moment on the grass. Seizing what he figured would be his one and only chance, Hill dived down the inside for the corner that followed almost immediately. Schumacher turned towards the right-hander. The two cars collided, the Benetton tipping on to two wheels before crashing back on to the track, its race over. Hill continued to the pits knowing that he now needed just two points to win the title, but he could see that his left-front suspension was bent. A quick check by the mechanics confirmed his worst fears: his race was over too. Michael Schumacher had become 1994 world champion while standing by the side of the track.

PATRICK HEAD

I have to say Damon was phenomenal through the whole thing. He knew the responsibility of leading the team rested on his shoulders. We had a very odd Grand Prix at Monaco. It was a very, very difficult race. I'd say we were very much on auto; we were still in shock.

In Japan Damon produced a phenomenal drive. Then he continued in Australia, where he drove out of his skin. Damon should never have any need to think, *Was I good?* He was brilliant. To beat Schumacher in a straight race in the wet at Suzuka was exceptional. In Australia Michael was recovering from a mistake when he saw Damon coming. He knew what he had done to his car and he drove straight into Damon. Immensely cynical. Damon knows it; I know it; Michael knows it. Having said that, it would have felt uncomfortable if we'd won the championship, although of course Damon would have happily accepted it. He'd done a great job.

SHERIDAN THYNNE

The first thing I actually did after Ayrton's accident was to talk to Damon because I thought how Damon handled himself in the coming weeks would be very important. I gave Damon a number of bits of advice, all of which he disregarded. The most important one was his habit of saying to journalists, 'I'm not happy about the way Frank and Patrick are treating me.' The first time he did it, I told him that it's not only ineffective but massively counter-productive. If he wasn't happy then do not discuss this at a race meeting but call Frank on Monday and arrange to come and see him in the evening and talk in private about it. You can say exactly what you like in private – but not at a race meeting. I was pissing up Niagara. He went on doing it for ever and that wasn't the right way to handle Frank and Patrick.

DAVID COULTHARD

There were mixed emotions when I got the drive with Williams. Yes, it was a brilliant opportunity but it had come under tragic circumstances. But when you're young, when people are killed around you – unless it's family members – then … With the greatest respect to Roland and with the greatest respect to Ayrton, I didn't know them personally. I was a test driver teammate to Ayrton and hung on every word he said. It was an incredible education for me. And then he was gone. And suddenly the opportunity was there for me to start.

For Damon's brief period on his journey to the world championship, he was always under immense pressure because he was the next big Brit after Nigel. But he also had come in after what had happened to Ayrton. I think he did a fantastic job, all things considered.

I don't think he is given the credit for handling all that. I have a lot more respect for him now than I ever did at the time because then he was someone I had to beat.

DAMON HILL

No doubt Suzuka was one of my best drives. It was an all-or-nothing race of the kind that I never again experienced. I didn't know they hadn't been able to change the tyre. I don't seem to remember them saying anything to me. In any case, what could I have done about it?

Because the race got split up, I had this cushion and I had to work out how to measure it out. It got to the point where there was no turning back. I never drove like that again. I was asked if I was aware that my reputation was on the line. Once you start thinking like that, you shouldn't be there anyway. In a way, it's a relief to be in that situation. You've made it like this. There's nothing else that matters except beating that guy. It's like boiling your whole life down to one task and throwing everything you've got, everything you've learnt. Everything you want to achieve is in this one thing. It's simple.

If you talk about climbing peaks, that was *the* peak for me. And it continued. When we got to Adelaide, it was like we just carried on the same race. It was amazing! You can't artificially induce that kind of thing. You get sucked up in it; everyone gets sucked up in it. You experience these incredible changes in performance and levels because you simply have to pull yourself up by the bootstraps and just go higher, higher, higher. It was intense and it was enmeshed with what happened to Ayrton; you couldn't disconnect it. There was a lot of emotion. It was a very special experience, pure essence of sport, a titanic battle for something; it wasn't just the race.

Afterwards, the team were pretty sick they didn't win. There was a little bit of anger as well because it was controversial. But most of those guys had been through this kind of thing before; they knew that's motor racing.

JOHN RUSSELL

The period after Imola was when the team got back on its feet, developed the car and ended up winning the constructors' championship. That nail-biter at the end of the year with Damon and Michael still stands out in my memory. To fight back from adversity is everything this team and Frank and Patrick are about.

Spain was a victory which we were handed as Michael had a technical problem, but you have to keep in mind what Damon had been through. We turned up at Monaco and the team was, psychologically, not damaged, but certainly suppressed. We still didn't have a concrete answer as to what had happened. We had a lot of pressure in Barcelona that year. After the last pit stop, which went very smoothly, Patrick wandered out to the pit wall and said to Ian Harrison, team manager then, and to me, 'Did all the fuel go in the car?' Ian and I looked at each other and said, 'Yes.' He said, 'It seemed a very quick stop. Are you sure?' All Damon had to do was keep going to win the race. It made us nervous, so we checked figures, checked everything and it was all there. But Patrick kept going on and on about this. Ian eventually said, 'Look, Patrick, it's not in the bloody rig, it's not on the floor, so it's in the bloody car.' Patrick was satisfied with that and wandered off.

DICKIE STANFORD

Massive pressure for Damon but also for everyone else on the race team. Our world had just been turned upside down. For me, with all these stories doing the rounds about the steering column and so on, the main thing was motivating the mechanics and reassuring them that they were doing a good job. 'Don't read the newspapers; don't listen to what people say.' I think we pulled together very well as a team, and that got us through the season.

Suzuka was probably one of Damon's best races. We couldn't get the right-rear wheel nut off during the one pit stop that we did. Karl Gaden tried to undo the nut, couldn't, and made the instant decision to nail the wheel nut back on. He knew we needed to be quick, and when he saw all the other wheels back on, he flicked the gun the other way and tightened it up. That was a really good race from Damon. By then he had really matured. We could see it. He had taken over from Ayrton and was pushed into the limelight. Everybody was waiting for him to fall over, so that they could turn round to Frank and say, 'Well, you should have got a decent number-one driver,' but he took the fight to Schumacher, all the way to that controversial race in Adelaide.

We had known that if we could keep Michael under pressure at that particular time he would make mistakes. We'd seen it in the past. He was on the ragged edge; he was trying to get away from Damon. And Damon was trying to stick with him. When Damon came into the pits after the collision, we could see it was going to need a wishbone change. How long was that going to take? On that car it was buried inside the monocoque; you would have to go inside to undo the bolts. We would lose three or four laps, maybe more. It was over.

JOHN SUTTON

The team was solid, but all the people were very sensitive and had of course feelings about the horror and the tragedy of the death of a driver, who after all, even though they're on a pedestal and paid loads, is a teammate and a colleague. Ayrton had come to see us, to tell us the car wasn't a dog, and it was going to be all right, and we were going the right way with some of the developments we'd been testing. He came and told us that after Brazil, when he'd spun off trying to stay ahead of Schumacher. So we were right with him, working hard to get the car right. And then he is gone.

It was also very unpleasant going through the year because of all the dodgy-looking things that were happening on the track with Benetton. Racing needle is fine, but Schumacher shaping up to do things like knock his main opponent off the road at the last race and so on; that wasn't good.

TWENTY-EIGHT
Stress and Success

Almost a year after the Ayrton Senna tragedy the Italian investigating magistrate Maurizio Passarini announced that he would need at least another six months before issuing a report on the findings of an investigative committee. Passarini made his announcement a few days before the 1995 San Marino Grand Prix, drawing more attention to an already poignant weekend for Formula 1 and Williams-Renault in particular. The media turned out in force at Imola, although what they expected to hear and see was unclear. The Williams team remained tight-lipped and typically focused on winning the race. The one tribute took place on Saturday evening, long after most people had left the circuit. Team personnel walked to the deserted Tamburello and paid their quiet respects. The fence was hung with numerous floral tributes and messages from fans.

After such a difficult 1994, Williams were looking forward to getting down to work with the latest car, the FW17. Coulthard was back on board despite Mansell having returned to win in Adelaide, giving the team some consolation after Hill's disappointment. Mansell wanted to do another season but Frank stuck with Coulthard, defeating McLaren in a legal tug of war over the Scotsman's services.

Hill led the first race of 1995 in Brazil until suspension failure intervened. Damon made amends in Argentina by giving Schumacher and

Benetton a hiding, setting himself up nicely for Imola. On a damp but drying track Hill bided his time until the anticipated change from wet-weather tyres to slicks was made. Lying third, he forced a mistake from Schumacher, who spun off and crashed. When leader Gerhard Berger made a pit stop in his Ferrari, Hill was through to another win to become leader of the world championship for the first time in his career. It went wrong in Spain, where Schumacher won and Hill fell back to fourth with hydraulic trouble on the last lap. Roles were reversed during Monaco qualifying with Hill taking a brilliant pole position. According to Hill, however, during the race the differential made the Williams only good enough for second place, Schumacher seizing his opportunity with another win.

Then Williams began to fade. Hill showed the pressure when he drove into the back of Schumacher while trying to regain the lead following a pit stop at Silverstone. Then he spun out of the German Grand Prix – due, he claimed, to a problem with the car – and Coulthard failed to stop Schumacher from winning. Patrick and Frank were less than impressed as the team slipped to third in the constructors' championship and Damon languished twenty-one points behind his arch-rival. He regained some ground by leading all the way to win in Hungary, only to fall back again when, according to Hill, Schumacher used ruthless tactics to win in Belgium. Coulthard had retired from the lead with a broken oil pipe caused by a thump from behind at the first corner, and had no more luck in Italy with a rare wheel-bearing failure. Damon, meanwhile, misjudged his braking and again went into the back of Schumacher as they disputed second place. Coulthard finally broke his duck with a convincing win in Portugal which took points away from Schumacher as the Benetton came home second.

Hill's last chance to stay in touch was lost during a miserable race at the Nürburgring, as Schumacher won and made his second successive title a formality: Damon left the road more than once and eventually spun off for good. The misery continued in Japan, where both drivers fell off the slippery track, ensuring Williams missed the constructors' championship for the first time in four years. However, an apparently reinvigorated Damon Hill turned up in Adelaide for the last race of 1995 and led from start to finish.

Frank, meanwhile, was busy thinking ahead. A test for Jacques Villeneuve at Silverstone in August had been impressive enough to have Frank sign the IndyCar champion for 1996. With Hill agreeing terms not long after, Coulthard was free to go to McLaren. But, looking further ahead, Frank had been sufficiently concerned by Hill's inconsistency to contact Heinz-Harald Frentzen about 1997. This was not the first time the two had spoken: Frank had enquired about the German's availability in the immediate aftermath of Senna's accident. Frentzen thanked Frank for his interest but said he was contracted to Sauber and would remain with the Swiss team.

When the 1996 season got under way it was immediately apparent that Hill's greatest threat would come from within his own team as Villeneuve took pole for his first Grand Prix and then led it until a leaking oil pipe forced him to finish a circumspect second. Villeneuve won his first race in Germany after Hill had taken the first three. With Schumacher making a shaky start at Ferrari, Hill and Villeneuve were having it all their own way. Villeneuve's confidence grew with wins in Britain and Hungary. When Hill finished fifth in Belgium, four places behind Villeneuve, thanks to confusion over pit stops, his championship lead was down to thirteen points with four races remaining. And then he was told he would not be required in 1997. The British media, recalling the Mansell saga, sharpened their pens. Frank scarcely batted an eyelid.

Upset and confused by the turn of events, Hill knew that if he won the next race, the Italian Grand Prix, the championship would be his. An aggressive overtaking move at the start gave him a lead that looked completely secure until he unaccountably spun and then retired. In Portugal Villeneuve strengthened his last-minute challenge by forcing Hill into second place and winning. There were nine points between them going into the final round in Japan, with Hill favourite – on paper, at least. The Williams pair shared the front row. At the start Hill took off like a rocket, leaving Villeneuve trailing. The issue was settled when Villeneuve lost a wheel after thirty-six of fifty-two laps. Hill could have retired there and then but he wanted to savour the moment. His twenty-first Grand Prix victory would be one of the sweetest for Hill and the team after almost three years of turmoil and tragedy.

ADRIAN NEWEY

The FW17 was, generally speaking, a bit quicker than the Benetton. But we just didn't get it together. Damon had got himself into a war of words, played out through the tabloids, with Schumacher. He should have come out the winner after what Schumacher had done to him at the end of 1994, but he came out the loser. He wasn't the driver in 1995 that he had been in the previous year. David did a decent job but he was pretty inexperienced and kept making stupid mistakes. So 1995 was a very disappointing year because we had a car that was at least quick enough to win the championship. We did have a few reliability issues but we also had drivers who didn't make the most of the car.

If Nigel had been in the car for the whole of 1995, I believe he would have won the championship. When he made a few guest appearances in 1994 he showed great speed but not the fitness and stamina to carry it through. I'd certainly pushed through the winter of 1994 to have Nigel in the car alongside Damon, but Frank wouldn't have that for whatever reason, so we had David. I have nothing against David of course; he's a great guy. But he wasn't very experienced at that point and he wasn't going to win the championship in 1995, whereas Nigel could have done. It also started to become apparent that there was a loophole in the regulations which, if explored, gave a huge increase in downforce, a big number that was worth over a second a lap. But to fully exploit that we needed a narrow gearbox. Patrick still wasn't happy with the longitudinal design, so he did a bit of a fudge-up by putting a step-up gear in the transverse gearbox. That took quite a while and didn't debut until Portugal. The car took a huge step forward in performance as a result. I was worried that we had showed our hand, but amazingly nobody copied it over the winter. So, that step-up gearbox, combined with a new diffuser and a few other developments, made the FW18 a very quick car for 1996. Damon got his head completely sorted out over the winter and came out absolutely fighting fit again.

I'd re-signed again and strengthened my contract's wording in terms of being involved with driver choice and all major policy decisions. If we were going to be battling with the FIA about things like active suspension being banned, I wanted to be involved in that. As I saw it, I knew I'd never be an equal partner with Frank and Patrick, but I felt I'd now earned the right to be involved with key decisions.

PATRICK HEAD

The FW17 was one of our better cars but we were operationally poor on the pit wall; Benetton and Michael were strategically much better than us in the races. They out-psyched us a couple of times during pit stops by doing short fills and seemingly pulling out a gap in the middle stint. There wasn't really a gap, but it demoralised Damon to see Michael look as if he was pulling away.

Damon turned up in 1996 a completely different man, completely self-assured and confident of his ability to beat Michael. You have to admire a sportsman who can turn failure into success by his own efforts more than somebody who is just naturally talented and blows everybody away. That's what Damon did. He turned a losing psychology of 1995 into a winning psychology of 1996. Damon's biggest problem in 1996 was Jacques, not Michael.

DAMON HILL

I was disappointed that I wasn't going to secure another season with the team through winning the championship, but again I had not got involved in anything to do with driver contracts for the following year because I just knew it was irrelevant. I assumed if I won the championship, that would be the best insurance I could have. It was a bit of a shock to realise that even if you win the championship it wouldn't be good enough to stay. I think I'd sown the seeds of my own downfall in 1995 because it was a poor year. At the end of the year it just fell apart. When I started racing in 1996, Frank asked, 'What have you done differently?' I'd just shed a skin and come back ready to go.

They don't understand drivers; that's the blind spot at Williams. They love drivers; they love the battle, the characters. Patrick loves seeing someone take his car by the scruff of the neck and wring every last drop. If it comes back and the wheels fall off and the engine blows up crossing the line, he's happy. That's their approach to it and not every driver is right for that.

Monaco is a hard weekend. It's full on, one extra day, a high-concentration event. I'd won pole position, got halfway through the race and the car stopped. We had testing the next day at Silverstone. I was bushed. I needed a break. I was driving the car at the test, thinking, *This is not good. I'm not into this at the moment.* Frank turned up and I said, 'I've got to go and recharge my batteries.' He said, 'Michael Schumacher will be pounding round Fiorano [Ferrari's test track] and we've got to keep going.' I thought, *You just don't get it, do you?* That epitomises Frank's approach. Somebody out there is doing more than us, so we've got to do more than them. Frank and Patrick are complicated but really positive people. If there's a difficulty, they will find a way to overcome it. That's their power.

I was part of Williams, if you include being a test driver, for seven years. So my Formula 1 career was more or less with Williams. Those guys were in my bloodstream. I'm not Italian; I didn't drive for Ferrari, but it might as well have been the same thing. To be a British driver, driving for Frank Williams and winning the championship, I think that's as strong a comparison as you're going to get to being an Italian driving for Ferrari.

DAVID COULTHARD

I remember Spa 1995. Someone had touched me at the first corner and the rear wing had come loose. They called me into the pits and of course I'm raring to get back into the race and I'm revving the nuts off the engine. The exhausts used to come out through the floor in those days. Patrick was right down behind the car, examining the wing, his hair getting singed by the exhaust. He gave the wing a bit of a shake before waving me out. The good old engineering eye: 'It'll hold! Send him!' It did stay on and you had a certain confidence knowing it was Patrick looking at it.

If you include the test team, I had a four-year period with Williams, a period when you're young and have a lot of time to spend at the factory, which means you get to know the guys. In many ways I knew the Williams guys better than at McLaren because by then I was into superstar mode – private flights, whizz in last minute, leave quickly, all the ridiculous stuff that you do.

I had a multi-year contract with Williams. When I became the race driver, they tried to impose that as a foundation for the race contract. My agents recognised that one couldn't become the other. When that was going through the Contract Recognition Board, Frank wasn't sure if he would be able to have me for the 1995 season, so he had to have someone serve me notice that he would be enforcing the contract.

We knew that at the airport someone was going to try and give us a letter. Tim – my agent – and I tried everything that we could to avoid this happening. I think it was Jamie, one of Frank's assistants, who eventually caught up with me. He wasn't getting on the flight to Brazil – it was the last GP at that time – but he got me at the door of the plane, threw an envelope at me and said, 'You've been served.' Then we had to go through the CRB. In the end they enforced the contract with Williams for 1995. My 1996 contract with McLaren was acknowledged at the end of 1994, so I knew that I was racing in 1995 for Williams and leaving at the end of the year. I remember seeing Patrick storming into

Frank's office, his neck red, after he had seen that IMG were challenging the contract. He said, 'You'll never drive for this team again!' And then he stormed out. He apologised later.

JACQUES VILLENEUVE

It was great to be with Williams because it was a team with a very impressive history and also at the time it was a very competitive team. I had won the Indy 500 and I was fighting for the IndyCar championship. In a way it felt like a natural progression. Maybe that was a young, stupid way to look at things because when you're young and things are going well, you always feel like you deserve it. That was only one small part of it.

On the other hand, I was so excited. Even on TV the cars looked fast. But going into a top team like that means you don't have any excuses. You have no choice but to perform, because you can't complain about the equipment. The first test was tough because I had just done a 500-mile race on an oval – very hot, and it wasn't a very good race either. Jump in a chopper, jump on a plane, land in the UK, go to the factory, have a seat made, go to bed and then test the next day. A bit of a hectic start.

The first race in Australia had a huge influence on the championship at the end of the day because it gave Damon a lot of confidence. The thing is, all through winter testing I had been quite a bit slower than Damon. I have never been faster during testing than my teammate – ever. It's only when the time comes and you have to do something special, that's when I've been able to pull something out of the hat. That's what happened when I got pole in Melbourne.

There was an oil tube that was connected in the wrong slot and got squashed beneath the floor of the car. It started leaking and that one little leak did the championship at the end of the day. Going into the last race, I was nine points behind. Quite a few races from the end I knew that I wasn't going to win the championship but I still wanted to make it hard for Damon. For race after race I kept on postponing his championship. It made it exciting. There was a very good respect between Damon and me. For me, Williams was the best team to start with.

DICKIE STANFORD

The 1996 car was quick from the start. I didn't think Jacques would be on the front row of the grid in Australia; I was expecting him to be somewhere in the middle. He should have won that race. Damon was quicker than Jacques but not quite quick enough to actually get past. Over, say, five or six laps Damon would have been slightly quicker than Jacques. I remember Damon coming on the radio and saying that Jacques was holding him up. Patrick sent a message, via the engineers, telling Damon to prove it by dropping back and catching up. Which Damon did, twice. Then the Renault engineers started to say that we were losing a lot of oil from Jacques's car. Looking at the two cars, you could see a blue and white one followed by a blue and pink one. Then Renault said they weren't sure whether Jacques would reach the end of the race. A few messages went to Jacques and he promptly ignored them. Then there was a very strong one – which he obeyed.

Jacques did prove that you could come from racing in the States and do well, but he did have the best car at the time. Jacques was okay. He was one of those people who, if he wanted to talk to you, he would. But he could go for three or four races without saying anything to you.

JIM WRIGHT

I joined in October 1994, working alongside Richard West, who was looking after sponsorship. In 1994 Segafredo had come on board as a sponsor. They had been involved with the Toleman team when Senna drove for them in 1984. When Senna died on Segafredo's home territory they stuck with Frank and didn't walk away. But Frank knew that we would have to work hard to keep them in 1995. It was December 1994 and we went off to Bologna to see Massimo Zanetti, the boss of Segafredo. I was surprised that Richard wasn't going but I think he was away talking to Sanyo in Japan. That gave me a boost of confidence because Frank obviously thought I was ready for this. I had already landed a deal straight away with a Japanese sponsor and that had appeared on the car in the Japanese Grand Prix in 1994. That was good money for the time and it got me off on the right foot with Frank.

So we set off for Italy on the private jet, which was a new experience for me. I noticed straight away that Frank has his routines when flying. He is passionate about aircraft and he talks to the pilots and always has a note made of exactly when he takes off and touches down. As we taxied in, Frank asked everyone to have their passports ready. The Carabinieri came on board and they were clearly thrilled to see him. Bear in mind that the Senna case was pending and this was still very big news in Italy. But it was clear that Frank is revered in Italy. He had taken on and beaten Ferrari. They knew what he had been through, plus the fact that he speaks fluent Italian and has had Italian drivers. When the Carabinieri officer saw Frank, he immediately waived the need to see passports. 'Please, Mr Williams, there is no need.'

We drove in the car to Zanetti's house. As we arrived, we saw TV cameras and lights. Mr Zanetti was waiting and said he hoped Frank didn't mind the media filming his greeting, then we would go into the privacy of the house. It turned out that Mr Zanetti was a local politician and having Frank Williams there did him no harm at all. Segafredo doubled their commitment for 1995.

STEVE COATES

One of the biggest worries for us after Senna's death was going back to Brazil. We had extra security laid on; we couldn't go into the circuit with our team gear on; there was concern about fanatics being hostile because of the loss of a national hero in one of our cars. How wrong could we be? The Brazilian people were totally the opposite. The sympathy was just unbelievable.

ANN BRADSHAW

Damon was a gentleman all the way through. I was left a bit in the lurch because, being the press officer, I wasn't party to all the things that had been going on. The news about Damon came out of the blue. But as far as I was concerned, what was done was done and I had to deal with it. People were saying that Frank was being mean. I'm not saying I agree with that, but as far as I'm concerned he can be whatever he wants because he has every right. He has got the team to where it is today. Patrick is a wonderful person and has played a major part in the team's success, but at the end of the day Frank took the risks. He generates a lot of business. Everyone at times like this seems to think they have the right to tell him what to do. I think they have no right at all. He hires and he fires. It's his choice.

I think my relationship with Frank was different to most because I have known him for so long and of course because I was a woman in a man's world. But even from my point of view, Frank was never someone who engaged in social chit-chat. He was not someone you would shoot the breeze with. He can be evasive – not indecisive – but evasive until he has made up his mind. Then, once that is done, you know where you stand.

PATRICK HEAD

Frank loves to see passion in people and in sportsmen. He's always been putty in the hands of outstanding drivers – not ordinary drivers but those he regards as outstanding. In 1991 Riccardo's contract had come to an end. I was talking to Frank in the motorhome at Spa and he said, 'I suppose I'd better talk to Riccardo about next year. Are you keen to keep him?' I said, 'He's a lovely guy. He's quick. He's shown himself to be a match for Nigel on his day. Maybe Nigel will beat him but you couldn't do better really. My vote is to keep him.' 'Okay,' he said. 'I'll do that, but probably I won't pay him a lot of money.' I said, 'That's up to you, Frank.'

I went outside and said, 'Riccardo, Frank wants to see you now.' He went in there like the schoolboy who was about to see the headmaster. About half an hour later Riccardo came out with a big smile on his face. He couldn't believe it. I think he'd screwed $2.5 million out of Frank when he was quite prepared to drive for half that.

But Frank can be very hard at times, and that's where Damon went wrong. He sent in this awful non-charismatic fellow Michael Breen, who was his manager or something. Breen went into Frank's office and didn't quite put his feet up on the desk, but he put his briefcase on Frank's desk, opened it up, leant back and said something along the lines of, 'We're opening negotiations at $15 million, Frank, so if you want to start bidding for Damon for next year, that's where it starts.' Frank left a long silence – his nurse was in there at the time and told me this – which was embarrassing apparently. It went on for more than two minutes. Then Frank looked up at him and said, 'Michael, when you come back with a sensible number and proposal, I shall be very willing to talk to you. Meanwhile, there's the door. I'd be very grateful if you'd take your briefcase off my desk and depart my office.'

If Damon had come in himself and sat down, he might not have got what Breen was asking for, but he would have got a lot of money. Sending in some charmless lackey was a big mistake. Frank's a sucker and Riccardo had him over like you wouldn't believe. But that was such a bad misjudgement by Damon. Breen didn't come back.

TWENTY-NINE
Rough Justice

It was not until 20 February 1997, almost three years after the accident, that the hearing into Ayrton Senna's death opened in a makeshift courtroom in Imola, the local judiciary too small to accommodate a case that had generated worldwide interest. Six people were charged with manslaughter: Frank Williams, Patrick Head and Adrian Newey as manufacturers of the car, plus the owner of the circuit, the circuit director and the race director who had approved the circuit on behalf of the FIA. The presumption underlying the prosecution was that fatalities could be eliminated from motorsport and that Senna's death was someone's fault. The reality was that Senna had been doing his job to the best of his ability in a car that the Williams team had designed and built to the best of their ability, and that mistakes and misjudgements are unavoidable – and in a sport such as Formula 1 may result in deaths.

On 16 December 1997 Judge Antonio Costanzo cleared all six defendants of manslaughter, ignoring the recommendation of investigating magistrate and prosecutor Maurizio Passarini that a one-year suspended sentence be imposed on both Head and Newey. In October 1998 Passarini lodged an appeal, stating that Head and Newey were 'ultimately responsible for the bad design and workmanship of the steering wheel modifications carried out on Ayrton Senna's Williams-Renault'. The prosecutor's appeal was heard in Bologna on 19 November 1999 and three days later rejected. In 2003 this verdict was overturned, only for that in turn to be rejected by the Corta Suprema di Cassazione, the court of last resort in Italy, on 27 May 2005, eleven years after the accident.

PATRICK HEAD

In order to make things legal we had to reduce the diameter of the steering column, but it was all done before the season, and all the cars had been modified identically. They were all modified to a properly approved drawing from the design office and the modifications were all done in the factory. Meanwhile, we had data showing the steering column was intact at the time of impact.

The final judgment of the court was that the car had crashed because of a failure in the steering column. They didn't explain the data; they just said they couldn't think of any other reason why the car had gone off the track. So it was an unsatisfactory final outcome.

It's without a doubt the biggest regret in Williams history, particularly for Frank, who was very friendly with Ayrton, and for the engineers, who quite apart from friendship have a responsibility to any driver. An engineer never wants to have a driver injured or killed in a car of their design.

ADRIAN NEWEY

The Italian justice system is such that, despite being a Catholic country, there is no such thing as an act of God. If someone dies, somebody must be guilty. If it's suicide, it's the person concerned. If it's not suicide, somebody else is responsible. So they take the approach initially of thinking of everyone that may be culpable. They then very quickly whittled it down to Frank, Patrick and me, and then Patrick and me.

A magistrate is appointed to investigate. Once he's investigated, he then becomes the state prosecution. Then another magistrate, whose desk is next to him, becomes the judge. It's a very strange system. I think one of the biggest problems was that it was a very technical case and we were struggling to understand what little data we had available. It was a combination of the circuit camera, the on-board camera from Schumacher's car and what we could drag out of the damaged on-board data recorder.

We were able to piece together something that seemed to fit all the facts, but what didn't fit was the implication that a broken steering column had caused the accident. The steering column did break in the accident and it did have cracks on it. The prosecution centred on that and didn't seem to be interested in looking at all the data that we could show.

Personally, I was very disappointed that Mauro Forghieri, despite being a designer who achieved great success in his day and who more than anyone must understand the difficulties of designing a racing car, became the prosecution's technical representative. In my view, he simply focused on the steering column, and perhaps being from an earlier generation he either didn't want to, or didn't understand the data that we were able to show from the data recorder. It was extremely difficult to get the magistrate, who was a non-technical person, to comprehend the basic concepts of things like understeer and oversteer, let alone try and understand how we were translating these squiggly lines. It went straight over the top of his head. It was a very frustrating case. It was chaotic, it really was.

STEVE COATES

I was involved in more depth because I looked after the tyres. What helped me were the details that came through – things such as the safety car not being geared up for its purpose. It was a family saloon car and the brakes were not up to the job. The guy driving it had a friend who had offered the circuit a Porsche for the weekend, but they declined. Damon and Ayrton were pulling alongside the safety car, telling him to drive quicker, but he just couldn't drive faster. The tyre pressures were critical to the sledging [bottoming] of the car and the pressures we calculated at the time of impact were low.

I went through quite a hard time. Being one of those that were charged originally, I had been affected by the thought of whether I'd contributed to the accident or not. Everyone else was going through the same thing, but Frank was very supportive – he would always ask how we were feeling. Of course we were all really only thinking about ourselves, but Frank showed he really cared about how everyone else was feeling.

Patrick is a totally different character. At the next race, Monaco, he was coming out of the motorhome. I went up to him to talk about the tyres at Imola. We'd had cracking on the side walls, something which we'd had for a while, and they looked horrendous. To this day I don't believe it was a tyre failure because we hadn't had any before, not even on the fast tracks such as Hockenheim. But I remember I wanted to talk to him to ease my mind and my conscience. I wanted to discuss what I thought it might have been, but he was irritable about it and wandered off. The same day, I talked it through with Frank; that's the difference between them. But that's the way they are; two quite different people and that's what makes it the perfect partnership.

IAN ANDERSON

The court case dragged on for years. What amazed most people at the factory was that Patrick, Frank and Adrian didn't have a nervous break-down. There was certainly a modification done to the steering in the workshop in order to get round the regulations; the cars were so tight and there was very little room in the cockpit. But the work was done under controlled conditions to the usual meticulous standard. I don't know where all that stuff about the modifications being crudely done outside the factory came from. The trouble was, we didn't get the car back at the time and, when we did, it was destroyed. We couldn't see what had actually happened, and meanwhile there was all this supposition and wild rumours. It was a bad time. It took a year for the team to get over it.

BRIAN O'ROURKE

Despite our best endeavours, we weren't allowed near the car. Things went on and on and on. At the end of February 1997 I was sent out with a photographer from Farnborough to Bologna to see the car. I had heard that bits of the car had been round every university in Italy, but I was surprised to find that it wasn't really like that. It was kept in a traffic police depot in Bologna because technically it was a road traffic accident.

The police chief had the steering column, which was the thing that was the bone of contention and photographs of which mysteriously appeared in Italian journals. The car itself was in a little corrugated iron lock-up in the yard. It had a big padlock on the door. They opened it up and we dragged out various bits of bodywork. The monocoque was a bit dusty but in pretty good condition. Everything was in place and the sight of the car brought events at Imola flooding back.

The way the prosecution worked, it wasn't an enquiry to find out what had happened; they had done that behind closed doors and then said, 'We know what happened and we're prosecuting you.' This company's approach had to be to demolish their case. It was not to say, 'We don't think that happened; we think this happened.' It became an engineering exercise and a lot of us were involved in it. It took the personal connection out of it, which I felt was very sad.

I went to the trial twice to give evidence. I thought Ayrton was worthy of better, quite frankly. The courthouse in Imola wasn't big enough so they rented a pensioners' social club or something with a dance-hall affair upstairs. I think the locals resented it being taken over in that way. I counted twenty-four legal people representing different groups: Williams, the FIA, the circuit owners. There were translators, the judge, two journalists and, I kid you not, a man and his dog sitting in a pew at the side.

It was a case of what was the primary cause of the accident and what was the secondary cause. People jumped to conclusions and said it was obvious what caused the accident. Two names from the team were released to the press as being responsible for the steering. Consequently, they were doorstepped, with paparazzi climbing all over their gardens. On the back of a Sunday tabloid there was the headline THE BOFFINS THAT KILLED AYRTON SENNA and a long-lens shot of two ordinary blokes from the design office.

JOHN SUTTON

When an aeroplane falls out of the sky, or two aeroplanes crash or whatever happens, the airframe maker, the engine maker, the airline and the CAA or the aviation authority in the appropriate part of the world get together and study all the stuff on the ground, pick it all up, lay it out in a hangar and do all the ballistic calculations to try and work out what happened. If it's a jumbo jet, then this is for the benefit of the many airlines running jumbo jets, all of whom have got some experience and might be able to contribute as well as learn.

The only people who had experience of how a Williams FW16 racing car performed were Williams, and we weren't invited. In fact, we were prevented from contributing. That said, we did a huge amount of work ourselves with what data we had and we did loads of work in the R&D labs, reconstructing and replaying recorded data from the instrumentation on the car, on steering systems, with and without steering wheels, to see whether it was even plausible that Ayrton could have left the road with a steering wheel that wasn't connected to the steering rack.

It was a very unhappy time because, aside from the loss of our driver, there was this insinuation and undercurrent of feeling that we were cowboys or we were concealing something. There were even suggestions that we had destroyed the data recorder on the car in order for the data not to be recoverable. It was very distressing to read that sort of thing.

JONATHAN LEGARD

I attended, on behalf of BBC Radio 5 Live, just about all the significant hearings in the Senna trial. The courtroom was a converted entertainment hall, with spotlights and a curtain behind the magistrate. Patrick and Frank were always remarkably dignified on their rare appearances, no doubt churning inside while the proceedings flowed in Italian, with lawyers on both sides performing to the gallery as much as to the court. It was a bizarre thing to watch.

THIRTY

Marooned

I n the midst of the courtroom drama in Italy Patrick and Frank had to deal with an important team issue. For some time Adrian Newey had been of the view that he ought to have a say in who drove the cars he designed. When Frank made the unilateral decision to replace Damon Hill with Heinz-Harald Frentzen, Adrian was not impressed. It made him more amenable to the ongoing approaches from McLaren even though his contract ran until July 1999. Newey insisted it was not about money, although he had been present throughout a period of impressive growth as the company's turnover jumped from £12 million to £36 million, and an operating profit of £6.6 million was registered for 1995. Frank remained the majority shareholder in the company with Patrick Head holding the other 30 per cent.

With 224 full-time staff, larger premises were again necessary. In 1995 the former headquarters of a pharmaceutical company occupying a thirty-two-acre site just outside the village of Grove in Oxfordshire was acquired for £6.7 million. It took months to move the team, lock, stock and wind tunnel ten miles west without excessive disruption to the racing programme.

In a typically pragmatic way, Williams put their vacated premises to good use. While rivals Benetton and Jordan staged high-profile launches for their 1997 cars at London's Planet Hollywood and the

Hilton Hotel, Williams chose the abandoned conference centre at Basil Hill Road to unveil the FW19. In what appeared to be the corner of an empty warehouse a blue and white Rothmans backdrop had been erected and a small stage constructed. Villeneuve and Frentzen removed a blue cover from a car dropped off for an hour en route to its first test in Spain. The photographers took their pictures; there was a question-and-answer session; then everyone was free to mingle and chat as the car was swiftly loaded back on the truck.

Frank and Patrick were in good form, Frank regretting the absence of Newey, who was on 'gardening leave' pending an agreement with McLaren to become their technical director. Patrick agreed that Adrian would be sorely missed but pointed out that the FW19 had been more or less completed before his unfortunate departure.

Whatever Williams's internal politics, Villeneuve was favourite to win the drivers' championship, and the team moved swiftly into the lead in the constructors' competition when Jacques won two of the first three races and Frentzen took the fourth – the German's only win during an increasingly unhappy season. Villeneuve, meanwhile, with a remarkable run of ten pole positions, put himself in contention for the title thanks to further wins in Spain, Britain, Hungary, Austria and Germany (the Luxembourg Grand Prix). However, a combination of circumstances – including a disastrous tyre choice by the team for a wet Monaco Grand Prix – allowed Michael Schumacher and Ferrari to close up. The championship would see-saw between the two drivers right up to the final race at Jerez.

In a repeat of Adelaide 1994 in almost every respect bar one, the contenders were in a league of their own as they drove like men possessed, with Schumacher leading much of the way. When Villeneuve attempted a daring overtaking move, it seemed to catch the Ferrari driver by surprise, and once again Schumacher turned in on his opponent. This time he did not achieve his objective: the Williams continued and the Ferrari did not. Villeneuve was world champion, Williams having already won the constructors' title for a record ninth time.

The double triumph marked Renault's withdrawal from F1, although the company agreed to supply Williams with their V10 for 1998 and 1999 through Mecachrome, a subsidiary which retailed engines to teams. So Frank's engines were no longer free; he would need to find somewhere in the region of £25 million for them. Money to pay for the engines came from carrying advertising for the Winfield brand, the result of the merger of Rothmans and British American Tobacco. That of course was Frank's department; Patrick and his technical team had to come to terms with changes in the regulations that meant cars with a narrower track and grooved tyres. Despite extensive testing with a 1997 car converted to suit the new rules, it did not take Williams long to realise that FW20 was off the pace.

In 1998 Williams played catch-up, except they never did quite catch up because the problems were embedded in the basic design of a car not helped by a garish maroon colour scheme. Three third places were the best that Villeneuve and Frentzen could manage in total, Williams holding on to third place in the constructors' championship by the skin of their teeth after failing to win a race for the first time since 1988. And there seemed little hope of improvement in 1999, particularly when the driver line-up did not include a Grand Prix winner.

Villeneuve had left to join British American Racing and Frentzen's brief and unhappy tenure had ended with a move to Jordan. Coming in after making his Formula 1 debut with Jordan, Ralf Schumacher would join Alex Zanardi, the Italian having limited Formula 1 experience between 1991 and 1994 before crossing the Atlantic to eventually dominate the IndyCar scene. Zanardi's free spirit and speed seemed ideally suited to Williams but it was another relationship that never truly got going.

The irony of 1999 was that Frentzen's performances in the Jordan would help push Williams from third to fifth in the constructors' series. Both Williams drivers struggled with the switch from Goodyear to standard-issue tyres from Bridgestone, while the customer Renault engines (now known as Supertec) were suffering from a lack of development and left Williams some 50 bhp behind Mercedes (McLaren) and Ferrari. Whereas Zanardi was a disappointment, Schumacher would have won at the Nürburgring but for a puncture. Long-term prospects also looked promising. Having run a Le Mans project for BMW, Williams and the motor manufacturer were going Formula 1 racing together. A return to former glory seemed on the cards.

ADRIAN NEWEY

Not that long after I'd been presented with the fact that Villeneuve was going to be signed for two years without my involvement at all, I made it clear to both Frank and Patrick that I was pretty pissed off. When I heard that Damon was being replaced by Frentzen, I was completely dumbfounded. At the same time, rows with the FIA were getting more and more onerous in terms of the technical spin-back because of an alliance between McLaren, Williams and Tyrrell. I'm not saying that group was wrong to take a stance; it's just that I wasn't being involved. And there were various other things that I wasn't a part of. McLaren had been ringing me once every few months since 1993 or even 1992, and finally I turned round and said okay.

I sat down with Frank and Patrick and told them that I thought I was being treated badly and I wanted to leave. Of course, they both said it wasn't as simple as that, as I had a contract. I said I appreciated that but I felt they'd broken it. I was already on very good money at Williams and McLaren had offered a fair bit more, but money wasn't the motivation for leaving.

Then Frank said, 'Don't tell Patrick, but here's more money than you'll get at McLaren.' I said, 'Frank, that's very kind of you but it's not about the money.' The whole thing became untenable and I started to take legal advice. I was told in December that I had a strong legal case because of the breach of clauses in the contract, but if I carried on work- ing there I would have what is known in legal terms as 'acquiesced': in other words, I would have rolled over and accepted it. Therefore my case would be weak. I needed to leave or stay – leave, as in going on leave and not going into work. So, rather reluctantly, I stopped coming in. I didn't just fail to turn up one day; there was some dialogue.

I felt guilty about not coming in, but, having said that, it was December and the design of the FW19 was done. It wouldn't have made much difference whether I'd left in December, January or February. We then got into a rather unpleasant legal battle which actually I quite enjoyed because for me it was a change of vocation. I appointed a chap named Julian Roskill from Rowe and Maw as my lawyer.

Patrick, I'm afraid, was very naughty, because he claimed that I had said unless they gave me more money I was off, which was absolutely not the case. It got a little bit unpleasant. By the time the court date had been decided I was quite looking forward to it as I thought I had a good case. I was rather disappointed when Ron negotiated with Frank and reached some sort of settlement. I was told that the court was off and I could start at McLaren at the beginning of August 1997. Having said that, it would have been a sad end if my strong and very enjoyable relationship with Frank and Patrick had ended in court.

PATRICK HEAD

Jacques [Villeneuve] was always a bit of a renegade – I'd say an odd character. He was a very appealing character but in many ways quite child-like. If he fancied a girl, he'd ask Ann Bradshaw to go out and chat her up for him. He was quite immature in many ways. His biggest immaturity was that he was a bit like Nigel in the way that he believed anybody in the team was either 100 per cent for him or they were against him. I probably made a lifelong enemy of Jacques when I was asked about my memories of him. I said everything positive but I also said I thought he made the championship in 1997 harder work than it should have been. I know Jacques hates me because of that.

He was very talented, a very strong character in many ways. Some of the things he did which are now forgotten parts of history, like overtaking Michael Schumacher round the outside of the long bend at Estoril, few people have any memory of that. It was an amazing move.

Despite being a strong individual, he had massive insecurities. In the environment of the team he always treated me as if I was not quite the enemy but as if I was not for him, which wasn't the case. My position is that I've always wanted Williams to be successful, not necessarily that I wanted solely a single driver to be successful. I don't look back on it with regret, but I know Jacques came out with a few bitter comments – not quite 'Patrick Head is an arsehole' but something pretty close to it. Maybe he's right!

The cars of 1998/9 were not Williams in that they were a horrible colour. They were red, the colour of the team that we had been desperately trying to beat for years! The FW20 wasn't that bad; it was quite a neat little car, a pretty car but for its colour. But the FW19 was a shitbox. To be fair to them, we were led up the garden path because we tested with Goodyear grooved tyres and they fell apart in a huge way. We designed a car with a rearward weight distribution. Then, two or three races into the season, Goodyear suddenly copied Bridgestone and came out with a wide front tyre. We didn't have much ballast on the car so we couldn't move the weight distribution forward. Now we had a wide front tyre that didn't suit our weight distribution. Meanwhile Michael Schumacher and Ferrari with Goodyear tyres gave McLaren a bit of a race for the championship.

As for 1999, the season was a considerable disappointment for Zanardi and for us. A Formula 1 car was very edgy on those tyres; it had very little low-speed grip and it was difficult for Alex to adapt.

JACQUES VILLENEUVE

I loved working with Frank because he is a real racer – his life is his team. He is willing to take risks – or he was when I was there – with drivers and give them a little bit of freedom. It was a little bit more difficult with Patrick. There was a lot of respect between him and myself. He is a very strong character: he knows what is right according to his views, in the same way that I knew what was right according to my views. We would both stick to our beliefs and that sometimes made it a little bit fiery. But he held his own and I held my own, and we worked like that.

It was an incredible season in 1997. But before it started Frentzen was signed, and he was touted as the next champion for Williams. So politically I was already in the wrong spot, and again in testing he was faster than me. But somehow he was not as strong mentally, versus Patrick. He collapsed as soon as the season got going. Often he would think he had pole, and then I would get him on the last lap; it killed him.

I'm just angry that the move I made on Michael at Estoril wasn't filmed properly. Most of the winter testing was done in Estoril. That corner reminded me of an oval corner. I told Jock and the rest of the team that during the race I would overtake someone on the outside; I never expected it to be Michael. We were behind a Minardi and I had to get by Michael to beat Damon to keep my championship chances alive. I had to take all the risks necessary, otherwise the championship was gone. It was better to crash then than to finish behind Michael and lose the championship. When we came up behind the Minardi, Michael slowed down a little bit so as not to get bogged down behind him and that's when I went round the outside. We were side by side and I ended up in the marbles. At some point our wheels intertwined a bit. I remember how angry he was afterwards. He said I was lucky it was him otherwise I would be dead. We would have banged wheels. He was really, really angry to get beaten like that. That brought a lot of pleasure.

Even though we got podiums 1998 was very disappointing. At the end of the day we managed to get what we could out of that car. We managed to do a few good races. We worked well together: me, Jock and the rest of the team. I always had the feeling that we managed to get more than we should out of the situation. Because the team were hard workers, it meant that you would think about what you were doing; that's the way it was in those days. It wasn't like someone sitting in front of a computer and saying within five minutes, 'Okay, that's the way it is. Just shut up. That's the way the car will be fastest.' You would still be given the option of trying something even if they did not believe in it, just so you could be proven right or wrong. Then everybody would accept whatever the answer was. It was great that you could work with a team like that in Formula 1.

I built up a very strong relationship with Jock; we're still the best of friends. I was a baby in racing terms. I came from IndyCars but my experience in motorsport was not that big, even though I had achieved a lot. So I was almost thrown into it. But I think being a baby like that helped me to not stress about it; to be a little bit carefree. When it is time to gamble a little bit and calculate the risk, you need to be a bit carefree and not to think about what it will bring you three years down the road.

DICKIE STANFORD

A lot of people were surprised that Frank had picked Alex. He hadn't done a great deal at Lotus although he'd gone off to Champ Car racing and done well. Alex knew what he wanted, but at the same time the car wasn't super-good. We'd gone from having the fastest car to a mid-field car. I think the drivers were given too much scope for trying to develop the cars themselves. Alex was always trying some weird things with his engineer. On paper they would work, but you knew that when they got to a racetrack they were not going to work. You would end up changing everything back to standard on the car after the first day of practice. I didn't get the feeling we were going to win races. The car was not that good; it's very rare that you remember the Winfield cars. They didn't look like a Williams.

ALEX ZANARDI

I had done well in North America and Formula 1 was pursuing me again. Frank began a series of long-distance conversations. He would conclude the conversation in the usual way: 'When you come to Europe, we'll sit down and talk about it.' There were discussions with other teams but I was only considering two options: stay with the Ganassi team in the States or go to Williams. Frank became very serious. 'Well, there is no reason to keep talking on the phone,' he said. 'Since you're always racing and find it difficult to come to Europe, I'll come and see you in Detroit the day after tomorrow.' I was very impressed he would do that.

As soon as I met him, I liked him and was immediately convinced I should race for him. We discussed the broad terms of a contract on the first day and the details on the following day. He agreed to more or less all my comments and we shook hands.

After the first test I wasn't very impressed with the cars, and I couldn't make them work on the grooved tyres. The Williams was completely different to anything I had driven in 1994, my last year in Formula 1. The new rules changed the cars completely. They were tricky and required a different driving style that was against my instinct.

JIM WRIGHT

I went over with Frank to negotiate the deal to sign Zanardi. The feeling was that it was a coup signing a guy who was just mega. At that time he was beating some good drivers, driving absolutely superbly. He could race from the front; he could race from behind. If something went wrong at a pit stop, he put his head down and charged. He was Frank's type of driver. We were elated that we had been able to go over there and sign this guy up for three years.

The other thing about Alex was that he was such a nice guy. He quickly realised that Frank had a keen sense of humour and Alex was able to tell jokes in perfect English – very, very funny jokes. Frank was just so entertained by this and he was delighted that we had signed him. From a marketing point of view, my focus was, 'Wow! This is great. He is a truly marketable guy, speaks three or four different languages, a double champion. This is just great!'

But it just didn't work out. I know that it was an enormous disappointment for Frank. I remember at the first race I was on the Rothmans sky bridge, looking down on the circuit in Melbourne. Alex got off to an awful start. He was behind the Minardis, and he couldn't find a way past them. I was just shaking my head.

There was a lot of head-scratching and I remember a lot of discussions between Frank and Patrick about why it wasn't working. Alex was struggling with the grooved tyres and had no experience of them in the higher temperatures.

JONATHAN LEGARD

I remember one incident of typical plain speaking from Patrick after Jacques was disqualified from fifth in the Japanese GP for ignoring a yellow flag. The race had been won by Schumacher. Afterwards the world was in ferment and I cornered Patrick with my BBC 5 Live tape recorder. He just went for it over Schumacher and Adelaide 1994. It was fantastic stuff, delivered in classic Patrick no-nonsense style, and made headlines all around the world on the Monday.

YVONNE DUNCAN

I trained as a physiotherapist at Kings College Hospital in London and then went to live in Melbourne. I started in the spinal injuries unit at the Austin Hospital in 1979. I was there for twenty years. I had a friend who had worked on Frank Williams when the race was in Adelaide, and when the race came to Melbourne I was asked to contact one of his people and set up appointments.

He was staying in one of the hotels on Queens Road opposite Albert Park. I got there early and was sitting downstairs when someone came down and took me to Frank's room. He had his team of carers. They put him on the floor. It struck me that here was this powerful man, leading a huge Formula 1 team, world champions, and yet he was so vulnerable

– being lifted out of his wheelchair and not coming in a power chair, where he would have had control over his movements. I had to make sure he had no stiffness in any of his joints, that he had a full range of movement, that he was not getting what we call shortened-in muscles. If you stay in one position for too long, then your muscles can get short and contracted. Then it gets harder to get dressed and all sorts of things. So you want to keep as flexible and supple as possible.

He had his stand-up chair, which they brought to Melbourne, and he stood in that every day. You don't actually need it but it's the best way of keeping weight going through your bones. It stretches some of your muscles so that they don't get tight. But psychologically it's important to be at your height and have eye contact so that people are not bending down to talk to you and you have to look up all the time.

He was so organised. Meticulous in every detail. He would say to me, 'You can push harder'. He couldn't feel what I was doing but he knew how far everything would move. I had such a workout for an hour, I was dripping at the end of it. I was exhausted. It was a hot day, and when you are spinal cord injured above a certain level, you lose all your temperature control. So the air conditioning was turned down. He was aware of everything, had every detail down. It was ten years since his accident and he told me all about it. The pre-morbid personality is vital. He is obviously a driven man with ambition, and that's taken him right through.

You need good people around you. The young guys he had with him were fabulous.

When it came to paying me, he opened his briefcase and there were just wads of money. 'How much do you want?' I was thinking, *This is crazy; these guys could do exactly what I'm doing*. I probably did talk myself out of a job.

I was warned that he was not the easiest man to get on with, to do my job and not try and have a conversation. So I was a bit thrown when he just came out and told me all that had happened to him and his wife and his children. He was a very impressive guy.

VIRGINIA WILLIAMS

There was an element of frustration in the first year after Frank's accident but I don't think there is any element of frustration now, because we've got it down to a fine art. When I say there isn't any frustration now, of course Frank would love to be jumping out of bed and getting in the shower. But there's more of an acceptance as time goes on. The first day that we came back from the hospital, it took me and the nurse about three hours to get Frank up.

His care is certainly routine. Luckily we've had some carers for a long time. The easier it becomes for them, then he's happy. We do have a small turnover, but all in all he's been very lucky.

I can remember one of the anaesthetists in the London Hospital saying to me that there isn't a great life expectancy. I don't think that anyone would have predicted at that time that Frank would still be alive twenty-three years later. I think the level of care definitely contributes to longevity. I found it very surprising that Christopher Reeve died as a result of a pressure sore. Frank would never have a pressure sore because no one would let that happen. Frank is very healthy and I sometimes find it quite annoying that he doesn't even get a cold from one year to the next – mind you when he does get one it's not fun – but I don't think Frank has had a cold or a chest infection for three or four years. There's not many of us who can say that.

JIM WRIGHT

Frank and Patrick aren't into landmarks very much. In 1997, just before Silverstone, most people knew that the next win was going to be the hundredth Grand Prix victory, which is a hell of a milestone. I seem to remember that we were a little bit lucky in the British Grand Prix because someone else was leading the race and they retired. Jacques inherited it and we won. I remember that Frank and Patrick were a bit miffed that on our home soil we were actually on for a beating when the car was very good. It was a great moment, a fantastic occasion, and everybody on the team was really happy. I went back to the motorhome to collect the trophies and take them over to the Paddock Club for the sponsors and the guests to see. I remember being stopped at some point and someone taking a photo. It was an amazing personal moment to be a part of that.

After finishing off the Paddock Club and coming back to the motorhome, Frank was there, standing up in his frame. I went up to him and said, 'Fantastic. Really, really well done. One hundred Grand Prix wins.' Frank said, 'Yes, thank you, Jimmy. But I remind myself that in ten days' time we're at Hockenheim and, fuck me, those Ferraris were quick today!' I said, 'Yeah, but come on, Frank, that's ten days' time. Now is now. A hundred Grand Prix victories, that is an amazing achievement.' He looked at me and said, 'Jimmy, it matters nothing. The next race is the most important and that's what we've got to focus on.'

Patrick was also miffed that those bloody Ferraris had been quicker than us. Patrick said, 'Yeah okay, I'm pleased. A hundred Grand Prix wins. But we could have been beaten today.' His focus was on what had gone wrong. He thought that they got the set-up wrong and that's why Ferrari had been quicker. That did annoy him, it really did. They expected Silverstone to be a home banker. It was, but by default. That simply was not good enough.

VIRGINIA WILLIAMS

I woke up one morning, and because Frank has nurses in his room we can't have the same bedroom, obviously. I turned on the radio and they said that there was a '... knighthood for Formula 1 ...' I immediately thought, *Bernie!* Then they said, 'Frank Williams', and I thought, *Well they must have got that wrong.* So I went next door to Frank and said, 'They've just said on the radio that you've got a knighthood. Have they made a mistake?' He said no, so I asked him why he hadn't told me, and he said it was because they instruct you not to tell anyone. I said that I was sure that didn't necessarily include me. 'So are you telling me you've been knighted?' He said he had.

It was extraordinary. I went out of the room thinking it was all quite surreal. Typical Frank. 'Sorry, couldn't tell you. Not even the wife!' It was quite odd. I just continued with my day thinking, *Wow!* I think it's quite special that he was the first in Formula 1. He deserved it. He showed enormous courage in the face of real adversity.

KATE BATTERSBY

Being a journalist, it was quite a story when Frank received his knight-hood in 1999. But from a female point of view I found it far more revealing that Ginny did not learn that her husband had been knighted until she heard the radio news on Classic FM on 31 December. Frank said the letter from Downing Street had said he couldn't tell anyone, and he claimed not to realise that didn't really mean your own spouse! I remember Patrick telling this story at a pre-season lunch, although he could scarcely get the words out because he was guffawing so much.

THIRTY-ONE
Extracurricular

For many years among the svelte single-seater racing cars at the Williams Conference Centre could be found the lumpy shape of a Metro 6R4 rally car. It was like finding an elephant among a pack of cheetahs. Of the three important projects taken on by Williams Grand Prix Engineering over the years, the Metro would achieve the least success. A touring car programme for Renault secured the British championship with Alain Menu in 1997; a Le Mans project with BMW would bring victory in the 24 Hours in 1999; a 6R4 crewed by Tony Pond and Rob Arthur would finish third in the 1985 Lombard RAC Rally, four years after the original concept had been created by Williams.

PATRICK HEAD

The Metro came not long after the so-called Winter of Discontent in 1978/9 when there was general unrest and widespread strikes. John Davenport, then of Austin Rover, asked if we would be interested in having a go at the installation of a Rover V8 engine in the front of a Metro. At that time we weren't even certain that we were going to be racing in 1981, so I said we'd take a look.

John Piper, Brian O'Rourke and Ian Anderson were brought in to start work on the project. We installed a Portakabin for the design group and a little flatbed in one of our small 5,000-square-foot factories. We did a mock-up of what they'd asked for and Tony Pond came along and sat in it. But he was so far back because of the engine in the front that he said he would never be able to drive it in a rally. So we obviously had to do something different.

I had been involved with Harry Ferguson Research some years before. It seemed pretty logical to make this car four-wheel drive and put the engine in the middle. We looked at one or two layouts. There was a chap called Mike Endean who was running the stores at Hewland gearboxes and he seemed to have a rough idea of what he was doing on transmissions. We mapped out the layout of the transmission and we got a good draughtsman from Austin Rover. We told them there was no way it could be a V8; the engine would have to be a bit smaller than that. Their man, David Woods, said they would chop two cylinders off it and make it a ninety-degree V6. It all happened from there.

Quite early on, in about 1983, we provided three prototype cars: one of them built and running, and the rest in pieces. I think that John Davenport had funded it through the spares sales at Austin Rover Motorsport. He then had to sell the idea to his bosses, and rather amazingly he did. But it took them an enormous length of time to turn it into producing 200 rally cars. They must have had the car for about four years before it actually went rallying. When it eventually got into private hands, it started doing very well. It's won over a thousand rallies, mainly national events, of course. So it has had a great national career, but never the international career that was envisaged.

IAN ANDERSON

I had stopped travelling at the end of 1980. I started a research and development section and built three of the 6R4 rally cars. The car itself was very good, but the series it was supposed to be for didn't last that long. Williams did the whole design. I was in charge of building it. We built a space frame, which was effectively the roll cage, and clad it with panels. We defined where the engine was going to go and it sort of evolved.

BRIAN O'ROURKE

I had trained in aerospace in the UK as a stress engineer on the Jaguar and Tornado. Then I worked in California at Northrop on F18 Hornets. I was wondering what to do next and had been chatting to my mates about maybe going back to the UK. Then I had this bloke on the phone saying, 'You don't know me, but I understand you're talking about coming back to the UK at the end of the year.' I thought, *Is this the CIA or what?* He said he was a recruiting agency in Bristol. They were wondering whether I might be interested in a job going at Williams. The technical spec for the job sounded great. I said, 'What aircraft programme is that then?' And he said it was Formula 1 racing cars. It had sounded really good until that point. I had never heard of Williams, never mind knowing that they were world champions. I had a couple of mates in the drawing office next door who were motor-racing fans. When they said Williams were the absolute best, I began to take it seriously.

A couple of calls later I was asked if I could get myself to the Las Vegas Grand Prix, where I had to meet this chap called Patrick Head in Caesar's Palace hotel. We chatted for no more than half an hour. That was it. I started a couple of months later, in January 1982. Knowing what I know now, having an interview with Patrick the day after he had lost the world championship by a point was perhaps not the best time!

I arrived to be told, 'We've got a job where we really need someone who knows a bit about structures to have a look at it for a few months.' 'Oh, what's that then?' 'Well, it's a rally car. ' I found myself designing the Metro 6R4. They had only the two units at Station Road. They took another two for a wind tunnel and a fibreglass shop. There was no office for me, so they used the car park for a Portakabin which evidently Patrick had lived in while his house was being built. I walked inside and found John Piper, a brilliant guy who I had been at college with and hadn't seen for about six years. And off we went.

It was pretty ground-breaking for rally cars in the UK because it wasn't just a stripped-down beefed-up chassis. The brief was to use as many standard panels as possible but it was pretty clear that all we would be able to do was use the outside ones. So from the ground up it was a completely new structure, and we had to fit this V6 in the back. I'm really quite proud of that car. We worked on it until the middle of 1983. We did the pre-assembly and then it went to Austin Rover at Cowley for completion. They didn't have any scales at Cowley for corner weighting or anything like that, so they rolled it out, John Davenport made a speech and it was arranged to bring the 6R4 to the factory at Didcot on a Saturday morning so we could do some calculations on weight distribution.

The FW08 had just been completed and some of the guys wanted to take photographs of it. They arranged to get all the old Formula 1 cars out on that same Saturday morning. Everyone was there with their cameras at a time when we were trying to keep this rally car quiet. We simply wanted to go behind closed doors and do some weighting. Patrick arrived, saw the 6R4 and said, 'Right! Let's give it a spin!' So we were running up and down the road on this industrial estate and David Wood of Austin Rover was wetting himself because all these people were taking photographs of a secret project.

PATRICK HEAD

The touring car project was a typical Frank thing. I think quite rightly he was wanting to help cement our relationship with Renault. They said they were not really making the breakthrough that they needed in their touring car programme and it needed elevating to a higher level. Frank at one of our lunchtime meetings said, 'By the way, I've taken on designing and operating the Renault touring cars. That won't take up much of your time, will it?'

We ended up with a fifty-five-man company at a racing facility in Didcot. John Russell, who had joined us as a race engineer and had done some engineering design when he was with us, went over to run the technical side of the touring cars. Tim Newton was taken on as chief mechanic before taking over as team manager on the touring cars after Ian Harrison had moved on.

We did have a lot on with Formula 1, but it was a question of needs must. It was part of the Williams business and we needed to do what it said on the tin, so to speak. Renault wanted to win the touring car championship – which we duly did in 1997. I think we did a reasonable job in 1995 because we picked it up quite late in November/December 1994. We had to run very much the car that we were given in the first year. It was a matter of trying to do it right.

JOHN RUSSELL

I had been a bit shell-shocked in 1994 when Damon said he wanted to switch to David Brown, who had been Ayrton's engineer. Damon and I get on very well now, but at the time it was an incredible hurt and a dent in personal pride. I'd put a lot into the four years, a lot of family sacrifice, because this was what I believed was probably my only chance in life of achieving a world championship as a race engineer. Personally, I felt I had been snubbed, but in the bigger picture I was completely sympathetic to Damon's request and demand to be considered the number-one driver and therefore have the number-one engineer. He had asserted himself and driven through adversity. Once I'd calmed down and buried the hatchet, I wished him nothing but success.

Renault UK was keen to do a racing programme for the Laguna. It was a Williams company. The team had the Williams ethic and went about trying to do the British Touring Car Championship by raising the bar but without bringing too much of the excesses of Formula 1.

I thought it was going to be a cruise. It wasn't. Patrick came to the odd race and was often in our factory as it was just round the corner. He took a great interest because this was a different challenge. It had the Williams name on it and he wanted it to succeed. He was a great mentor at the time as it was a complete change of direction for me. I'd run a racing car but had not been responsible for the engineering of a programme.

We started by cobbling up what we could from the original cars and won some races. We got the constructors' but not the drivers' championship. The following year we completely designed our own car and made a few mistakes, which I hold my hand up to. The concept was pretty good but it was flawed in a few areas, and the engine manufacturer had some big issues as well, so 1996 was not a great year for us. Alain Menu finished second in the championship but it wasn't what we had hoped for. I was pretty determined to put that right in 1997.

We had a great team: Mark Ellis was the lead race engineer; Gerry Hughes ran the other car and Jason Plato came on board as one of the drivers. We went to Jarama to shake down the car and run it without the 1997 aero kit on it. It looked nice, and Alain was happy with it. Then we put the 1997 aero kit on it. Alain did five laps and came in with a massive grin on his face. He said, 'Job done.' Sure enough, it was. We'd ticked every box.

PATRICK HEAD

We had signed our Formula 1 deal with BMW in June 1997, but a few months beforehand we had done the deal for Le Mans. The Le Mans programme was going to be a seven-year deal and involved setting up a facility which is now our conference centre but was actually built as a base for BMW Motorsport.

In the first year it was quite honestly not very good, although there were all sorts of reasons or excuses, whichever way you look at them. There was too little time and too big a culture change because we didn't know anything about Le Mans. The second year was good. The car was designed and built under John Russell's stewardship, along with Graham Humphrys. To be fair to BMW, after we had made a bit of a mess of it in the first year they were very good and said, 'Well, okay, let's do it right now.' They were insistent that the car should be ready in January, and they were absolutely right. We managed to get it debugged and it won Le Mans in 1999.

About a month before we went to Le Mans BMW decided that they couldn't afford to continue with this and Formula 1. Which was disappointing because we had to close down the Le Mans activity and make most of the people redundant.

JOHN RUSSELL

We started the BMW programme massively late. It was a courtship programme for Formula 1, and they asked us to do Le Mans. The car wasn't very pretty as BMW had wanted to put some styling effort into it, which they did, but we never had the time to dial out the compromise between aerodynamics and their styling input. It wasn't a lemon, but we had a technical issue with a wheel-bearing seal which I considered to be potentially dangerous, so we pulled it after six hours racing. That was bloody embarrassing for Frank and Patrick and for BMW management given the Formula 1 commitment they were making.

However, they gave me enormous support, and we filled the team with other key people like Graham Humphrys as chief designer. I became chief engineer and Dave Williams, who'd been factory manager, helped out massively on the commercial, financial and political side. The 1999 car was just great. They had decided to stop the programme to concentrate on Formula 1, so the fifty people in the building realised their jobs were gone or certainly at risk, but everyone just dug in, did the job and produced the cars.

Patrick took a lot of interest. He occasionally came along and asked, 'Are you sure about that?' We had a good understanding, particularly after having done the Renault programme. He was instrumental in making sure there was the right strength to back me up in the second year of the Le Mans project. It was just terrific. Winning Le Mans is the pivotal point in my career.

IAN ANDERSON

Because I had already done sports cars, Patrick asked if I would be interested in being works manager. Unfortunately, the first car wasn't very good. We had a lot of wheel-bearing problems with it – it was just done too quickly.

By that point BMW had realised their Formula 1 engine was going to be horrendously expensive. They didn't really want to carry on. Frank was in the process of building a facility for them; it was quite expensive and BMW had already paid masses of money for it. They decided to do another year. It was pretty stressful, I must admit. Horrendously long hours. I decided to bail out of that because I didn't think it was really me.

The company had got so big that Patrick asked if I would be interested in becoming involved in the whole site, looking after security, health and safety, the general infrastructure of the company, central heating, air conditioning and so on. I did that for three years. The company was so big that I would be walking round and thinking, *I wonder who that is?* It became extremely impersonal. It was being run like a modern factory with modern systems. Frank and Patrick had brought in people from various companies that had operated in that manner. It was production-orientated; the team feeling had been lost. I went to the Christmas do and there were so many people, you just did not know who they were. That's the way modern Formula 1 is.

The BMW facility – I think it was 40,000 square feet – became filled with spare parts, carbon fibre, bodywork, Formula 1 stuff. There was nowhere to store it. Patrick went over there one day and said it was crazy. It was decided that John Cadd would take out the bits he thought we would need and everything else would be destroyed. I ended up hiring a road roller. We filled five skips, those forty-cubic-metre huge great things. We just kept crushing the stuff and putting it in. Lord knows how much money went in there. An undertray cost about £10,000, and we must have crushed twenty or thirty of those. A lot of the stuff we had left over, we auctioned off to people in the company, so they got a wheel or something like that. Then I had to hire three other units, off site, just to store all the rest of the stuff. You simply wouldn't believe the amount of stuff that gets generated and is never used. That's not a criticism of Williams; it's just the way of Formula 1.

THIRTY-TWO

Not Quite the Ultimate Driving Machine

G iven the team's lack of success during the previous two seasons, Williams attracted a surprisingly large audience to the launch of its FW22 at the Circuit de Cataluña on 24 January 2000. The majority of the media were British, but their interest had little to do with Williams commencing a potentially fruitful relationship with BMW; there was a major story brewing that the team might make a relative unknown the youngest ever British Formula 1 driver. Jenson Button had completed just one season of Formula 3, finishing third in the championship, and had done little else of note. But his test drives for Williams had been so impressive that the nineteen-year-old now found himself the focus of the Fleet Street hacks assembled in the paddock at Barcelona. Even with the launch only hours away, no one knew if the drive alongside Ralf Schumacher would go to Button or the Brazilian Bruno Junqueira. Frank seemed to have been dithering for most of the winter.

It was no surprise when rumours began to circulate in early December that Zanardi was to be let go. It was not that he was demanding too much money, but because he had done little to deserve the modest amount he had been paid – seventh at Monza had been his best result. But Williams did not have a suitable substitute. BMW had made it known they would like to see Juan Pablo Montoya, Zanardi's successor as Champ Car title holder, come on board, but the Colombian was under contract in the United States for another season and would be expensive to buy out, the last thing Frank needed as he hammered out a settlement with Zanardi for ending his contract two years early. Hence the test shoot-out between Junqueira and Button. The Briton was marginally quicker, but no one could be sure which way the decision might go. Finally, Frank gave Jenson the nod, and the British media went into overdrive, wheeling out every known cliché incorporating 'button'.

The FW22, developed by an engineering team including Gavin Fisher and aerodynamicist Geoff Willis, hardly received a second glance. To those who did look, the most obvious change was the disappearance of the ghastly Winfield maroon and the arrival of BMW white and blue. Of course for Patrick and Frank how the car went was more important than how it looked.

It would be another difficult year, unsurprisingly, given all the changes. After a shaky start, Button secured an outstanding third and fifth on the grid at Spa and Suzuka – his best actual result being fourth in Germany at the end of July. By then, Frank was bringing Montoya into the team; Button, on a five-year contract, would be leased to Benetton for two years. Schumacher, who had made it to the podium three times, would stay on. Williams finished third in the constructors' championship. While that was an improvement on the previous two years, Patrick was quick to compare Williams-BMW's meagre 36 points with McLaren's 152 and Ferrari's 170. There was clearly much work to be done.

Williams finished third once more in the standings at the end of 2001. There had been progress – 80 points against McLaren's 102 in second place – and Williams had won four of the seventeen races – three to Ralf, one to Juan Pablo – but the team had been held back by mechanical unreliability and the learning process involved in a tyre switch from Bridgestone to Michelin.

The start of 2002 looked much better when Schumacher and Montoya finished first and second at round two in Malaysia. Juan Pablo then put his FW24 on pole in Brazil and Ralf finished second. But after that the Williams effort was torpedoed by the 2002 Ferrari, which made its debut at Imola. Michael Schumacher was starting a roll which saw him finish no lower than second in the remaining thirteen races; those he did not win generally went to Rubens Barrichello in the other red car. Williams may have moved into second place in the constructors' championship, but 92 points to 221 for Ferrari told its own sad story, and the relationship with BMW had shifted. Instead of Williams calling for more power, BMW were asking for a car capable of matching what had become one of the strongest engines on the grid.

The 2003 season was summed up by Patrick Head immediately after the final race in Japan. A journalist, either brave or extremely stupid, asked if Head was disappointed. The answer was quick and to the point: 'Of course I'm disappointed. What sort of question is *that*?' A very silly question in view of what had just occurred. Montoya had been leading when his FW25 stuttered to a halt as its hydraulics packed up. Meanwhile, Ralf Schumacher, forced to start from the back of the grid instead of his anticipated pole position because of rain during qualifying, had spun his way to twelfth place. Not only had BMW Williams Formula 1 failed to score any points for the first time in 2003, the battle for the constructors' championship had been lost to Ferrari. A fortnight before, Montoya had been eliminated from the drivers' championship. A golden opportunity had been lost. Ferrari had been struggling most of the season and McLaren had shot themselves in the foot with a 2003 car that never actually raced. Of course Head was disappointed! It was not as if Williams and BMW had been sitting on their hands. The recent disappointments had prompted Patrick to take what he described as a critical look at the team and how it operated. Sam Michael, who had come from Jordan to take up the role of chief operations engineer, had worked alongside Head to reorganise internally and sort out the FW25 when it had proved disappointing at the start of the season. By Monaco

Williams had got going as Schumacher took pole and Montoya scored a flawless victory. This had partly compensated for a missed victory for the Colombian at the previous race in Austria, where a water leak had caused an engine failure. The promise had been fulfilled by two wins in succession for Ralf and one for Juan Pablo. The momentum, which had been with Ralf, then switched to Montoya so much that he was within one point of Michael Schumacher going into the penultimate race at Indianapolis. There an aggressive move by Montoya brought a collision with Barrichello's Ferrari and a drive-through penalty at the precise moment the Williams needed to switch to wet-weather tyres. The time lost had effectively ended his championship chances.

Montoya had been talking about joining McLaren. His relationship with Williams had nosedived at Magny-Cours. Wrongly believing he had been shafted by pit-stop tactics, he fired off a volley of abuse over the radio. Montoya was recalled to Williams HQ at Grove, where he was reprimanded verbally and then in writing just to make sure he had received the message. Juan Pablo may not have liked his telling-off but for the rest of the season he exploited the excellent combination of Williams, BMW and the continuing rise of Michelin. The objective for Head – once he had dealt with journalists and their dumb questions – was to make sure the package was effective from the very first race of 2004.

Williams were then rocked by the news that Montoya was indeed leaving, but not until the end of 2004. McLaren's announcement meant Williams could not involve Montoya in development ideas that might carry into the following year. For the team, especially the mechanics, there was also the demotivation of working on a car that, if it won the championship, would allow Montoya to take the coveted number 1 to McLaren.

Williams were one of the first teams to reveal their 2004 car, on 5 January. The FW26 caused quite a stir. At a time when regulations discouraged innovation and encouraged uniformity, the Williams sported a short broad nose with two pillars descending to hold the front wing, an arrangement immediately known as walrus tusks. By round thirteen (of eighteen), the tusks had gone, replaced by a more conventional nose. That was the most obvious sign of a troubled season with the team taking wrong turns on three or four fronts that more or less covered all the important aspects of the car, while the BMW V10 was a little short of its customary front-line power. In the middle of all this Patrick brought forward his plan for Sam Michael to become technical director while he assumed the title of director of engineering.

All told, it was a difficult season, not helped by Montoya and Schumacher racing in the knowledge that they would both be leaving at the end of the year, and in cars that secured them fifth and ninth in the drivers' championship, to make Williams fourth on the constructors' table. Ralf Schumacher's season was interrupted by a puncture which sent him into the wall at Indianapolis and caused hairline fractures of two vertebrae, his place being taken by Marc Gene and Antonio Pizzonia for the next six races. There was some consolation at the final race, Montoya marking his farewell with a brilliant win. It would be the last for Williams for a considerable time.

PATRICK HEAD

The year 2000, the first with BMW, we did as well as could be expected. It was a big engine, quite heavy, but it was not without power. BMW's Paul Rosche was a wonderful person, a lovely character with a motor-racing heart. It was a difficult time: there was a lot of politics at BMW. Mario Theissen was moved in and another guy who'd never designed a racing engine in his life became technical director. He was a clever guy, but he didn't know anything about racing engines. They pushed Paul Rosche out. That was in 2000, the year his engine was running.

Rosche had taken on a chap called Andy Cowell, who is now with Mercedes and is the architect of the current and last year's championship-winning Mercedes engine. He's a very bright young lad, but because he was a Rosche appointee he was sort of *persona non grata*. Mario Theissen brought in Heinz Paschen, who to his credit could see the work that Andy Cowell was doing in laying down what would be a very good engine. Paschen maybe made one or two areas of it a little bit more robust, but in detail he just carried on producing Cowell's engine, the P80, which in 2001 was a brilliant engine. Absolutely fantastic. We should have won the championship in 2001 and 2002. It wasn't totally reliable. We did have half a dozen engine failures, so that was part of the reason. But in truth the car wasn't good enough.

We went into 2001 with a determination to close the gap to McLaren and Ferrari and get ourselves into a position where we could win races. We did that, but then you ask yourself at the end of the season, 'Why didn't we do better?' We'd had eighteen retirements from the thirty-four car starts. Eight of those retirements had been driver inspired – not necessarily always our drivers, thanks to impacts from behind and suchlike – with the rest shared between car and engine. In total, that was greater than 50 per cent, which obviously wasn't acceptable. There was still a long way to go.

In 2003 we started to get our act together, but we didn't win the championship because we weren't ready. When we ran the FW25 for the first time, it was disappointing. For a time we lost our way because of confusing data from tests and uncertainty over which way to go with the rear suspension. We started the season weakly and then were strong in the middle. But Ferrari managed to throw in a curved ball after Budapest, where they challenged the Michelin tyres, and we spent most of the Monza test on long runs for legality for the Michelin tyres. We allowed that whole business to upset our process.

We were eight points ahead in the constructors' championship before the last three races and only one point behind in the drivers'. Between Ferrari and the FIA, they created the sort of upset that generally has been symptomatic of what occurred should anybody in that period threaten Ferrari's dominance. We should have been tougher and been able to deal with that and still win the championship. But we didn't. It wasn't as if we were being pathetic; we were still quick but we didn't win in 2003. And then Juan said he was leaving.

He'd got very steamed up about that incident during the French Grand Prix. He had been lying second to Ralf when he decided he wanted to come in a lap early. He knew what lap Ralf was coming in so he thought he would be able to jump him. He came in and returned with a very fast lap. But Ralf on that lap asked if he could come in early, and Sam could hardly say no when we were in a position to do so. When Juan came round and found Ralf coming out of the pits, still in the lead, he became very upset because he thought that in response to him coming in early, we'd said to Ralf, 'Oh, you'd better come in early, otherwise Juan's going to get you.' But that wasn't the case. It was Ralf who had initiated it.

We produced that rather stupid tusk car in 2004. We had Ralf and Juan, both in different ways very macho drivers but like oil and water, and their biggest interest was to shaft each other. Neither of them were team drivers.

JENSON BUTTON

It all happened very quickly. I had just finished the Formula 3 season and had one test in a Formula 3000 car. I was thinking that would be my next step, so when I got the Williams drive it was amazing. It wasn't a shock because I knew I was quick, but it was a big step at a relatively young age and with very little experience. I had to learn quickly but Frank and Patrick gave me the time I needed to gain that experience through racing.

Out-qualifying Ralf in only my second race was a memorable moment. I used to watch him on television and he had a few years' experience, so out-qualifying him was strange. I had a great race against Verstappen in Brazil, an awesome experience. I finished seventh in the race but I was on my way to the airport when I found out that I'd been given sixth place after David Coulthard had been disqualified. I had just earned my first point.

To qualify third at a circuit like Spa was also pretty amazing. It's such a long circuit with such demanding technical corners. It's a circuit I'd always loved in Formula Ford and Formula 3, but in a Formula 1 car it was very different. When I crossed the line in qualifying I was behind only Hakkinen and Trulli, and in front of Michael [Schumacher]. It was a great feeling. I also got my first taste of a Formula 1 press conference that day. It meant a lot to me and I realised that was exactly where I wanted to be, fighting at the front.

The British Grand Prix in April 2000 was an incredible experience racing in front of my home crowd. The build-up was massive, not just because of me but because DC [Coulthard] was starting at the front of the field and had a real chance of winning. I remember going round the outside of Michael and got a round of applause. I came home fifth running on only nine cylinders. I remember crossing the line and seeing the Union Jacks. DC won the race, which was also a very emotional moment and a great day for British fans. Every time I go back to Silverstone, I always get that same feeling, no matter how good the car is. It's great that fans stick by you through thick and thin.

Williams was a really happy place to be. As I gained more experience, we spent more and more time together. I had, and still have, a lot of respect for both Patrick and Frank. I was very sad to have to leave the team but they gave me a lovely farewell, and even though I've had a few contractual issues since, Frank, Patrick and I have remained good friends.

DICKIE STANFORD

When I heard we were getting Ralf, my first thought was that this must be off the back of Michael, or is he just naturally quick? He is quick but he suffered from having lots of outside distractions. Everybody compared him to Michael. Given a good car, Ralf would be as quick as Michael. Sometimes I believe that he was actually quicker than his brother. Michael worked harder, but if you put them in the same car I'd put money on Ralf. Michael would be thinking all the time, looking for the angle to help find an advantage. Give Ralf a quick car and he could be as fast as anyone else.

I had a lot of time for Montoya, but the problem was he wanted to do everything his way. He was always against anyone who wanted to do something different. He was so prone to outbursts that you wanted to say to Juan, 'Just be quiet and get on with it!' He had to have his say, whether he was right or wrong. If things were going his way, he was great – fantastic in the car, full of fun, having a joke and a laugh. If they were going against him, then the world was against him.

MARC GENE

There is no one who lives for Formula 1 as much as Frank. There is no one else who works in the factory on Christmas Day and New Year's Eve. And then there is no one with the personality of Patrick – so outspoken with things, and told direct. I think they are the last ones remaining in Formula 1 of the old school. They like and want real racing drivers. They don't mind drivers who like to take risks. I didn't have many accidents. I had only one big accident, once at Silverstone. I remember Patrick called me, and after asking if I was okay, he wanted to make sure that it wouldn't happen again. But his main concern was that I was okay.

I had always been aware of Williams when racing in Spain. They were of relevance to me because of the drivers they had and the titles and races they won. I had raced in Formula 1 with Minardi before becoming the Williams test driver. In 2003 I replaced Ralf for the Italian Grand Prix at very short notice. Sam Michael called me at 5 a.m. on Saturday morning and said, 'Get here quickly! Ralf is not feeling well.' So the adrenalin was pumping that day and it went very well. I finished fifth in the race, but only twenty seconds from the winning car. I scored some points which helped Williams finish ahead of McLaren in the championship.

I did three Grands Prix in total for Williams. And then Frank wanted to change *all* the drivers. He wanted to change the two race drivers and the two test drivers. Luckily for me, it was good timing because then I joined Ferrari. I had four years with the team but sometimes you need to change the relationships, and it was perfectly fine for Frank to do that. In my career I have to say it was good because I then went to another top team. I know that Williams are very proud to be a British team. Maybe that is one of the reasons why the BMW relationship was becoming difficult. I could see that the two sides worked in different ways.

MARK HUGHES

It was the summer of '02 and we journalists were writing that the Williams-BMWs were setting the tracks alight in qualifying, with Montoya taking pole pretty much a given. But just as surely on race day their challenge would fade along with their Michelins, and the Ferraris would disappear up the road at a canter. It had happened again like that on a blisteringly hot day at Magny-Cours. Monty had stuck it on pole, then limped home fourth while Michael Schumacher took yet another victory. Both Montoya and Ralf had experienced the usual problem of preventing their tyres going off after just a few laps. Williams seemed to be making no progress in curing the problem.

So after the race I went to find Patrick to try to get an insight into what they thought might be at the root of the problem, whether they had any idea of what avenues to pursue. Patrick's a fantastic bloke but getting him after a bad race can be like meeting a bear with a sore tooth. I got down to the Williams motorhome to find it was already being staked out by Peter Innes of *Motoring News* and the Colombian radio guy whose job it was every weekend to report to the Colombians why their man Montoya had failed to win again after blitzing everyone in qualifying. Patrick was inside there, they told me. Had they tried going in? I asked. Yes, but Patrick would just disappear into the debrief room as soon as they did that. He clearly didn't want to talk.

He used to come down to Magny-Cours on his BMW motorbike, and after a few minutes of the three of us waiting – two of us at one end of the motorhome, one of us at the other, so we had both exits covered – he appeared at the top of the steps in his motorcycling leathers, took a peek out, saw we were still there, grimaced, went back inside. It went on like this for about half an hour, with Patrick appearing ready to go, then going back inside. Until eventually he obviously decided he could wait no longer. He strode out, helmet in hand, staring straight ahead, making for the paddock exit. We converged on him asking our questions. He didn't break stride, didn't stop looking straight ahead. 'Yep.' 'Don't know.' 'No.' 'We are looking at it.' 'No,' he answered to each question in turn.

By this time I was beginning to get the giggles, and I'm sure that didn't help. Then finally we were given a break. Toyota's transporter was reversing towards us at an angle, apparently blocking his escape route. He was going to have to stop. To the right was blocked by the truck, to the left by some bushes. But it made no difference. Patrick wasn't stopping. He continued to stride towards the bushes, then just swiped them aside as he made his way through in his leathers. I gave up at this point mainly because the image of an angry Patrick swiping bushes aside while chased by two nervously polite journalists was just too funny for me to keep control. My shoulders were shaking uncontrollably. To Williams's great credit, after I wrote an affectionate column describing the scene, from the very next race they began a policy of making sure Sam Michael was available at a set time post-race to answer any questions.

A year or so later, it was one of those BMW dinners in the parallel motorhome – they never used to share motorhomes, which was significant, I think. The night was well into its swing as Patrick was leaving next door and popped his head in to see all the drunken hacks. He then proceeded to pull up a chair and join in. I got chatting to him about his racing exploits, and he was telling me that he'd done a couple of Honda CRX races in 1988. A friend of his owned a car and got

Patrick along to share it in a couple of two-driver long-distance events. I'd done a CRX race under similar circumstances at Donington, and now that Patrick mentioned it, yes, I did recall him being there at the driver briefing. Anyway, he was telling me how at Donington he took the first stint and had made a good start and was up the front half of the field and feeling quite pleased with himself when, two cars in front of him, someone spun at Old Hairpin. He had to stand on the brakes to miss it and most of the field passed him in the process. That was me! In my defence, I'd been nudged by the guy behind. Patrick still seemed so disappointed by the incident fifteen years later I don't think I was brave enough to tell him.

JONATHAN LEGARD

I remember in Brazil when talk of cost-cutting was all the rage in Formula 1 one year, probably in 2002, as the effects of 9/11 began to take hold. Frank was asked about the chances of teams working together to make changes, and he came out with this.

'We will always spend what we have in our budget to make ourselves competitive, to do what we can to win. Because we're racers, we're competitors. That's what makes us what we are, what we do. We race to be first off the plane; we race to be first to the baggage carousel; we race to the car hire to get the best cars; we race to be first to the track; we work late into the night to make our cars go fastest. That's what we're about and you tinker with that at your peril.'

It was all said with minimum fuss but it carried maximum impact. He may be sat in a wheelchair but the racer's mindset was still set to fast forward.

JUAN PABLO MONTOYA

A great four years racing, and of course I had been a test driver with them the year before. I have great memories, particularly of Frank. We still talk a lot on the phone; we get on really well. I have a lot of respect for Frank and we had a lot of fun; we had a good relationship right from the start. We had good times and our bad times, as you do anywhere, but I can't complain.

BMW always seemed to think they were superior and had better engines. Don't get me wrong: they did a really good job but they were overconfident about what they were doing and they gave the impression that what they were doing was more important than what Williams was doing. It was pretty clear that they always thought they could get more by doing it themselves, and I think they came in for a bit of a surprise.

Monaco and Brazil wins were both very special – I have the Brazil car at home. It was very special to win my last race for Frank and to close that chapter with a win was pretty huge.

As for the incident at Magny-Cours ... Funny, but I think our relationship improved after I told them I was leaving. It wasn't as good as it could have been at that time. A lot of things changed and I think the pressure went away from them. Everything happens for a reason; that's the way I feel. It never affected my relationship with Frank.

JIM WRIGHT

Patrick was invited by Mario Theissen to go on the Mille Miglia. Mario had got a BMW out of the BMW Museum, a very rare BMW, and Patrick was his co-driver. It was going to be a story for various publications, and stuff was being filmed and photographed. Patrick knew that and went along with it. He thought this would be a good opportunity to have some off-time with Mario over a period of a few days.

Then Mario, who was driving, had a sizeable shunt. Patrick had seen it unfolding in front of him and had said, 'Mario, slow down. They are about to pull out. Slow down!' Bang! They crashed at 50 miles an hour, which in a 1950s car – no seat belts or anything – was a sizeable crash. Patrick ended up in the footwell. He was okay, but in a heap in the footwell. Mario's first reaction was not, 'Oh my God. I'm really sorry;

are you okay Patrick?' No. His reaction was concern about how he had damaged this priceless car and what that might do to his career. I think Patrick's respect for Mario at that moment went down into the footwell.

In 2003, in the Austrian Grand Prix, Williams were on for a good result when there was a big bang as the engine blew up. There was a huge hoo-ha over this and the subsequent press release which said there had been a mechanical problem. It was very clear what had happened – the engine had blown up. There was obviously an investigation as there was for any car failure. It turned out there had been an O-ring failure, and as a result the radiator had burst. BMW took the position: 'Ah! The radiator. Williams make the radiators therefore a Williams fault.' I said, 'Hold on a second. Let's see what's cause and effect here.' Williams believed the O-ring was a BMW responsibility, which then led to the failure of the radiator. Whatever, it didn't matter. What was important was that the fault was corrected even though there was a lot of discussion, a lot of finger-wagging going on.

Next was Monaco, which was a fabulous race which Juan Pablo led while under huge pressure. Then in the last six laps Juan Pablo was on the radio saying, 'There's no fucking power, no fucking power.' They said, 'Yeah, we know. We've got some temperature problems; we're decreasing the revs.' A few laps later Montoya is under enormous pressure: Kimi Raikkonen is all over him. Juan Pablo says, 'If you don't give me some more fucking revs, I'm going to stick it in the fucking wall.' This was typical Juan Pablo. He meant it; he was driving the wheels off that car. So they agreed that they would give him a burst of power through the tunnel to protect him down to the chicane. Meanwhile the temperatures are still climbing and everyone is sweating in the pits. This thing is about to let go at any point. But somehow everything held together and we won the race.

The car arrived in *parc fermé* and there were puddles of water under it. Everyone in Williams knew it was the same problem that had happened at the previous race. There was the realisation within the team that we were within an ace of throwing away a win at Monaco. It should also be pointed out that four weeks before Monaco, at the Spanish Grand Prix, there had been the discovery of a drawing in the BMW truck of a snail, and it had in German a caption, 'The new Williams car'. It had deliberately been leaked to the media to make Williams look stupid. The car was poor in Barcelona, but two weeks later in Austria it was capable of winning the race. And now the win, fair and square, at Monaco.

Patrick went up to get the trophy and everyone from Williams was there, chest out. It really was a massive moment because they knew the history of this continuous pressure from Munich and then the denial in Austria over what had happened. Then to be within an ace of it happening again in Monaco. There were a lot of victories during the time I was there but Monaco 2003 was amongst the biggest because everyone had been under the cosh, really under the cosh. The atmosphere between Williams and BMW really had become very difficult.

ROBS LAMPLOUGH

Frank wanted to get land. He had this passion to become a landowner, have a chunk of England, and he ended up with a property near me. I'm a farmer and I have a business in Grove, so we're not only physical neighbours now, we're business neighbours as well. I've got Grove Technology Park, and that's the biggest commercial estate in his immediate area.

I have a Spitfire, which is kept at my home. I know that Frank likes them. He always asks me about aeroplanes, and if I'm up I'll try and fly past the factory. In fact, he asked me to do a fly-past when the BMW people were over signing the contract, I believe. So he had me do a fly-past in the Spitfire at the appropriate moment. He loved that.

THIRTY-THREE
Auf Wiedersehen, P1

Heading towards the thirtieth anniversary of their first win (first place is known as P1 in Formula 1 vernacular), the team's resilience would be tested to the limit. Finishing positions in the constructors' championship between 2005 and 2008 would swing from fourth – considered a disappointment in the heady days of a decade before – to eighth.

Sam Michael continued the process of realignment within the company during the winter of 2004/5 while at the same time preparing for two new drivers. While Mark Webber's signing had been publicised before the 2004 season was over, the choice of second driver was a typically long-winded affair as Frank appeared to dither over Antonio Pizzonia, a known quantity as test driver and occasional substitute, and Nick Heidfeld, whose career at one point had seemed on the rocks. And in the background rumours continued to surface that the relationship between Williams and BMW was no better – indeed probably worse – than before. But all these were minor issues compared with two events which had far-reaching consequences for Williams: the commissioning of a new wind tunnel at Grove and the late introduction of rule changes affecting aerodynamic and bodywork configurations for 2005, which would put BMW-Williams on the back foot for the best part of the season.

There seemed cause for optimism when both cars were running up front at the second round in Malaysia, Heidfeld making it to the podium after Webber got himself tangled with Fisichella. Then the boys in blue and white finished second and third at Monaco a few months later. The FW27 was on the pace at the Nürburgring, and there was evidence of the necessary speed at Monza in September. But those were just four of nineteen races. Elsewhere, it was a constant struggle for balance and grip – unsurprising given the technical team had almost no data to work from thanks to the decommissioning of one wind tunnel and the slow introduction of the new one.

At least the facilities were ready for 2006, but the team would lose Heidfeld, whom BMW had taken with them in their switch from Williams to Sauber. The season would turn out to be one of the most disappointing in the team's history. Finishing eighth in the constructors' championship pleased Patrick and Frank about as much as learning that Webber and Nico Rosberg had crashed into each other on the opening lap of the final race. This was a sad way to end the team's two-year relationship with Webber and single season reunited with Cosworth engines, but had also been the final opportunity to salvage something from a year in which two sixth places had been the highlights. There had been flashes of potential, but with third place at Monaco within reach Webber had been let down by yet another mechanical failure. The FW28 was rarely on the pace. Performance shortfall was one thing, but the spate of breakdowns was galling for a team which prides itself on attention to detail.

Williams had taken a gamble by signing Rosberg. The 2005 GP2 champion scored two points in his first race but then showed just how difficult it is to step up to Formula 1. None the less, the team had no hesitation in keeping the son of their former world champion on board for 2007. Meanwhile, Sam Michael was implementing a series of reforms focused on improving reliability and introducing new blood. Jon Tomlinson arrived as head of aerodynamics; Rod Nelson moved from Renault to become chief operations engineer; John Russell returned with sole responsibility for reliability and moving Williams on from the eleven mechanical failures that had contributed to such a poor track record in 2006. All this took place in the context of Williams changing engine supply to Toyota and the introduction of a revised seamless-shift gearbox.

Early indications that Williams might be back on course came when they started the 2007 season having already completed several race distances; in 2006 the team's first completed race distance had been at the end of the opening round of the championship in Bahrain. Sure enough, fewer niggling failures allowed the technical team to focus on making the car faster rather than simply a reliable runner for Rosberg and Alex Wurz, the test driver having been promoted to the race team. Going into the Japanese Grand Prix, Williams were eleven points behind Renault and hoping to close the gap in the final three races. It did not happen because of Renault's strong showing at Fuji and an electronics problem for Rosberg, but the fact that the team had entertained the thought of beating the reigning champions marked a step up in expectation as well as performance. Williams finished fourth in the constructors' championship.

The 2008 car, the FW30, was a step forward, but this was one of the closest seasons of all time. Less than a tenth of a second could mean the difference between the third and eighth rows, and the Williams cars were all over the place: eleventh on the grid one weekend, sixth the next, then fifth, followed by fifteenth and eighteenth. The FW30 was competitive on tracks with slow corners but struggled on those requiring good high-speed aerodynamics. Rosberg summed it up by taking his first podium in Melbourne but then finishing fourteenth two weeks later in Malaysia. Kazuki Nakajima's first full season for Williams did not go much better. The team had slipped back to eighth on the constructors' table by the time the final round was over. Part of the reason for the mediocre showing was the decision to focus on the 2009 car, which would have to conform to the most wide-ranging changes to the technical regulations since 1983. The fresh approach might just give Williams the opportunity to get back to where they belonged, particularly as steps were being taken to drastically reduce budgets in Formula 1.

It was appropriate, if unfortunate, that money should dominate the news on 26 February 2009, the day Williams invited the media to Grove for a pre-season briefing. The previous evening the Royal Bank of Scotland, a prime Williams sponsor, had announced a staggering loss of £24 billion. BBC News naturally led with this story but then got their facts wrong by saying that RBS were pulling the plug on Williams, thereby spelling the end of the team, Formula 1 as a whole and probably the world as we know it. Frank was not slow to put them straight: RBS had simply said they would not renew on expiry at the end of 2010. Williams would fight on.

FRANK WILLIAMS

The deal with BMW was done for all the right reasons, but it just didn't work out. It was agreed with Mr Pischetsrieder, the BMW chairman, as far back as 1998, but then they got into trouble financially. In the meantime they put the programme back to 2000. Then in 1999 the loses rose to €3.4 million, a massive loss, and Bernd had to resign.

In the meantime he had just appointed his buddy Gerhard Berger to be team manager, and Mario Theissen, whom I didn't know. And those two worked to get everything under their control. The first meeting we had, we were accused of having broken the contract in some way. We hadn't, and they backed off. It was just a small thing about who was going to pay for testing and it set the scene for what was to follow. It was apparent that BMW were being aggressive from the start. It was not a partnership of respect and friends.

Mind you, we were no longer very good then. Adrian had gone; Patrick had gone off the boil a little; the guys we had weren't up to it. It didn't work properly downstairs. BMW got a bit unhappy about it, and they were right, from that point of view. The engine in 2001 was in a league of its own, phenomenal. The only thing that saved the car was the horsepower. I could understand their frustration. BMW is a very proud company; they were spending a lot of money, but show the car a lot of corners and it was not up to it.

I loved Juan Pablo Montoya's spirit. He had wonderful car control, but he was a bit too emotional at times. I was sorry to see him go and I think he regrets going, although he likes the USA very much and racing there means it's easier to get back to Colombia. Ralf was very fast but moody. He did it for the money and I really got the impression that he wasn't nuts about Formula 1. He was in his brother's shadow; he never quite seemed at ease with himself. He had good days but he was not consistent.

SAM MICHAEL

It was looking quite good at the end of 2004, and we thought we were back on track. Then the regulation changes hit us quite hard, and we didn't recover from them as well as we would have liked to. At the same time we commissioned the new tunnel and decommissioned the old one, so that was out of action for four months as well. It really hurt us. We didn't get as much development as we would have liked and spent the year playing catch-up.

There were points during the winter where we were getting one run per day in the tunnel and you are normally getting twenty-five to thirty runs per day. It was terrible. We were having to make design decisions on the car with no data. You can look back in hindsight and say it was bad timing, but actually it's amazing how long it takes to commission a tunnel.

Then it suddenly seems worthwhile. The best thing is when you can see progress. And the changes we had towards the end of the season were massive. We signed off the last piece of development on the FW27 just before Brazil and both tunnels were totally focused on the FW28, the 2006 car.

PATRICK HEAD

The Bridgestone tyres were excellent in 2006, but we gave ourselves an added difficulty initially because we were not familiar with the range of compounds thanks to having no carry-over experience from the previous year. When we were testing over the winter, we were extremely slow, well off the pace. Our long runs didn't look too bad but our single laps and first laps were very poor, and generally the winter running on cold tracks did not teach us very much. That improved when we got to hotter climates, but you could see quite clearly from Michael Schumacher's performance that the tyres were excellent and fully capable of winning a championship.

Once Cosworth got on top of an early problem, the V8 returned to being an extremely good, fully competitive engine. I have no doubt that it would have been capable had our car been a match. The FW28 had a poor handling characteristic at the rear, particularly entering corners. It's about the worst characteristic you can have because there are all sorts of follow-on problems. For example, it causes you to put on more wing, and of course that makes you slow on the straights.

Monaco was a particularly low point. Mark was in very good shape. He could see that Alonso in front was in trouble with his rear tyres whereas our Bridgestones were just getting stronger and stronger. Monaco is a bit of a special case in terms of the engine cycle and traction control, which gives the exhaust a bit of a hard time. But this type of unreliability went on all year. Some of those problems came from design, some from quality control, and some from maybe trying too hard and taking risks that didn't pay off. It caused us to take a very good look at ourselves. We identified areas of weakness and reorganised ourselves internally. We restructured the design office under heads of departments who had to deliver to the chief designer. We promoted internally and we took one or two people from other teams because we felt we needed a bit of fresh blood.

DICKIE STANFORD

You hear the rumours and we rated Paul Rosche as a top guy who knew what he was doing. The feeling was, *Now we're going to go places. BMW aren't coming in just to make up the numbers.* They came in with a lot of new people who hadn't done Formula 1. It was quite hard work for the test team, bringing everyone up to spec, ready for racing. There were different ways of thinking, and even before the first race you could see the management changing at BMW. Slowly but surely we could see all the original people being diverted somewhere else.

They had a goal – I wouldn't say it was unrealistic – but they wanted something within a very short period of time, and it didn't seem to be coming from here. There was the clash between BMW and Frank and Patrick, which I must say was kept out of the garage. Franz Tost was team manager of BMW, and I was his counterpart on the race team. We made sure that whatever was going on outside stayed there. The guys from BMW and Williams working in the garage actually had a really good relationship with each other. It was a very good team that just didn't work out – one of those things that should have but never did.

JOHN RUSSELL

I was back for the first year of Toyota. It was different. I knew it had changed. I'd been out of circulation full time as an employee really since 1994. I jumped back briefly, but only for three months before going to Jaguar. Then I went to Australia. Bernie Ecclestone once said that Frank and Patrick run the best grocery store in the business. But it's no longer a grocer's shop; it's a supermarket. But you can still get a pound of bananas if you know where to look. It's got the veneer of a ruthlessly organised supermarket, but if you go behind the scenes the grocer's shop is still there, which is the nice thing about Williams.

MARK HUGHES

It was not long after I first began covering Formula 1 regularly. I'd spoken to Frank a couple of times but didn't really know him. I was then at one of those Saturday 'meet Frank' mass-interview sessions that BMW used to lay on. The session was about ten minutes in and I'd not yet asked a question, was just listening. There was a gap of a second or so when no one was talking and Frank looked at me and said in perfect Geordie, 'Whey man, yi've not asked any questions yet, like, ya daft bugger,' much to the puzzlement of the assorted Italians, Germans, Brazilians, etcetera. He sees so many faces I'd no idea he'd even recall ever seeing me, let alone remember my accent. We now regularly converse in Geordie.

In 2005 I was talking to Patrick in the Williams motorhome about nothing very important when Mario Theissen came in the door and approached our table. He very politely said, 'Excuse me,' to me and then asked Patrick when he could come and discuss 'what we were talking about earlier'. Patrick seemed very irritated, looked up and just said, 'When I've finished doing this.' Theissen visibly bristled, said, 'Okay,' and walked back next door to the BMW camp. Seemed all was not going well in that relationship.

JIM WRIGHT

I could speak to you for two days about BMW. The one thing you have to remember is that the original deal was done between Frank and Bernd Pischetsrieder, and Pischetsrieder had a guy called Karl-Heinz Kalbfell as his commercial guy. He wasn't a board member but he was as close to a board member as you could possibly get. He was in charge of marketing for the whole of BMW. Pischetsrieder left or was ousted; Kalbfell was still there, but there was a lot of politics going on, and the original deal that was done between BMW and Williams was not being carried through. A new regime was in place, which was Mario Theissen and Gerhard Berger. It was clear that although there was a signed contract between BMW and Williams which said X, Y and Z, Gerhard and Mario didn't approve it and didn't want it.

Frank could have said, 'Well, I'm sorry there's a signed contract; get on with it.' Frank being Frank said, 'Well, although we've got a signed contract, we want to work with these people over five, seven years, whatever, so it's best that we build a relationship with them.' So, he tore up the original contract and we started afresh. At a very early stage it became apparent that Mario's ambition was to be a team principal, and I think that created an unhealthy tension throughout the relationship. Frank and Patrick bent over backwards to try to make that relationship work. I wouldn't be critical of Mario and Gerhard: they came into something at a later stage and they wanted to do it in the way they believed was right. They believed that what other people had committed BMW to was wrong so I don't criticise them. They had their own views, and it was right that they should implement those. You can't take over something and be responsible for it if you are inheriting something you fundamentally don't believe in. There were issues there from the start.

ALEX WURZ

My first memory was an International Touring Car race at Silverstone. I'd had a pretty spectacular win, and when I finished they called me on the radio and said, 'First of all, you have to go to the stewards of the meeting because they want a word with you, and after that Frank Williams is waiting for you.' I had to go to the stewards to keep my first position and then I went to Frank. He had waited more than one hour because there were a few drivers at the stewards, so I'd had to queue up. But he waited all that time and just said that he'd had a really great time watching me be so aggressive. That was my first contact. That was about 1996. The next encounter I had with him was when I was in my first season with Benetton. He wheeled past me in Australia and said, 'We spoke about you, but now you are too expensive, and I should have picked you up when you were cheap.' After that we always had friendly chats. The real contact came when he called up and offered me the driving position in 2007.

I didn't really know what to expect, because you hear so many different things. I had a mega two years at Williams from the first to the last moment. I respect everyone there for what they're doing. I still have a very good relationship with all of them. When I am in England sometimes I drive by to see Frank. I stop and talk, not only about motorsport but about life and stuff.

I was from the first moment on very deeply involved with the car development and building up team strategy, and for me that's the field I'm interested in. It was extremely rewarding that from the word go I was right there and they wanted to talk to me and hear me. After the first test I gave feedback and mentioned something about the suspension geometry, and in my second test we had different front geometry. I thought, *Wow!* It took the other teams half a year to be convinced, yet Williams made it right away. They really involve the driver much more than other teams, which can be an advantage and a disadvantage, depending on who your driver is and who is guiding your development.

You feel very clearly that this is a team with tradition. There is a point when you feel that the tradition is weighing too heavy and is a burden. You have to accept that this is a fast-moving business and things are changing, and when you're not in a position of race winning you have to leave your history aside and concentrate on that moment. Even if you achieve 100 per cent and you're only seventh, then you should be at that moment happy that you achieved all you could. You shouldn't be happy about not finishing first of course, but you can't be completely destroyed – and sometimes that was the case at Williams.

NICO ROSBERG

I first became aware of Williams when they were invincible in the early 1990s. When I switched on the TV for the first time in my life to watch

Formula 1, they were going to win, whatever happened. I started watching in the early '90s. I was thirteen, and for all of my youth they were unbeatable. Mansell, Hill, Villeneuve, Prost, the whole bit. Of course, my father had told me a lot about the team. When I joined Williams in 2005 they had won their last GP in 2004 and were just behind Ferrari. I was joining the number-two team at the front. The fact that it had been my dad's team didn't have any bearing.

MARK WEBBER

I was very, very excited about going to Williams, but it didn't really turn out as we would have liked. It was a tough situation for the whole team then. So they're not the memories I had in mind. I particularly enjoyed working with Patrick. You always got a straight answer. That was good and socially it was very good as well. Frank is an inspiration in many ways. To have been what he's been through, he's absolutely incredible, and that was another reason to lure you there. There is an absolute uniqueness about how Williams run as a team. It's a total one-off, and no other team could do what they do or how they do it. I worked with some good people there. I enjoyed working with Sam and some of the engineers. We had some fun – we had to in the middle of some of that – but most of it was toil and not as nice as we would have liked.

We had a chance to win Monaco. I was cruising really, doing really well, and the car was very quick there – we got the most out of it. We had a lot of reliability problems that year. We gave away a lot of points and podiums.

Patrick remembers every failure rather than every win. He was like that, straight from the hip, mate. When I was there, his motivation was high but probably not as high as when he was in the 1980s and 1990s. Whereas Frank probably hadn't changed all the way through. He was mentally always there, whereas Patrick probably did go through a bit of a different stage. It meant a lot to me when Patrick put his head in the cockpit at Brazil for my last race and said, 'Sorry it didn't work out for you.' He knew I was on my way and I still remember that. I got pissed off at times and so did they with me, but it was good for Patrick to say it to me. I liked his style.

But Frank's passion is phenomenal. If he can, he still loves going to Becketts at Silverstone and watching the cars going through there. He had a stopwatch in his road car. He used to love seeing how we were doing against the clock, preferably kicking the opposition's arse.

THIRTY-FOUR

The Odd Couple

Sir Frank Williams and Patrick Head are unique in every sense. There never has been, and probably never will be, a motor sport partnership that has worked so successfully and endured for so long. Patrick and Frank are united by a love of motor racing and the narcotic draw of competing at the highest level in such a dramatic sport. But the fact that they are such disparate characters has allowed their personal chemistry to bind this collaboration of pragmatism in their respective departments. Only Formula 1, with its mix of driving on the edge of human endeavour and the urgent need for solutions to complex technical questions, could have brought these two men together. And, arguably, only Williams and Head could have made it work.

Frank and Patrick have their procedures and their foibles, just like anyone else. But the majority of those quirks, combined with matter-of-fact methods, simply encourage a profound sense of endearment which permeates the observations and anecdotes that follow below. No other personal alliance in racing – and arguably within the wider context of sport – generates admiration and affection fashioned by many years of sometimes getting things wrong but always operating with dignity and honour.

Williams and Head are the core of this team. Their ethos of winning correctly rather than at any cost is a template, not only for the Williams

F1 workforce but also anyone struggling to cope with the fact that finishing first is the preserve of just one and the frustration of many. The knowledge and experience accumulated through thirty seasons of racing was apparent during a press conference at the fifth round of the 2009 championship in Spain. Asked about his disappointing season thus far, Patrick did not dodge the question.

'We have had some fairly unusual races,' said Head. 'In Australia we messed up a pit stop for Nico. Then, when he was on the option [softer] tyre his race engineer encouraged him to push very hard as I think they thought he might be able to get Rubens [Barrichello]. But the option tyre was very delicate and it fell off a cliff really for us. We have not made the best of the Grands Prix. In Malaysia and Shanghai, with the wet and the wet-dry conditions, which is an opportunity for everybody, for various reasons we did not make the best of that.

'In Bahrain, although Nico made a good start, he lost a lot of places going into turn one. He started ninth and finished ninth, nobody broke down. [Felipe] Massa broke down but Kimi [Raikkonen] got Nico going into the first corner, so it was not a very special race. We are certainly disappointed with the results but there are a few teams in that position and there is no point in kicking the dog or anything like that. You just go back and work that bit harder and try and not make the same mistakes. And there is no point in complaining that we are an independent team up against the big guys. I think we have got the resources. We haven't got maybe as big a budget as some teams but I don't think we think we are budget-limited in developing the car. It is up to us to keep up.'

Two weeks later in Monaco, Frank was typically clipped but to the point when asked why his drivers, Nico Rosberg in particular, appeared to be competitive during practice but not in either qualifying or the race.

'If you are quick, the race will tell you – or the public – that you are quick,' said Frank. 'In practice, you can fool people, including your-self. The best way to review anything is to look at the results after each and every race. That's why we're here. Formula 1 always finds out the truth pretty quickly.'

Here, then, is the truth about Frank and Patrick by those who know them best.

NEIL OATLEY

I count myself really lucky that Williams is where I started my career. Frank and Patrick were great people to work with and learn from. It's probably not so obvious nowadays, but Frank had an incredibly expressive face. If something was going well, it was like a cartoon mouth with the lips curving up; if something was going badly, it really was upside down. You didn't need to ask; you just knew. One glance at Frank's expression was enough.

He was an incredible enthusiast about anything he did. I used to live in the same village as him, not far from Didcot, and probably two or three times a week he would decide he wanted to run home. So I had to drive his car back and pick him up in the morning, no matter what I wanted to do myself, so he could do his five-mile run. I acted as his taxi service.

In those early days Frank had some deal with Fiat – I think he had a mate there who got cars really cheap. Fiat brought out this sport model with an R engine and a spoiler on the back. It probably wasn't any quicker, but just looked as though it might have been. When this car arrived, Frank was jumping around the office with joy because he'd got this racing car and he could pass on the boring one to Patrick. He was just over the moon.

HOWDEN GANLEY

I really do admire all he has achieved, particularly in the face of such adversity. In my next life I would like to come back and drive for Frank again, but I would like to know he'd have Patrick there as well! His determination is incredible. He is a winner. But the thing that always struck me was that big winning smile; he could melt everybody with that. You would be pissed with him and he would just give you one of those smiles – and that would be it. No more argument.

NIGEL MANSELL

Very few people are legends in their own lifetime but Frank is quite an exception. Very few people would have been able to cope with the trauma and fighting for life as he did for so long and come out of it on top.

ALAIN PROST

I was sure the team would go on. But I never ever imagined that Frank would be so involved for more than twenty years now, the way he is at the head of his team. He really has set an example. Frank is really unbelievable. I remember when he was running the team when I was there and he had some difficulties, you really need to have the passion and to trust in yourself and in your team. I tried to run a team but I was four times world champion and having success as a driver is different.

BERNIE ECCLESTONE

I'm absolutely sure if it had happened to me what happened to Frank, I wouldn't have been able to do what Frank has done. It's not a case of wanting to physically; it's wanting to mentally. Particularly when you remember what he was like before the accident, running everywhere, never sitting still. He is exceptional. He has done everything the hard way but he's never changed.

DEREK DALY

Sam Schmidt was an IndyCar driver who was paralysed in an accident. I was at the US Grand Prix and I met Sam and his wife. I said to Sam that I would like him to meet Frank Williams and that he was in a wheelchair like himself but had completely got on with his life and put it behind him and moved on. I went to see Frank and said, 'I've got a friend of mine; he's in a wheelchair. He's a race car driver, paralysed; he's thinking about starting a team. Would you take a minute to come out and talk to him?' He said, 'Of course I will.' Before Schmidt arrived, Frank said, 'Derek, I'm happy to talk to him. I'll tell him to do it because look at me Derek, I'm in a wheelchair but before that I did everything, won everything, and had a good time. So moving on in the wheelchair was no big deal because I'd already done everything I'd wanted to do.'

I said that if he could convey that to Sam, then it would help him. They had a great chat and Sam started his own team the following year and he's been one of the most successful Indy Lights teams in the States.

PETE FOSTEKEW

And apart from being in a wheelchair, Frank has never really changed. Yes, he's slowed down a bit, doesn't rush around so much obviously, and of course the trouble is now you can't hear him coming. Before, you could hear him clip-clopping about the place, and you knew he was coming, but now he creeps up behind you and you don't know he's there. But his ability remains, and I suppose that must have been the saving grace for the company because I can't honestly see it would have survived without him.

In my working career, which is knocking on fifty years now, the two men I most admire are Frank and Patrick simply because of what they've achieved between them. History states that we've won all these world championships, and I for one am very proud to be a part of that, but if those two hadn't got together, it wouldn't have happened. Frank will tell you he's no engineer but he can drag money out of the back end of a donkey. Patrick, on the other hand, couldn't do that but he's a bloody good engineer. This has been like a marriage made in heaven from a motor-racing point of view.

STEVE COATES

If you're in trouble one way or another with Frank and you've got a clever answer, he'll appreciate that more than grovelling or apologising profusely. I became chief truckie responsible for freight and logistics. Frank's always had a thing about the grass and the bushes around the factory: everything has to be impeccable. Frank had a sign made by maintenance, about two foot square on a solid square post, saying KEEP OFF THE GRASS. One night we got back late from a race and this guy had gone up on to the grass and put two massive furrows, right outside the factory: six-inch-deep ruts which I couldn't do anything about. Not only had he gone up on to the grass, he'd also hit the sign and bent it at a ninety-degree angle, which I couldn't pull straight.

I came in the next morning thinking I was going to get it. If I was in trouble or knew I was going to get a bollocking, I'd play cat and mouse – hide and keep out of Frank's way for as long as possible. After about two weeks I thought he'd forgotten, but then we got to the next race and he'd not been there two minutes before I was summoned. He called me into the motorhome and said, 'You truck drivers are supposed to be the best truck drivers in the world, the most professional truck drivers in the world. Your cargo is worth millions and millions of pounds, so how is it that you can't keep off my fucking grass?'

I said, 'Frank, I quite agree, we are the best drivers in the world, but unfortunately we haven't got the best equipment. The trucks are not state of the art with heated mirrors; we have these cheap old trucks with mirrors that keep steaming up. So unfortunately it doesn't matter how professional we are, we still can't see your effing grass.' He just pissed himself laughing and said, 'Go on, bugger off.' He gives you a ticking-off, but he'd never ever lay into you. He has never lost his sense of humour.

When I used to do the tyres, I got a bit more responsibility over the years – to the point where I would be totally left alone to make all the decisions about picking the race sets, doing the pressuring, the lot. I cocked up quite a few times. If Patrick was involved, I'd go down to the

Goodyear lads to get the tyres stripped at the end of the race. They'd greet me with 'So you got a bollocking then?' When I asked how they knew, they'd say they could hear it! If Patrick was delivering a bollocking, we reckoned you could hear it four garages away. Frank, on the other hand, would just have a quiet word.

If Patrick has made a mistake, he will apologise. People have accused him of being arrogant and rude but he's not; he's simply got so much going on in his head. I can't think of anyone who is more forgiving than Frank or more trusting in your work. He has complete faith in his staff around him, and that's where that loyalty comes from.

SIR JACKIE STEWART

You could say Frank's accident was character-building, and it surely has built a character in him. But here he is still with the strength, the dignity and the presence. You don't hear Frank talking badly of people or being abusive of people. Frank Williams has an amazing mind-management programme. He's not Mr Personality but he has a dignity that is very British – no one more proud to be English, though of course his whole success has been based on his Scottish education! He's proud of the monarchy. The Princess Royal is one of his heroes and he carried 'Save the Children' on his car for years for nothing.

There isn't a union like Frank and Patrick anywhere else in motorsport. Both of them carry a dignity with them; both of them think before they speak. The two are a similar mould. Patrick comes to a race occasionally on a motorcycle. He comes in the morning and changes in the motorhome. After all these years in the business and being such an icon, he doesn't feel that he should wear the team kit until he's in the paddock.

DAMON HILL

When you know the amount of work they put in, the effort and the time and the rest of it that goes into producing a car that can win a Grand

Prix, you realise how priceless that is. To have it thrown away by some silly engineering mistake or driving error, you cannot imagine how frustrating that must be. You can understand why they pop sometimes.

They're like a married couple: Frank loves Patrick and Patrick loves Frank, and they go racing together. They can't use the word love; they're big men, they'd never go there. But that's what it is. These stories unfold and it's watching them deal with it which is the beautiful part.

FRANK DERNIE

Being at Williams was the best time of my life. We were a small group of people. Patrick and I meshed very well. What I was good at, he wasn't and vice versa. We had total confidence – I hope – in each other. If I went into the machine shop and saw something being made that I didn't like the detailed design of, I was probably the only person who would say to Patrick, 'Do you think that's all right?' and he would listen.

LADY SARAH ASPINALL

Frank's first win in 1979 was wonderful. He really deserved it because he had put his heart and soul into it. He almost sold his soul to the devil. But that's what you have to do. He could be a selfish bastard, make no mistake. Very tough. If he likes you, he is the most wonderful friend. But I wouldn't like to cross him.

KATE BATTERSBY

I do think he's easily the most interesting person on earth to interview. Celebrity is just anathema to him – the idea of slashing your emotional wrists in public for the benefit of a goggle-eyed public would repel him. When the journalist Robert Philip asked, 'What do you think of being a paraplegic?' Frank replied, 'I don't give a fuck.'

He also once told me an off-the-record story which I love because it really captures a savage humour which can be (a) fabulously funny and (b) often against himself. Lots of people only ever see him on TV hunched over a monitor in the garage with that rigid expression on his face. The idea that he is incredibly funny escapes a lot of people.

I was trying to engage him – hopelessly – in a questionnaire-type interview, in which one of the questions was 'Who would you have dinner with if you could have dinner with anyone at all?' He's just terrible at those kind of questions, and first he just said, 'I don't eat dinner,' or something a bit literal like that, deliberately missing the point. Then he asked me to turn off the tape recorder. 'It would be that ugly tennis woman, the really rich one, whatever her name is.' I said politely, 'Do you mean Martina Navratilova?' and he said, 'Yes, that's her. It would be a perfect dinner, because I could get her to give me all her money to sponsor the team, and also she's so muscly she could carry me around all the time.' Patrick was also standing nearby for that one, and snorted his head off. But then so did I. It's always grieved me not to be able to use it.

I didn't meet him until 1994, i.e. long post-accident. But what I remember especially from that first meeting was the way he likes to look at you if you happen to be a woman. Obviously we know that he is, shall we say, a chap who has always enjoyed female company, but I think he liked the game of slightly discomfiting you by looking at you in a kind of flirtatious – not leery or yucky or anything – manner, because he knew you were thinking in your leaden way, *Hang on, this guy's in a wheelchair so I must be wrong*, which is of course a terribly patronising way to think. I felt uncertain about it for a while, thinking, *Nah*, but then I mentioned it to Jane Gorard, who worked in the PR department. She grinned in instant recognition, saying he definitely liked to do that. His accident diminished him physically so much that sometimes it can be hard to imagine him as the chap of pre-crash legend who ate up life. I never knew him as an able-bodied guy, but sometimes it's possible to peer through the two-way mirror of time and be able to see through it back to the day when he must have been a powerfully attractive bloke. I don't know if he'd like to know that, or if it would piss him off more than ever.

He said he crashed because of his own 'hooligan driving ... The stupidest thing I ever did was disregard the laws of physics regarding adhesion to the road. Every corner I could see around was a challenge.' He's not much given to introspection, as you know, but when he talked about his life of 'fantastic privilege' in Formula 1, I asked what he'd think if he got to the pearly gates and was told by St Peter that the accident was the trade-off for this life of fantastic privilege. He didn't hesitate. He said, 'Yes, fair enough. I'd ask for another deal in my favour, mind you. I'd ask to meet one of the great composers – Beethoven, say – so I could shake his hand. But if that was the deal, I'd say yes.'

ROSS BRAWN

I never saw them fall out. It was like a marriage. They were always bickering but they always stayed together. I remember Frank used to come in and say, 'Tell me something technical, Ross. Patrick hates it when I know anything technical about the car, so just give me a snippet about the car that I can go back and wind him up.' So we used to feed him. But they always had a very strong relationship.

MARTIN BRUNDLE

I drove their car in 2007 for ITV. I had a fitting at the factory, and I have to say that of all the cars I've driven for ITV the Williams team gave me the most professional service. It was almost like I was signed up for the season. I had a seat fit and was constantly asked what I needed. They ran two cars for us: a halfway-house 06/07 and an 07 for us to do some overtaking features. They really went to town and did a good job.

DICKIE STANFORD

You have McLaren, say, where Ron Dennis was pushing for the ultimate this or the ultimate that; we tend to get on with it. I'm not saying

McLaren don't get on with it – they obviously do – but we go about it in a different way. Williams more often than not have been in McLaren's shadow and everyone likes the underdog. We don't have multi-million-pound motorhomes, or whatever they're called now. Yes, it looks good and the sponsors probably like it, but, as Frank says, it doesn't actually make the car go any quicker. I think if Frank had his way we'd have a caravan out the back of the garage.

We don't make anything for anyone else. We don't have an engine manufacturer behind us. But we can generally keep up with everyone else with what we've got. All our technology is the same as everybody else's. It's beginning to show that we don't have an engine manufacturer behind us, but that's life – we've got to make a better car.

JOHN CADD

The big thing for me is that Frank's a fighter. After his accident it would have been so easy to throw in the towel, but he's carried on. I've got a lot of respect for him and for Patrick. I've been here for thirty years. I could have gone to other places. But in my heart it's racing and it's this team.

STEVE COATES

Frank still comes down to see us, but we're more tucked away. There are so many more departments and the chances of bumping into him are less. I don't think Frank is aware of how many people are working for him and not Team Williams. He just won't have it. He doesn't realise that when you get down to the nitty-gritty, we're here for him, out of respect and loyalty.

ALAN CHALLIS

If you wanted a question answered, just go and see Frank. His door was always open. 'If I'm not there, just make an appointment and I'll see you as soon as I come in.' Patrick's door was always open too. I was unfortunate enough to lose my wife a year ago. They treated me very well over that. I've been given an open invitation to come whenever I want to come. I haven't done, but the invitation is there.

SAM MICHAEL

Frank lives around half an hour from the factory, and not long after I'd joined I'd been over there with my family. We'd been in two cars because I had to go back to work. Frank and I left the house at the same time. I was just in front of him and had to stop for fuel. He kept going, and after I had finished and paid I called Frank and asked him why he was taking so long to get to the factory. He said, 'What do you mean? My driver's flat out, like he always is.' So I bet that I could beat him to the factory.

I was in a BMW 330. I caught them about 400 yards before the factory and overtook going into the roundabout. I won't say what speed I was doing, but I had everything timed just perfectly. I just caught the apex of the roundabout to turn left and right at the last minute. I had all the brakes smoked up going into the roundabout and had to push Frank into the gutter. I thought I'd just got away with it. Then at the last minute a farmer comes round the roundabout in his Land Rover and I thought, *Oh God, I'm about to have a massive shunt in front of Frank*. I didn't know whether he'd be angry or laughing his head off. I stopped in the middle of the roundabout, in front of this Land Rover, which had to stop as well, looked up and waved, got into first gear and drove off. When I got out of the car, Frank thought it was the best thing since sliced bread. He said he was praying that I was going to run into the side of the Land Rover, just so he could embellish the story more.

Frank is your racer's racer, he really is. Frank will ring me up when we're testing and ask me to take the mobile phone out on to the pit lane so he can hear the cars going past. This is someone who has been listening to them for forty years but will get me to leave my mobile phone on the pit wall for a couple of minutes so he can hear the noise of the cars ringing through the grandstands. One of my favourite sayings he has is 'Racing is a state of mind. You're either in or you're out. There's nothing in between.' And he's stuck by that since I've known him.

I have loads of funny stories about Patrick too, but unfortunately you can't print any of them – not because they're dirty or anything like that, but because they're so politically incorrect. Which is what endears him to people.

VIRGINIA WILLIAMS

It's good that Frank and Patrick are so different, otherwise it would be too clinical. If Frank and Patrick were similar in their control, then it wouldn't be as much fun. They're quite an odd couple, and that's why it works. I've often thought that it's the day marriage, because Frank and Patrick are virtually married, aren't they? Frank and Patrick's relationship is thirty years old and Jackie Stewart gave a dinner two years ago to celebrate it. There aren't any other relationships in Formula 1 that have lasted that long – nowhere near, not even close. I remember Alexander Hesketh talking at a function to celebrate Frank's hundredth race win and saying, 'We won *one* race, and that was hard. To win a hundred … It's quite an extraordinary achievement.'

GERALD DONALDSON

The opinions expressed by veteran insiders in response to my queries as to what so-and-so was really like were a shock to the system when I first ran away with the Formula 1 circus as a journalist some four decades ago. According to the prevailing wisdom nearly everyone involved in the sport was an appalling human being. Certain character traits were seen as redeeming virtues. 'Decent blokes' were much appreciated, and even the most dastardly villains could be forgiven if they were considered to be 'real racers'. Very rare were those who enjoyed the distinction of being regarded as both decent blokes and real racers. Chief among them were – and still are – Frank Williams and Patrick Head.

The Williams team principals remain highly likeable, hard-nosed competitors who share a fighting spirit tempered by an engaging sense of humour. Even when Patrick shouts he has a twinkle in his eye, and Frank, ever the enthusiast, gets as much from his sport as the keenest Formula 1 fan and loves to talk about it. I once asked him what made a top driver. 'The best of them,' Frank said, 'are driven, motivated, pushy, won't-accept-second-best, immensely competitive people. This is what makes them good – because they're bastards!'

ADRIAN NEWEY

Frank has tremendous determination: he lives for his motor racing. One of the things he measured people by was how many hours he thought they were doing. He had a tremendous regard if he thought people were working on a Saturday. Some of the guys got smart to that. They knew that Frank would arrive at around eleven o'clock on Saturday morning, be wheeled in through the race bay, look at the cars and then disappear upstairs. Then he would come back down at about five o'clock. So they would come in and make sure they happened to be walking through the race bay at eleven o'clock, then go away again after having been in the factory for about ten minutes, and then happen to be walking through the race bay at five o'clock.

There was an amusing incident for everyone else but me at Magny-Cours in 1991. A local motorbike dealer had decided it would be good publicity to lend Nigel and Riccardo a couple of Suzuki 1100s. Patrick decided that was far too dangerous for the drivers and he and I should have the bikes. It was a lovely sunny weekend, perfect for a bike, particularly as we stayed in a chateau some distance away, and it made a great ride to and from the track. Come Saturday evening, we were feeling pretty chuffed because we had qualified on the front row. It was in the days when all mechanics ate in a central canteen affair colloquially known as the roach coach. The Williams motorhome was parallel with where I was about to set off on the bike, and opposite was the roach coach, with all the Williams boys having their supper. At the end of the alleyway it was necessary to do a ninety-degree right by the Camel hospitality area.

I set off on the bike, pulled what I thought was quite an impressive wheelie, but I had underestimated how quickly the Camel motorhome was coming up. I made the fatal basic mistake of getting on the front brake before the front wheel was back down, at which point, when it did land, I went straight on my side, skidding along on my arse and my elbow, and then impaled myself in the lower awning of the Camel motorhome, with the bike alongside. I got back on my feet, looked around and could have sworn I'd seen people eating in the Camel motorhome. Then, one by one, dignitaries and VIPs covered in red wine and cream pastries rose from beneath their tables.

The boys of course gave me a fair old cheer and a jeer. Nigel had been chatting to Frank and he told me later, 'I saw you coming into view on your rear wheel and I saw you going off on your arse.' But Frank, who can't turn his head very far, had seen this slightly blurred vision and he'd said to Nigel, 'Is that one of ours?' 'Yeah, I think it was Adrian.' 'Did he damage his uniform?' 'Oh yes, it's totally shredded.' 'Andrew, send Adrian a bill for the uniform, will you?'

And the bill duly arrived, but it came with a watch. It was the hundredth race for Longines, and because we won it Williams were given a special watch to commemorate the event. And Frank and Patrick had very kindly given it to me.

In 1992 we decided that if the car got too hot we needed a means of re-pressurising the water system. We had a dry break on the water pipe and then a little oxygen bottle that discharged air and water back into the system. So, if it boiled on the grid, we could recharge and refill it.

Dickie Stanford had carefully set this up. Just before qualifying at Kyalami, Patrick decided that this needed testing, and that he was going to be the tester. So he looked at the regulator setting which Dickie had carefully worked out and said, 'No, no! That needs to be much higher.' He gave five turns of the regulator, plugged it in, and the water pipes just went 'Pfffftt!' Riccardo was strapped into the cockpit. Hot water and shit went everywhere, and one of the mechanics was scalded. Patrick took one look and, his navy background to the fore, simply said, 'Oh well, never mind,' and walked off in the other direction, leaving behind all this chaos, a broken car and a late start for Riccardo in the session.

If the car came in and the driver reported handling issues, Patrick would get on the radio immediately. He was always very quick on the button. He would then pontificate for the next ten minutes. We managed to get MRTC, the radio suppliers, to put a time-out button on the system so that you couldn't talk for too long – it would cut you off. The first few times Patrick carried on talking, not realising we could no longer hear him. He wised up to that after a little while. There must have been a little beep that told him he'd been timed out but, completely unfazed, he would come off the button and back on it and carry on before anyone else could get in. It became a quick-draw competition and he would win almost every time.

Patrick was very good to me because I had no track record. Right from the start he gave me a lot of freedom to design the car, and I'll always be grateful for that. Apart from that slight thing over the gearbox, technically he let me do anything I wanted.

He and Frank are a pair of eccentrics. Working for Williams and then going to McLaren was a fascinating contrast: two extremely successful teams that could hardly be more opposite in the way they are run. Frank and Patrick run it very much as a sort of big model shop, a big hobby shop. In those days nobody knew about management school; you just got on with it. It was great. It was also very honest, because there was no spin to it. What you saw was what you got. Whereas in McLaren it was very slick, very corporate. Neither Frank nor Patrick are control freaks. Eccentric in many ways maybe, and Patrick's never afraid to make a point, but he's absolutely not a control freak. If you earn his respect, he's happy to give you space and let you get on with it.

BOB CONSTANDUROS

I had only been a freelance journalist/commentator for a year when I had my first brush with Frank Williams. Saudia had begun their sponsorship of Williams in 1978. The late Gordon Procter, the father of an old girlfriend, was advertising agent for Saudia. He hired me for the princely fee of £500 to act as his temporary PA for that year's Monaco Grand Prix. My first duty was to meet him in Monaco when he arrived late on Wednesday evening. He immediately demanded to know where his passes were. I could only guess that Frank had them. 'Ring Frank,' I was commanded.

I knew enough about Frank to realise that ringing him after about 10 p.m. was not a good idea, and the time was well past that. But better to incur the wrath of Frank on the end of a phone than the man standing over me. So I made the call. Frank answered. Where were Gordon's passes? I enquired. To his everlasting credit, Frank did not go off the deep end, blasting me for ringing him at that time of night, but curtly and briefly explained in words of one syllable where I could get the passes in the morning. 'And goodnight,' he concluded.

Since his accident Frank's often been accused by those who don't know him of not showing any emotion when he's been filmed during practice and qualifying sessions. Frank can be as enthusiastic and animated as anyone, as Gerry Donaldson and I discovered after Juan Pablo Montoya put his Williams on pole at Spa in 2001. Post-qualifying, Gerry and I went to see Frank, who was in raptures over Juan Pablo's performance. 'Did you see the car through Eau Rouge?' he asked, eyes gleaming. 'Did you see the way it was moving through there? Fantastic! Hard-on time!'

Frank isn't always so good with the press of course. I've had the job of asking him lots of questions in FIA press conferences and elsewhere over the years, but I've gained respect for him blanking those enquiries that he hasn't wished to answer. How often have we seen people babbling away when they should really have just held their tongue? But if Frank doesn't want to talk about something he won't. He won't be impolite; he'll just explain that he doesn't want to say anything on such-and-such a subject. It may not be very helpful to journalists, but at least they know where they stand with him.

CLAIRE WILLIAMS

I think I'm always surprised by my father's level of passion for racing. To have that commitment is just extraordinary. The determination and the single-mindedness to do what he has done I find a bit incomprehensible because I couldn't do it myself.

When Dad was growing up, there was no room for self-pity. His mum was a steely character and you didn't walk around feeling sorry for yourself. Also, because he never really had anyone caring for him when he was young, that didn't bring any expectation of having someone care for him later on. So while he had plenty of love and care after his accident his prevailing attitude would have been, 'You get on with that; that's what you do.' We've been brought up like that: there's no self-pity and you get on with it.

When Dad says 'I couldn't give an eff about my disability' I sincerely believe that he thinks that. Obviously there is other stuff associated with it that means he does care, but overall his attitude is, 'This is it. Stuff it. This is what I've been lumbered with – or lumbered myself with.' He's in a very lucky position because he had the team to focus on. I don't think he'd be like he is if it weren't for Williams F1.

There was a strange, strange situation when I went to a race and Dad said, 'Can you come with me tomorrow to the team principals' meeting?' I was, like, 'What?' He said, 'I need you to take minutes because I can't understand anything that Mark or Gordon' – or whoever his assistant was – 'writes.' He said he had asked Bernie if it was okay. I walked in there, and I've never been so terrified in my entire life. You see everyone in the motorhome being reverent towards Dad – they come in quite nervous. I don't like that. Whenever I see people being a bit nervous, I want to say to them, 'It's only Dad! He's cool. Don't worry about it; he'll make you feel very welcome.' But at the team principals' meeting, even among those people, I couldn't believe the amount of reverence they had for him. I was really surprised. Dad would keep quiet for quite a long time, but if he made a move to say something everyone shut up. Okay, he speaks very quietly, but there was immediate silence. He was sitting on the right-hand side of Bernie, and there was definitely a pecking order. But it was very revealing to see that. And they are quite protective of him.

JONATHAN WILLIAMS

Flavio [Briatore of Renault] is very fond of him. Of all the team principals Flavio is probably the one he is closest to. When Flavio turned up from the world of fashion, he is on record as saying that Frank was the only one who gave him the time of day.

CLAIRE WILLIAMS

I remember when we used to be taken to Silverstone in the car, and as soon as people recognised Dad sitting in the front seat, they clambered all over the car. I would be sitting in the back and thinking, *My God. That's my dad. Look at this.* The sense of pride is just ... Well, I'm a bit pathetic about it and it makes me well up a bit.

JONATHAN WILLIAMS

It is a bit weird for us when we have a no-fuss relationship and access to him. It's one thing for that to happen at a racetrack, but when you are away from there and people recognise him, it's strange. About two years ago in a hotel in Hampshire a woman came up to him and was all over him. She was Scottish and said, 'I can't believe I'm shaking the hand that's shaken David Coulthard's hand.'

CLAIRE WILLIAMS

There is the father relationship in that he is always careful to look after us and make sure that we are fine and that we're well and we're healthy, our cars are safe and roadworthy, and our houses are warm – he's big on warm houses and central heating. But there's not that kind of father relationship – he's not your normal dad.

JONATHAN WILLIAMS

There isn't a father relationship in terms of routines, in that when we were younger he would not always put aside time for, say, karting or football or horse riding or cinema. Most fathers do that on a weekend because they have a more routine job at work, and then they relieve the mother at the weekend because she has had the kids all week. But of course Dad couldn't do that.

CLAIRE WILLIAMS

I used to get the bus to school and Nanny would take me to the bus stop. One day Dad said he would take me. I've never been so proud in my life because Abingdon Boys School used to go on the same coach. I knew all the boys, and they knew who my dad was. That morning when Dad dropped me off at the bus stop I've never been beaming so much in my life. It was one of the few times he did it. I was so proud, but it made me forget my lunch. I was in a state for the rest of the day. It was pathetic. He was only able to do it a few times. He only went to one parents' day, but I'll always remember it because he had made the effort and it was a surprise that he was able to come. It wasn't that he didn't want to do it; it was because racing and the team took so much of his time. There is no resentment whatsoever about him not being a normal nine-to-five dad. I much prefer him to be the way he is; I wouldn't change anything at all.

I would much rather he is happy at what he does and maybe not be around so much. I had a conversation with Sam Michael when he first started. He's got two young kids and he was saying that he was worried that he was missing stuff. I said, 'Don't worry about it. When they're older they'll be so much more proud of you for who you are and who you have become as technical director of a Formula 1 team, rather than have you at every single parents' day.'

JONATHAN WILLIAMS

One thing that my mother said is that Dad and Patrick are very protective of each other. If they see something derogatory about themselves, then they pass it off. But if they see something derogatory about the other, then they will immediately confront the source. Apparently some journalist in recent years had quite a bawling out by Patrick because he had written something about my father.

CLAIRE WILLIAMS

I think the relationship is quite cute. Every day at bang on two o'clock Patrick brings his little lunch pack up to my father's office and will go in even if Dad hasn't come back from pushing – going round the factory floor in his wheelchair. It's almost as if it's Patrick's place to go there.

JONATHAN WILLIAMS

You will see Patrick at my father's desk when my father is at a team principals' meeting somewhere. They always want to know if something is afoot, what this means to the other. Do they support this? What insights do they have? It is a true partnership. Between them they have provided the complete set of skills that we have needed as a company to exist and evolve to where we are now.

CLAIRE WILLIAMS

We were saying that Dad is in awe of drivers, but he is in absolute awe of Patrick. He says he is the most gifted person he has ever come across. Brilliant engineer. Brilliant brain. It works because, as everyone knows, they have totally different sets: they stay out of each other's territories and that's how it works. They are quite sensible normal people.

JONATHAN WILLIAMS

I wanted to absorb motor racing the whole time when at school. I spent time at the factory in my teens. Iain Cunningham took me to Formula 3 races. I decided I didn't want to go to uni. I drove vans for this company from autumn of 1993 to the late spring of 1994. I worked for the Madgwick International team and met a lot of people. Then I heard there was a job going with the company that distributed spares for Dallara. I was there for about a year and a half, and that taught me a lot before coming here in early 1996. The admin side of my role here began to kick in and evolve in 1997. I am managing the cars as soon as they are finished racing. We decide if it is going to be a museum car, a show car or perhaps on loan to a private museum. I do a lot of work with driver development and the identification of young drivers. I also work with any current driver with the supply and configuration of their fire-proof safety wear, working with Sparco. I do whatever research my father may need if he is going to a FOTA [Formula One Teams Association] meeting. I try and get into the political or commercial history of whatever the subject may be.

CLAIRE WILLIAMS

My father doesn't really understand people who have weekends off or holidays – he doesn't get it. Dad has never been on a family holiday with us, ever. Every year Mum and I always go to Marbella. It's always been a family thing – same place every single year.

I never knew when I left uni what I wanted to do. I think it was probably a logical course for me but Dad never ever wanted me to work here. 'Don't get any ideas into your head that you can come and work for me. No way I'm having it. Your brother already works there; go off and do your own thing.' He was really quite stern about it. So I was a bit confused and upset as to why Jonathan was allowed to work at Williams and I wasn't. It was understandable though, because everyone who works here had come through the proper channels and not through the back door.

I went off to Silverstone and got a job there. I really lucked in. I absolutely loved it and thought, *Brilliant. I don't have to work for Williams; I can show Dad.* But then I was made redundant. I had always come in my holidays and helped Donna booking hotels and so on – she's the race team secretary – so while I was looking for another job I came and helped her. During that time the press officer decided to leave, so Jim Wright called me and said he would really like me to do the job. I said, 'You've got to be joking.' I asked if he had run it past Dad and he said he hadn't. I said there was no way he was going to agree. Jim said not to worry; he would sort it out and call me once he had spoken to Dad. Jim called me and said, 'You're right. No effing way!' I think it took a couple of months to have him agree. Dad is quite right: it's quite inappropriate to have all your children working for you. It's a difficult position for him. He did succumb, but he put me on the most pathetic salary ever and a six-month probation period. I really had to work my backside off. He gave me a bit of a hard time. Fortunately, he decided I did an all-right job and kept me on.

We have quite a laugh. We're very lucky that we get to see our dad every day. He's such a great boss because he gets on with everyone and he cares about everyone. It's such a nice atmosphere when he wheels around marketing, which is open plan. He starts whistling at me to go and make his tea. It's so chilled out and relaxed. I sit there at my desk and think, *That's really cool; that's my dad.* And everyone thinks he's brilliant. And everyone works their arses off because he is that inspirational character.

A friend of mine works in the City with John Varley, the CEO of Barclays. My friend said, 'Your dad came to see my boss the other day and he was a bit of a nervous wreck that morning. When they asked what was wrong, he said he was going to meet Frank Williams and was excited by the anticipation.' When Dad left, my friend obviously asked how it went, and John Varley said actually meeting him in reality far outstripped the anticipation. He had never been so overwhelmed by someone. He was in awe.

I really want to get across how instrumental Mum has been, being there in the background. I really think, in a lot of areas, if Mum hadn't been there Dad wouldn't be where he is today after his accident. I went into his office the other day and he was having this quite gooey phone call. I was quite worried for a minute – then I discovered it was with Mum. It's quite amazing to have that relationship and be that sweet after thirty-two years, even if it did take her a long time to pin him down. He is very proud of that.

STEVE COATES

One final point, and this is something I really want to say: when Frank goes, I shall miss him like hell. I've often thought what I would put with the flowers because a card would never be big enough to let everyone know what he's like.

ACKNOWLEDGEMENTS

I am extremely grateful to everyone at Williams who took the time to pass on their thoughts and make this book what it is, but I must single out Liam Clogger for his unstinting support and hard work marshalling many of the contributors. Quite simply, I could not have done this without him.

Thanks to: Ian Anderson, Lady Sarah Aspinall, Kate Battersby, Matt Bishop, Barry Boardman, Thierry Boutsen, Ann Bradshaw, Ross Brawn, Martin Brundle, Johnny Bute, Jenson Button, John Cadd, Michael Cain, Alan Challis, Liam Clogger, Steve Coates, Bob Constanduros, David Coulthard, Iain Cunningham, Nicki Dance, Derek Daly, Ron Dennis, Frank Dernie, Tony Dodgins, Gerald Donaldson, Mike Doodson, Yvonne Duncan, Bernie Ecclestone, Giancarlo Faletti, Malcolm Folley, Pete Fostekew, Steve Fowler, Howden Ganley, Marc Gene, Bernie Goble, Diane Hamilton, Patrick Head, Alan Henry, Damon Hill, Sylvia Hoffer, Melanie Holmes, Mark Hughes, Alan Jones, Rick Jones, Linda Keen, Jules Kulpinski, Jacques Laffite, Robs Lamplough, Niki Lauda, Jonathan Legard, Charles Lucas, Nigel Mansell, Ryan McGlashan, Cathy Metcalfe, Sam Michael, Juan Pablo Montoya, Adrian Newey, Marigold Newey, Neil Oatley, Mansour Ojjeh, Brian O'Rourke, Riccardo Patrese, Nelson Piquet, Alain Prost, Nigel Roebuck, Keke Rosberg, Nico Rosberg, John Russell, Dickie Stanford, Sir Jackie Stewart, John Sutton, Stuart Sykes, Sheridan Thynne, Jacques

Villeneuve, Johanna Villeneuve, Mark Webber, Claire Williams, Sir Frank Williams, Jonathan Williams, Jonathan Piers Williams, Virginia Williams, Peter Windsor, Viv Woods (nee Orriss), Jim Wright, Alex Wurz, Alex Zanardi.

Special thanks to the team of transcribers included above for turning around more than sixty interviews efficiently and quickly.

I am indebted to Andrew Goodfellow and his team at Ebury Publishing, plus the ever-patient and supportive David Luxton, for making this happen.

INDEX